Praise for D

"Men for years have struggled to define e   ave
shared that frustration not knowing what to look for when they seek a 'real man.'
David G. Evans's most recent book, *Dare to Be a Man*, provides an in-depth look at
what that description looks like, up close and personal. It is a read I thoroughly enjoyed and wholeheartedly recommend to men and women!"

—BISHOP T. D. JAKES, *New York Times* bestselling author of *Before You Do* and *He-Motions*

"Bishop Evans's dedication to his work and to his mission in life to help people become better is remarkable. Not only does he talk the talk with his writings . . . he walks
the walk."

—STEDMAN GRAHAM, *New York Times* bestselling author, entrepreneur, and educator

"David G. Evans's latest book, *Dare to Be a Man*, is a powerfully relevant examina-
tion of God's role and authority in reestablishing the proper dynamics between men,
women, family, and community. *Dare to Be a Man* challenges its readers—male and
female alike—to interrogate their own misconceptions, false assumptions, and mis-
placed priorities in forming preconceived and faulty stereotypes of manhood and
masculinity. David G. Evans writes with clarity, insight, and sensitivity—and is ever-
mindful of the sovereignty, guidance, and truth of God's original, biblical intention
as the basis for defining authentic manhood. This is a must-read—both for today's
Christian men striving to regain their sense of power, purpose, and vision—and for
the women who love them."

—PASTOR PAULA WHITE, author of *Move On, Move Up*

"Speaking into the lives of men is not an easy task. I can think of no one more qualified to do that than Pastor David Evans. As a pastor, teacher, mentor, motivator, and
friend, he knows how to challenge men to unlock their potential, and how to show
women how to motivate the men they love. This book is a must-read for every man who
is ready to be all that God has planned for him to be and for every woman who wants
to see her man soar! Get this book. I dare you!"

—MARTHA MUNIZZI, award-winning singer/songwriter

continued . . .

"*Dare to Be a Man* is a call to action for every man to become the person God created him to be. Women will also find valuable lessons within these pages and will learn how to support all the important men in their lives. It is a must-read for men and women."

—THE REVEREND DR. SUZAN JOHNSON COOK, author of *Praying for the Men in Your Life* and immediate past president of the Hampton University Ministers' Conference

"For too long our culture has reduced manhood to a very few, very distorted role models. David Evans sets the record straight by reminding us that men need to be both caring and strong, able to listen as well as to stand up for what they believe, and above all, emotionally open people who can express themselves not just through their fists. The guidance he provides in *Dare to Be a Man* is invaluable not only for men, but for women who want to have better, more fulfilling relationships with men."

—WILLIAM PATRICK, coauthor of *Loneliness* and editor of *Iron John: A Book About Men*

"Coming to terms with masculinity in the twenty-first century requires wading through the many 'images,' both true and false, offered and marketed to the male population. There is a desperate need for a recovery of our true rites of passage into manhood, and a courageous pursuit of what it means to really dare to be the unique man each man is called to be. I am deeply appreciative of the groundbreaking approach my dear friend David G. Evans has taken to this necessary and pressing issue in his newest book, *Dare to Be a Man*. To every man and woman who wants to explore the rich possibilities both active and dormant within every man, I invite you to explore the insights and guidelines offered in this practical and powerful treatise."

—DR. MARK J. CHIRONNA, overseer of Mark Chironna Ministries

"Filled with insights on the unique challenges men face in today's world . . . and advice on ways to connect with the godlike qualities that lie deep within us . . . Both men and women can benefit from this book."

—JEANNE STAWIECKI, two-time Guinness World Record winner

DARE TO
BE A MAN

The Truth
Every Man Must Know...
and
Every Woman
Needs to Know About Him

DAVID G. EVANS

BERKLEY PRAISE
New York

THE BERKLEY PUBLISHING GROUP
Published by the Penguin Group
Penguin Group (USA) Inc.
375 Hudson Street, New York, New York 10014, USA
Penguin Group (Canada), 90 Eglinton Avenue East, Suite 700, Toronto, Ontario M4P 2Y3, Canada
(a division of Pearson Penguin Canada Inc.)
Penguin Books Ltd., 80 Strand, London WC2R 0RL, England
Penguin Group Ireland, 25 St. Stephen's Green, Dublin 2, Ireland (a division of Penguin Books Ltd.)
Penguin Group (Australia), 250 Camberwell Road, Camberwell, Victoria 3124, Australia
(a division of Pearson Australia Group Pty. Ltd.)
Penguin Books India Pvt. Ltd., 11 Community Centre, Panchsheel Park, New Delhi—110 017, India
Penguin Group (NZ), 67 Apollo Drive, Rosedale, North Shore 0632, New Zealand
(a division of Pearson New Zealand Ltd.)
Penguin Books (South Africa) (Pty.) Ltd., 24 Sturdee Avenue, Rosebank, Johannesburg 2196,
South Africa

Penguin Books Ltd., Registered Offices: 80 Strand, London WC2R 0RL, England

PRINTING HISTORY
Putnam Praise hardcover edition / September 2009
Berkley Praise trade paperback edition / September 2010

Berkley Praise trade paperback ISBN: 978-0-425-23645-1

The Library of Congress has cataloged the Putnam Praise hardcover edition as follows:

Evans, David G. (David Gregory)
    Dare to be a man : the truth every man must know . . . and every woman needs to know about him /
David G. Evans.
        p.   cm.
    ISBN 978-0-399-15494-2
    1. Christian men—Religious life. I. Title.
    BV4528.2.E915   2009   2009017110
    248.8'42—dc22

PRINTED IN THE UNITED STATES OF AMERICA

10 9 8 7 6 5 4 3 2 1

Some names and identifying characteristics have been changed to protect the privacy of the individuals involved.

While the author has made every effort to provide accurate telephone numbers and Internet addresses at the time of publication, neither the publisher nor the author assumes any responsibility for errors, or for changes that occur after publication. Further, the publisher does not have any control over and does not assume any responsibility for author or third-party websites or their content.

ACKNOWLEDGMENTS

THERE IS NEVER a successful anything without the participation and contribution of people who unselfishly bring their unique abilities and perspectives to the process. I have been blessed with extraordinary people who not only encourage but have the unique ability to allow me to be myself.

My greatest concern is not listing everyone and giving each the proper credit so richly deserved. So I want to thank everybody who loves and cares for me for everything.

First and foremost, I thank God for the opportunity to do so many things I never thought possible. This book represents another one of those God moments in my life. I thank Him for the wonderful network of family and friends who continue to encourage me that I have something to say worth writing. Your importance to me has not diminished. You continue to push me, through your expectations, to greater things.

To my grandmother of ninety-six years, Leola Elizabeth Prince, I thank you for the decades of powerful prayer, perspective, and wisdom you have provided for me during the past fifty-seven years.

To my grandfather, the late Albert Q. Prince, who modeled what a man should be without reservation when I needed a caring and loving example.

Special thanks to my family, Lisa, Blair, Henrietta, Marva, Lori, and Deb, for your love and support. Daddy loves Blair.

To the David G. Evans Ministries team, Crystal, Lisa, Valerie, Yalonda, for pushing me to my first book four years ago; along with Jack, Gary, and Emmanuel, for your diligent support. Thank you! Here we go again.

To the young men I have mentored during the past eighteen years, Craig, Derek, Shaun, Terrell, Tre', and to their mothers—Darlene, Crystal, Yolanda, Lisa, and Charlotte—for trusting me to dare your sons to be men. The labor has not been in vain.

To Lois de la Haba, the super agent, for your guidance, patience, passion, and incomparable experience; thank you.

Special thanks to the Putnam family. Joel Fotinos, for your belief in my approach, ideas, and message, and that I can do this a couple more times. To Denise Silvestro, thank you for your patience, guidance, and strategic handling of the manuscript, along with my schedule and the challenges of the past year. I want to thank Meredith Giordan along with the rest of the Putnam team committed to the success of this project.

Of course I can't forget Adrienne Ingrum and Olivia (Silver) Cloud for all of their help and guidance.

This book is dedicated to my mother, Wilma Evans Robinson, a woman of extraordinary grace and demonstrated love. You had the difficult task of raising a man as a single mother. I thank God for giving you the job. Thank you for your wisdom, strength, and love. Thank you for believing there is nothing I can't accomplish and showing me by example that all things are truly possible if we believe.

Thank you for being my shield, fierce defender, adviser, cheerleader. I miss your face, your voice, your company, our time, sharing the events of my life, and the light that entered the room every time you arrived.

I thank God for the privilege of being your son.

CONTENTS

INTRODUCTION
The Hidden Life of a Man

"I have seen a son of Jesse of Bethlehem who knows how to play the harp. He is a brave man and a warrior. He speaks well and is a fine-looking man. And the LORD is with him."

—1 SAMUEL 16:18, NIV

DARE TO BE SUCH A MAN.

As a man, you may have some difficulty deciding who you really are or who you truly want to be. In the "being" process, you may imitate your personal hero or, amazingly, you may become the very man you despise. You may often appear to be one person with your friends, another with your coworkers, and yet another with your loved ones. Then you add to these complex behaviors the fact that you don't switch roles as well as you should, and like many men, you may be unable to make up your mind who you want to be.

The title "man" is full of expectations that quite often change with your varying social contexts. Definitions of acceptable masculinity have changed significantly, and amid evolving cultural and even reli-

1

gious expectations, it may be difficult for you to grasp a consistent definition of manhood. You may have become frustrated trying to model yourself after a changing prototype that invalidates the historic view of a man.

Today, the way a "real man" is supposed to look, act, and think is being defined using a feminine perception of manhood, partly because so many males are raised in female-headed households. We are bombarded with media portrayals of men who are either silent or so sensitive that they emulate women. (Such men often attempt to be a woman's girlfriend rather than her man!) Men, we are suffering from an identity crisis!

The first step to becoming a man who dares is self-discovery. Until you discover who you were created to be, you cannot possibly know where you are going.

Reflection is often a very harsh reality. For years, the man I saw in my bathroom mirror didn't reflect an image of God, but rather a brokenhearted boy who had come home daily to a father who abused substances. My reflection had been shattered by all the negative, destructive behaviors that particular man, disconnected from his purpose, brought into the lives of all those around him.

Hurting people hurt people. Shattered men shape contorted images within boys, who become men living in clouds of confusion. While caring women like my mother often try to balance these negative influences, no mother can fix her son and no woman can fix her man.

But God's hand was firmly behind my distorted image. God's purpose and destiny for me would eventually overpower the confusion inherited from my father's legacy. Ultimately, I have not been shaped by my broken, human father, but rather by my healing Heavenly Father.

For years I didn't know who I was supposed to be. In an arena as critical as identity, I was open to suggestions from a variety of sources. The problem was the suggestions were either from men who were secretly not sure of their own identity or from women whose suggestions were based on disappointment and failed relationships. I needed to figure out who I was.

There was no class addressing my issue but there was a blueprint. Much to my surprise, the Bible contained the information I needed—ancient truths about what is right, good, and wholesome concerning relationships, responsibility, fathers, and manhood.

Through my grandfather, Albert Prince, I saw the image of my Heavenly Father and heard a call to manhood. Because of him, the image I saw in the mirror reflected hope rather than hurt. *I had been dared by His image through a mighty and valiant grandfather to be a man after God's own image.*

Your past doesn't have to shape or define your manhood. Instead, you will discover that you are *fearfully and wonderfully made.* Deep within the heart of every man, beyond the hurts, lies a marvelous destiny designed by a loving Father.

There is a "man" God wants to release inside of you and every man. Within every man is a "man" of confidence, purpose, strength, destiny, consistency, power, sensitivity, accountability, and loyalty. A man who is spiritual and loving—a problem solver and a leader.

At your core, your manhood is not defined by who others think you are, or even by who *you* think you are. A man is who God says he is. God made every man to be a profound and complex, marvelous, mighty, valiant, prudent warrior for truth.

Men, allow me to show you who God has created every man to be. This book is a daring challenge to men and a celebration of what men can—indeed, should—be according to God's design, and instruction for what a woman should look for and know about a man.

As children, we often dared one another to do something we

thought extreme, impossible, or incredible—even dangerous! I am daring you, each and every man reading this book, to be the man God designed and destined you to be.

FOR WOMEN

SUSPICIOUS ABOUT HIS FEELINGS

Many women have discovered the hidden life of men. Perhaps through painful experiences, you have learned that a man can be very frail. Men are sensitive. We get hurt, but we often won't cry. No tears may be visible, but we weep inside. A man's hurts will cause him to be present and absent at the same time. Our inner scars may be hidden by pretense and denial. Women, you've experienced this but weren't sure what to do. Machismo is the shield in front of a man's hurts. But deep within the heart of every man hidden by hurts is a deposit of marvelous destiny imparted by a loving God.

Ladies, you are about to learn the secrets of understanding how to deal with us men and how to relate to us. Men are extremely important to you. Whether with your father, brother, son, boyfriend, or husband, your relationships with men can be great sources of joy, confusion, and, at times, pain.

The significant men in your life can stretch your emotional, physical, and spiritual strength to the limit at times. An anonymous woman's prayer says, "Lord, I pray for wisdom to understand my man, love to forgive him, and patience for his moods, because Lord, if I pray for strength, I'll beat him to death!"

A man is predictably complex. Predictability gives the impression that we are simple—easy to read and to understand. We are not. This is just one reason we can be so confusing to the significant women in our lives. Understanding a man is often like trying to hit a moving target. Getting us to open up emotionally can be like trying to open a can with your teeth—extremely hard and often painfully futile.

You probably have experienced caring for a man who was attempting to head in more than one direction at a time, while expecting your full support in each direction. Makes you feel crazy, doesn't it? You finally tell him, "Just make up your mind!" He is insulted because you have figured out he's not sure which way to go.

The reason your man seems to change with every new idea is that he hopes he has finally discovered the thing that will reveal his identity. He is hoping that *this time* will be *the time*. A man who does not know who he is usually has little more than his imagination. The success he admires and wishes were his own often belongs to another man.

But take heart, ladies. There is "a man" within the significant men in your life—"a man" created to fulfill his role in society as well as in your life.

Ladies, I am thankful for the opportunity to speak to you in this book and to share with you this prayer to pray for the man you are thinking about as you read.

Woman's prayer:

God, I thank you for the chance to see revealed to me in this book things my father should have told me, characteristics about men that may be confusing to me. Help me to be as open and transparent as possible. Help me understand the words that will bring knowledge and help heal old wounds that loving a man can produce. Bless _____, I pray.

This book is written to men and for men, but it is also written for women. I'm going to share some man secrets with you—stuff your daddy should have told you. My purpose in writing this book is to challenge both men and women. I hope and believe this book will help many men, but also the women in their lives. I am grateful to the women who will read *Dare to Be a Man* in an effort to understand the significant men in their lives—spouse, father, son, brother, relative, professional colleague, team member, or friend. Read this book knowing that many of the feelings, issues, and experiences cited are common to both genders.

As you read, I invite both men and women to abandon the cultural myths about manhood that you have unwittingly adopted as dictated by your past, or subtly absorbed from the media, misguided relatives, religious legalists, frightened men, and wounded women. Men and women need to be healed without scars. This book is an adult conversation with men and women concerning the difficult subjects and problems we men face and the problems men and women encounter in relationships. I am especially addressing the negatives most people avoid, the areas where we men are hardly challenged, our problem areas. I don't avoid the negative in this book. I see this book as an opportunity to get to the nitty-gritty!

Choose to believe the truth of God's purpose for manhood. Dare to be a man!

Dare to pray this prayer:

God, I thank you right now for the awesome opportunity to be called a man. I bless your name for your goodness and your mercy. I thank you that I have come to this book to celebrate being a man. I'm about to learn some things, God, that are worth celebrating. I am about to learn some things, God, that I should have known a long time ago. So thank you right now for what you're about to do as I read this book.

As you talk to me through these pages, I will talk back to you honestly and openly. I open my mind, my heart, so I can receive what you have to say. I thank you now for another opportunity to speak to you. Right now, God, I pray to know you better and for the pardon of my shortcomings.

God, I've been hanging out in the world long enough. I need to come back to my home. I need to come back to you. I ask you now, true Spirit, to lead me, to unite me to you, God.

Thank you for the ability and the anointing that you have placed upon me. Give me your words for my life. In Jesus' name I pray.

I dare you to read on.

DARE TO BE A MAN OF VISION

~

Vision is the ability to see past
your present into your future.
Vision pulls you toward success.

A MAN MUST DARE to center his vision on duplicating the image of God. What I as a man am looking for is God to imitate. A woman is looking for a man whose vision for himself is to imitate God. We understand that when God made humans, our Creator made us—men and women—in his image. We are to reflect the Almighty's image—to act, think, and represent God fully on the earth. When I want to find out what a real man is all about, I must begin to look at the things God says a man should be. Job 1 says he is an upright man of substance and prayer, has a relationship with God, avoids doing the wrong things, and takes responsibility for others.

God has uniquely equipped you as a man to dramatically affect your surroundings and personally impact the people to whom you relate. Every household is affected either positively or negatively by the presence or absence of a male. Strong vision that shapes godly character enables a man to bring order and peace to his environment.

If you lack vision, you will lack structure, and this lack can lead to disorder and dysfunction. A visionary male brings a spirit to the household that contributes to a positive atmosphere.

In the Hebrew home of Biblical history, the father was primarily responsible for the life education and discipline of his children. It was his job to teach his children the law, how to interact positively with neighbors and friends, and the fundamental principles for managing money and life. As the head of household, the Hebrew man gave most of the instruction; his wife was there to support him in that impartation to their children.

Fatherhood was created by God, and men are assigned to develop and protect their children and propel them to fulfill their God-given purpose. But something has changed radically.

Jesus warned us that a house divided against itself cannot stand (Mark 3:24–25). Contemporary men and women, fathers and mothers, husbands and wives are often out of alignment with God's blueprint. Men are abdicating the roles God designed for them. Women are taking on responsibilities that men were designed to fulfill. Too many mothers find themselves giving most of the instruction to children, with fathers acting as assistant. Mothers have had to take on the role of chief giver of wisdom and knowledge, casters of vision for children. Children grow up confused by faulty and often conflicting family dynamics. The family unit becomes dysfunctional when the parents are misaligned.

A Biblical principle found in the first chapter of Genesis has universal impact and relevance regarding the relationships between men and women. The man and woman, the father and mother, can be compared to the sun and the moon. The sun and the moon are both created with specific spheres of authority in the same sky. Because of their designed courses, the earth enjoys stability—days, seasons, tides.

When a man and woman structure their relationship for success, they agree on the process necessary to achieve economic, social, relational, and spiritual success. They commit to a plan, and the family enjoys stability and seasons of fulfillment, as well as economic and spiritual success.

I call that plan a vision. Your family should have a vision statement. Each family member should be able to articulate it and restate it at various milestones—birthdays, graduations, weddings, and the passing of loved ones. These important events are optimal times to restate the education, economic, social, and spiritual beliefs and goals of the family. These can be poignant times of reflection, gentle correction, and inspiration to both your immediate and extended family. A man of vision takes the lead in shaping his family's vision.

If you are a single man reading this book, I envy you. It is imperative you develop a vision for your life *before* responsibility for family forces you into catch-up vision mode. The earlier you create a vision map for yourself, the greater opportunity you will have for success. If you are single, look into the future and determine who you want to be and the life you want to build. A man with a vision can make a plan and avoid wandering through life. A man with a vision can construct a path to success. You want to live on the road to success. Remember, vision is always inclusive of others. The sooner you become a visionary, the greater chance you have for success.

VISION ENABLES STRUCTURE

Structure is a key element in the success of any endeavor—and that includes relationships. Love in and of itself will not guarantee the success of any relationship. Love and work are like the faith-and-work equation in the Bible in James 2:17. The Bible says faith without appropriate action is useless. I usually say intention without action leads you nowhere. Vision leads to structure, which leads to a productive, satisfying relationship. Good happens. Excellence is intentional.

Structure is the road map for your vision. It keeps the vision in order and relatively close to the timeline you have set for yourself. When your vision is well ordered, well structured, and well communicated, you will engender a sense of security in those whose lives you touch. One of your keys to success will be a well-ordered vision and a commitment to its fulfillment.

Traditional elements that once brought cohesion to our society seem to have lost their place. The more advanced our culture becomes, the less there appears to be a need for structured personal interaction. This lack of personal interaction hinders relationship-building and accountability among peers and families. It fosters an unbalanced view of life and produces superselfish people whose only sense of responsibility is to themselves. Creating a vision for structured personal interactions will have a profound positive impact on those you are responsible for as a man.

THE IMPORTANCE OF CASTING A VISION

Your vision is just an idea unless it is cast or communicated to those it includes. I must remind you, real vision always includes others. When you cast your vision correctly, those included will begin to understand your purpose in their lives and their productive participation in yours. Once your vision is well thought out and cast, you will become more secure in your personal purpose, while those around you, who love and depend on you, will grow more secure in that relationship. Vision reconnects you with your innate role as a leader.

Too many of us have abdicated our role as leaders and vision casters. A number of factors have contributed to this anomaly, but mainly it is the misguided belief that we need to give up our position and role in order for women to fully exercise theirs.

The media trend is to portray men as weak, whining individuals, superficial and unable to handle the challenges of life. Extremes, not balance, are the standard media portrayal. These depictions are not to be confused with reality. Trends should not be adopted as lifestyle choices, especially when they distance us from responsible interaction with others.

The principle of being your brother's keeper still has merit today. It is a precept that demands more than superficial concern for someone other than you. Being your brother's keeper is a reminder of the human need for social interaction and responsibility. As a man, you accept responsibility for "keeping" those to whom you are accountable—spouse, children, family, and other significant relationships—making provisions for their well-being and sustenance. One of the ways you do that is by casting a vision.

My aunt Maggie's funeral presented me with an opportunity to cast a vision for my extended family. Aunt Maggie was an extraordinarily beautiful woman in her youth. She was always beautiful on the inside—enormously talented, gifted with multiple abilities, energetic, intelligent, and full of life. Yet at the time of her death, she had not reached her potential, her talents and gifts were largely untapped, and she was economically unfulfilled. Her countenance was that of a person who had lived knowing there was much more she could have achieved.

After the funeral, family members were gathered in the airport and concerns were voiced regarding Aunt Maggie's life. I began to talk about choices. I said, "Adults have the right to make their own life choices. Many of you will disagree with them, but the decision is ultimately theirs. Sometimes you want something for a loved one or friend that they don't desire for themselves. The challenge is *not* to get emotional about a choice you ultimately have no jurisdiction over." Needless to say, I had their attention.

The circle included several generations: my grandmother was in her eighties; aunts and uncles were in their fifties, sixties, and seventies; cousins were in their twenties and thirties. All gathered around. It was a great moment. I began to recast the family vision. I said, "Many of the women in our family have achieved success, but Aunt Maggie became disconnected from that legacy. The choices you make in life are never casual but have destiny in them. Life choices are critical. Remember, part of legacy is staying connected to family and friends who have made a positive impact on your life."

As I talked about the expectations of our family and the outstanding legacy of our females, I realized there are no incorrect times for casting or reinforcing family vision. In tragedy, vision sharing to reinforce the possibilities of a generation is part of your responsibility as a man. Vision casting is a seed sown for the future.

In the weeks following, I had conversations with almost all of those in attendance, reiterating the need for strong male examples and the importance of choices in the fulfillment of personal and family vision.

Becoming a man of vision gives you direction and reveals personal purpose. Vision casting always begins internally. Your sense of what you wish to accomplish in any facet of your life is the seed of any vision. You must decide what your legacy will be. Write that down. The question will produce an emotional answer, which must be translated into words and action. The key to successful vision building is to pick your goals. Do that first. Then work your way back to your present position in life.

At first this method will seem strange. Why not start where you are, then work toward the goal? Vision requires you begin where you want to *end*. Using this method will make the steps to completion more evident. Try this method right now. What you need to do to transform your future will become evident.

There is another benefit for the man who casts positive vision. When you cast vision, a natural benefit is that areas of strength and weakness are naturally revealed during the process. What you need to do to break the negative habits of the past suddenly becomes a non-negotiable. Vision casting stretches the mind of a man to such an extent that it becomes difficult for him to return completely to an old way of doing things.

This vision-casting role of males is often compromised in our society. Perhaps you are one of many men who does not fully comprehend your potential, unable to actualize all you have been created to be. Sit down and cast a new vision for your life.

VISION CASTING IN SINGLE-PARENT HOUSEHOLDS

The rise of female-headed households and the changing nature of relationships between fathers and mothers do not mandate a termination of generational goals, especially for the children. The family's vision principle can remain intact even though the familial structure has changed.

Never united in matrimony does not mean never united in terms of goals for your offspring. Divorced does not mean detached. Immature behavior displayed during and after the divorce process will only serve to impede the development of your children, leaving them victimized by the breakup. If dissolution is inevitable, your children's welfare, future, and sense of well-being should remain the priority.

THE STRENGTH OF A WOMAN

I was raised in a single-parent household. My mother is proof a woman can become the strong leader necessary to influence and ensure the generational success of her family. My mother raised my brother and me in a low-income housing development in Chester, Pennsylvania, called the Fairground Projects. It began as a safe place but changed radically as we grew older. It used to be said, "Nothing good came out of the Fairground." My grandparents also lived there and helped to raise me. They were excellent role models in a rapidly changing environment. Divorce carried a stigma in those days, but our extended family was extremely supportive.

Mom was committed to providing a positive environment for both of us. She was breadwinner, visionary, coach, educator, and disciplinarian of the household. Our home had begun to take on a new dimension of optimism after her divorce, and she discovered she was equipped to handle a dual role when necessary.

She learned how to do things that were not customarily female and became interested and conversant in the things that interested my brother and me. Consequently, we were raised with a nontraditional view of a woman's ability, role, and position in society.

Mom's circumstances pushed her into uncharted life waters. She struggled but swam and stayed afloat. She went back to school and excelled scholastically and vocationally. I saw her work two jobs and run a catering business to support us. I learned a work ethic from my mother that I retain to this day.

Ironically, she was my example for achievement. Her divorce from my father did not cause her to divorce herself from casting a generational vision and instilling values for success in her children.

Mom knew she could tell me how to be a man but she could not show me. My mother made it her mission to surround my brother and me with the positive male role models in our family. My grandfather provided us with a strong and loving male role model. With positive male interaction and vision casting, boys raised in female-headed households can mature into men of strong identity. A woman must center her vision for the men in her life on seeing that the characteristics they possess reflect the image of God.

When you cast a vision, you give a child, or anyone else close to you, a mental picture of his or her possibilities in life. This includes your plans for that person as well as a road map for what it means to be successful. It includes vocational aspirations, educational goals, and the seeds for a developing a well-rounded perception of life. Give your children a mental road map for the future that includes establishing a standard of excellence, disdain for average performance, and assistance in discovering their passion. Your vision starts with a personal transformation.

When you cast a vision, you are sharing your desires and the methods for making your forecasts become reality. The blueprint for that transformation is duplication of the character and love of God. Your new vision demands a departure from the negative images of your past. Your prototype is God. Your journey into a new type of manhood is beginning.

Take the dare. Decide today to be a visionary.

Take the dare. Decide to be different. Set the goal. Look into your future. Create the legacy you want to represent you.

I dare you to center your vision on duplicating the image of God.

- Begin internally.
- Identify what you wish to accomplish—pick your goals. (These are the seeds of your vision.)
- Decide what your legacy will be.
- Write these down.
- Write down the questions you ask yourself during this process.
- Write down the emotional answers that will arise.
- Translate your words into action steps, working your way backward to your present position.

2

DARE TO
HAVE A VOICE

A man's conduct gives life to his words.
Men are deemed great because their words
and intentions are followed by action.

I WAS LISTENING TO A group of women venting about the men in their lives. The conversation was both interesting and troubling. They were complaining about their brothers' failures in contrast to the successes in their own lives. They said the male family members had justified their lack of productivity based on a variety of external factors; none of the males admitted personal responsibility.

These women held a festering disrespect for their brothers, which gave them a negative framework for relating to other men in their lives. This collection of attractive, accomplished women were disappointed, confused, and even a little angry. They had unmet expectations of these men who had not figured out who they were supposed to be.

Men, the roles you are expected to fill are varied and lifelong, with little, if any, room for a break from the expectations. Even when you are in recreational mode, you face expectations from your peers. You are always expected to be a man. You must be one kind of man with your friends, another with your coworkers, and someone else with your loved ones. Expectations of you are set by a number of sources. The women in your life have set expectations for you without fully understanding what it means to be a man. Mom has her expectation, your sister has hers, and the woman you love has yet another. And all three may be different, even conflicting. Having attempted to respond to them all, you may have simply given up.

Mark was the only male in a household of females. His mother is very proud of him for running a successful business. His sisters are proud of him as well, and so is his wife. Yet the three often cause Mark a tremendous degree of stress, as their expectations of him conflict. Because she raised him as a single parent, his mother feels entitled to his supreme loyalty and expects him to provide for her in her old age. His sisters, Jane and Liz, lacking relationships with good men, expect him to find them prospects for dating or marriage from his pool of friends and business associates and to be a surrogate father to their children. His wife, Michelle, feels she is always competing with his mother and sisters and wants him to clearly demonstrate his loyalty to her above anyone else.

You may have set your own expectations and operate from self-imposed stereotypes. George was raised by his paternal grandmother in Texas during the 1950s. His parents were absent from his life and his paternal grandfather was incarcerated. Absent any male role model, George developed for himself the criteria of a real man, coupled with his grandmother's expectations. George managed to earn advanced degrees and has been married for over forty years. Nevertheless, his interpersonal relationships are shallow and his behavior toward his wife was abusive for many years. And though his relationship with his son has improved, there is still a great chasm between them.

With the swell of media images, many young men are emulating images both unreal and undesirable. Rappers brag in their lyrics about going to hell, as though they are so hard nothing can intimidate them. Other young men emulate the behaviors of these men, who are celebrated and idolized by the media but are not examples of true manhood—impregnating women irresponsibly, abusing them with no sense of accountability.

The absence of authentic role models can leave you feeling pressured to perform, even though you are not exactly sure what you need to be doing. And time after time, you miss the target of expectation.

Many men are unsure of themselves, disillusioned by what supposedly constitutes a real man. Too many of us are trying to model ourselves after a prototype that invalidates historic manhood but does not show us how a real man looks, acts, and thinks.

We know it is incorrect to try to fit into a woman's idea of manhood, rather than become secure in our own identity and add the necessary skill sets to produce positive interaction with a woman. But identity confusion and personal identity crisis are at the root of the manhood dilemma. It is extremely difficult to figure out *who* you should be when you are not sure *what* you should be. Even after you figure out who you should be, the right idea of manhood, you will continue to struggle with what you should represent as a man in various situations.

MAN'S VOICE IN HIS HOME

Have you ever felt displaced in your own home? That may be because there is a distorted societal view of a man's position in his home. You are expected to conduct yourself with a sense of ownership and involvement that you may never have felt you possessed. You may feel as though the house you are working to pay for is not really your domain. Man's sphere of influence has effectively been moved outside the home. Ask yourself:

- Is my domain outside my family unit?
- How much influence do I exercise inside my home?
- How can I have passion for something from which I have been effectively excluded?
- What are the cultural norms of household leadership in which I was raised?
- How can I learn to lead my household according to God's purposes and design?

Listen to this about a man in ancient times (Exodus 3:1–5). God calls Moses to a mountain. A mountain is often seen in scripture as a place of hindrance, a blockade, something standing between man and where he wants to be. God calls Moses to a mountain and Moses comes up to the mountain and several significant things happen.

We look at the mountain as a problem, but a mountain is a sanctifying, identifying, maturing place for a man. A problem helps set a man apart in his manhood. So a mountain, to a man, is a place where he hears God. God uses a mountain for a man to sanctify him and to attune a man's ears to the voice of God. A man must learn the voice of God in his life. No one else can recognize the voice of God for you. You have to learn it for yourself. And when you learn it, you will then have a voice of your own.

Your inner voice reflects who you are. It also demands to be obeyed. It is influential and persuasive. The fruit of your life is directly related to your decisions; decisions dictate character, and both of them impact your future. When a man of vision begins to change his future, reflecting the image of God as his vision becomes clear, he becomes a man with a real voice. The defeating voice of negativity is replaced with a "can-do" voice of accomplishment. Your inner voice will change. An inner voice change triggers an outlook change. A new outlook gives you a new perception and perspective. Your leader voice is born, and you take a new position in your home and in significant relationships.

GOD'S PLAN VERSUS OUR REALITY

We have strayed far from God's plan.

I believe the problem began with two important misunderstandings: first, a lack of clarity about God's plan concerning the leadership role of men, which I'll discuss in the next chapter; and secondly, an erroneous understanding of submission, which I'll tackle in Chapter 4.

The Biblical loss of man's voice begins in the book of Genesis, with a picture of a man and a woman in a place of productivity with the ability to maximize the expanse they have been created to occupy. God placed them in a place of opportunity and gave them the skill set to succeed if they observed a few fundamental principles—cooperation, fulfilling role expectations based on their abilities and gifts, strategic planning and execution, discipline, accountability, and responsibility.

They were given the authority to rule their environment and fulfill their destiny together. Then a crisis in leadership is revealed in the story. There was a breakdown in discipline, which led to a lack of accountability and responsibility. The strategic plan was interrupted; the gifts and talents failed to produce their anticipated result. Both the man and the woman lost their places, their strategic advantage, and their prosperity.

The divisive factor is given a place of influence rather than put in its place. The serpent, which they had authority over, was given a place of influence and authority. Eve listened and responded to a voice she had been given the authority to reject. She did not exercise her authority, which would have preserved her position and authority in her environment.

Meanwhile, the man was silent in this situation. He was present but silent! He had lost his voice and abandoned his responsibility to be an influence in critical situations. He watched instead of speaking.

God told Adam to call the animals by name. It is safe to assume God knew what the animals should be called. God was giving Adam an image test. Would Adam agree with God by agreeing with Him concerning their names? It seems so. God doesn't disagree with any of Adam's name choices. At this point, Adam is aligned with the image of God and saying the things God says.

A sure way for a woman to figure out whose image a man is living in is to listen to what he says. Is he saying the things God says? A simple image test but effective nevertheless.

Adam's agreement with God signaled the beginning of a productive, responsive relationship—God with man and man with his environment. Ladies, the test worked then and it will work now.

Both men and women need to be able to successfully interact with their environment. Men, God has put something in your voice that He has designed to produce cooperation. Your voice has been designed to generate a response. It is a reality advertising executives have known for years. You may have noticed most of the major ad campaigns feature a man's voice. Automobiles, alcohol, tobacco, or athletic wear—the majority of the campaigns feature a male voice.

Over the course of any given week, I will counsel approximately thirty-five people, many of them men who have lost their voice in their own home and in their relationships. They feel as though their voice has no influence and is not welcomed. In an attempt to "try to keep the peace," they keep silent, feeling only major issues are worth the aggravation of a confrontation. They believe that opposing points of view will often lead to a negative outcome. They resign themselves to the situation, feeling, "It's no use."

The problem stems from the difference in male-female methods of processing and articulating information. We men receive information, then process, contemplate, and articulate, while women receive, process, articulate. This accounts for the difference in response rates during conversations between men and women. Add to that the universal estimates on the different rates at which men and women think and speak. No wonder there is a gender communication gap!

Women, as a rule, respond at a faster rate than we do. Most of us respond with silence because we just can't keep up. The exception is usually the man who has been raised in a female-headed household and has been conditioned to respond at a faster rate. All this comes from men being raised in households where the father was not aware of his responsibility or position and the woman stepped in to fill that void.

As Jesus finished the parable about a house divided (Mark 3:25), he says, "No one can enter a strong man's house and carry off his possessions unless he first ties up the strong man. Then he can rob his house" (Mark 3:27–28, NIV). Take away a man's influence in the home and you have basically tied him up and left the home vulnerable to subtle but serious attacks.

When you rediscover your God-given voice, it allows the woman in your life to stop trying to fulfill both roles. When your woman's understanding of you is regained, the two of you can return to the kind of mutual admiration and fulfillment God intended. Determine to become a presence reflecting God's image and embracing His assignment. Without this reconnection with God to regain your voice, your woman may find herself aiming at a moving target because you may have become contextually inappropriate. She may be unable to connect with the man she needs to communicate with. You cannot take on with your woman the persona you assume with your friends, in the workplace, or the fellas on the basketball court or golf course.

When you have a problem with your sense of self, it is a compounding problem. You discover a deeper sense of inner confusion with each new challenge you face, you have difficulty comprehending what is expected of you, and you may speak in a manner that seems inappropriate or irrational.

It is time to rediscover your voice. Here's how you do it. First, the greatest potential strength you have is not physical. It is your potential for influence. Like salt, you can flavor any situation once you become aware of how it works. Salt's influence is not released until it comes into contact with something.

Man, you have already experienced this influence positively or negatively. You have influence. Now that you know this, you must decide to reverse some old negative behaviors and become a positive influence on those around you. You must become the solution in each situation. Your reputation as a man will change.

A man's reputation is vital to his influence. If you are reading this and need a change in reputation, realize that it is accomplished by a retooling of your voice and the effects of your presence. As you build a new history of positive constructive input, the expectations of those around you will change. This takes a little time and reflection.

Take a serious look at the expectations you have created in those you love. It is probably a mixture of positive and negative for most men. Habits, actions, and character of the past must be brought into line with the prototype. Positive influence will change the expectations of both you and those with whom you interact. When positive respectful expectation is exhibited, your reception in all facets of relationship will change. It all begins with a reconnect to God.

FOR WOMEN

LEARNING TO SPEAK THE SAME LANGUAGE

You are often so descriptive that men lose your point. Here's a tip for you: Sometimes a man will give up trying to understand the issue and begin to grunt and say "Okay" continually. It may be a sign that he is losing interest in the descriptive part of your concern. Don't circle the airport too long. Land the plane. It has begun to sound like nagging, blaming, and complaining to him. Add to that the emotional challenges, dysfunctional family effect, and other painful experiences in relationships and you may have a man who cannot hear your heart.

So what do you do? Think as though you are making a presentation at work or applying successfully for employment. Boil down the details so the important points of communication are not lost in the explanation. Guard against being overwhelmed by your feelings and failing to express yourself clearly. Over-the-top emotionalism often reduces the integrity of the issue in a man's mind. You may think it adds to the explanation, but it doesn't, and repeated displays usually are regarded as contrived even when they are not.

Your greatest misstep, however, is when you fail to plainly ask for what you need or want but expect him to figure it out. He usually will do nothing, because the field of possible mistakes is too wide, especially if you are discussing an issue that historically has caused conflict.

If you have thought or said, "If he really knew me, he would know what to do without me having to say anything," you are certain to be hurt or disappointed. Articulate the full emotional message clearly. It is so essential for complete understanding.

Both men and women must learn to unlock the nonverbal message behind spoken questions. When the two of you are in a conversation, especially a tense one, understanding is essential. Always remember that the burden of understanding is on the speaker. The listener is not responsible for the speaker's message. It is your job to make yourself understood. Don't start the conversation based on assumptions about another person's mind-set, opinion, or experience.

Men and women do communicate differently, and you must understand this dynamic. You can have a conversation with another woman, leave out certain details, and still comprehend the entire dialogue. It is the context of being a woman that gives you an accurate sense of what was communicated. It is no different for men. It explains a lot about why we don't understand one another. At times it feels as though we are speaking two different languages, especially in times of conflict or emotionally driven conversation.

Men and women need urgently to reconnect and realign their positions. As we look at the state of relationships between men and women, it is apparent we are in a desperate search for relationship answers. Divorce, unhappy family situations, coexistence rather than relationship, and broken family bonds are responsible for the musical-chairs approach to relating.

The first vulnerability occurs when the voice of influence starts to come from outside your home. Role models and heroes different from the mother and father foster a rejection of the discipline and structure of the immediate family. The lack of these strengths creates vulnerability in the child-parent relationship. Positive voices outside of the parents do exist; however, trouble arises when those voices overrule parental influence.

Outside voices are usually people who are ill-equipped to offer solid assistance to the child or adult they are influencing. I call it "influence without responsibility." This type of vulnerability usually ends up culminating in a family member who rejects your counsel in a crisis while trying to apply "sterile" influence from outside. By "sterile," I mean advice lacking a full understanding of the circumstances.

Men and women are not sure what to do or which way to turn, so they try a variety of approaches. We all have little idea how to engage in productive relationships. Men and women must become reacquainted in a fundamental but productive way of relating, using the basics outlined in God's Word.

Men and women do articulate in remarkably different ways. A good analogy of this difference is that men paint word pictures with broad strokes while women draw in minute detail. Therefore, to begin to articulate more effectively, men have to be a little more detail-oriented, while women must realize that too much detail obscures the issue when communicating with men.

Often the vocabulary used in a conversation can cause miscommunication, because words often contain different shades of meaning. For instance, when a man says he understands something, it does not necessarily mean he agrees with it. Understanding doesn't necessarily communicate agreement.

To a man these are entirely different phases toward a solution. He can understand what is being said but disagree wholeheartedly with the other person's conclusion. Not understanding how vocabulary and expression differ between men and women can cause huge communication gaps between them.

Bridging the gap between these two styles of communication requires effort from both parties. A man tends to communicate in a way that makes sense to him, with an expectation that the woman will understand what he is thinking. Miscommunication can happen when he assumes the woman has received what has been said in the way he intended it to be received.

Taking the time to ask if the other person has understood your perspective saves a great deal of unnecessary conflict. Without the use of the questioning step, you may leave yourself open to misunderstanding and unrealistic expectations. Learn to do this and get past the fear of appearing vulnerable or incorrect. Your woman needs to understand that you may not say what's really on your mind until her last word has come out of her mouth.

Responsible Communication

Men and women look at responsible communication from different perspectives. A man feels part of his objective is to bring to light the woman's part in the issue they are discussing. The woman will often respond to this by accusing him of trying to turn the situation around, so she in turn reminds him of his part. This dynamic occurs primarily when a man and woman are discussing an emotional issue. Unresolved, the conversation goes round and round, seldom dealing with the real issue at hand.

To move past this cycle and on to effective communication, both parties in the exchange need to look at the way they communicate. Often the problem is not what has been communicated but rather the manner in which it has been delivered. Men, having the warrior bent, want to isolate the problem, handle it, and finish the conversation rather than seek to uncover what caused the problem in the first place.

Too often a man is more concerned with "winning" the discussion and doesn't take the time to really understand the situation. Meanwhile, the woman is circling the conversation like an airplane over an airport. She feels she is making progress, but to the man she seems to be simply going over the same ground. The man just wants to get to the bottom line so he can resolve the thing. A more effective strategy is to allow the woman a couple of rotations around the airport and then remind her that a circling plane needs to eventually touch down at the designated location. She needs time to paint her detailed strokes in a meticulous, detailed fashion.

For example, if asked to describe a room, a woman's description will include the colors, the style of the furniture, the texture of the fabrics, the coordination of the drapes to the furniture, and what she likes and dislikes about the room. A man will simply say, "It's a great room." They have described the same room but articulated what they have seen in very different styles. To be effective at cross-gender communication, men have to become experts at listening to the minute details of a woman's communication, even though the average man really does not want to hear that much detail.

To facilitate meaningful communication, a woman has to learn to listen to a man based on the broader strokes he paints and ask the right questions in order to fill in the details she needs in order to understand what he is really thinking.

A woman will generally say what she is thinking and what she is feeling, eventually. A man needs to realize that a woman processes information through her feelings. A man measures the impact of his words on the woman's feelings. The woman is more likely to say what she feels and then assess the damage afterward. Men try to assess the possible damage ahead of time. Not understanding this process causes the breach in a man and a woman's desire to effectively communicate with each other.

Men have to learn how to speak "Woman" and women need to learn how to speak "Man." Each must learn how to speak the other's language, acknowledging that both sides want to bridge the communication gap.

A final characteristic of communication that needs to be factored into gender communication is the unspoken message.

The Mystery of the Unspoken Message

One of the things that men must become adept at and that women need to become attuned to is the unspoken messages being sent within the other's responses. Because men paint in broad strokes, they have a tendency not to hear small increments of information. On the female side, important information can become bogged down in the need to communicate details.

A woman may get hung up on a minor detail that has no cognitive effect on the outcome. Seeking to generalize the situation, men often miss a significant detail that is vitally important to the outcome. A common meeting place must be found where the woman does not anesthetize the man by giving him details he doesn't need and the man willingly listens to the details, learning to sift through them for relevance.

You and the woman in your life probably want many of the same things, but a communication breakdown makes it seem that the two of you are positing opposing points of view. Often, following a protracted and highly emotional conversation, after tempers have flared and cooled, you and she will realize you both missed something critical to understanding the exchange or said something that did not accurately convey a thought. What's hilarious is this: Have you ever had an argument and, after about an hour, arrived at the conclusion that you basically were saying the same thing?

Many times you will not fully understand what she wants from you. She hears your words but not your heart. Sometimes this misunderstanding is a product of the male "bilingual" style of communication. That is the way many of us have learned to communicate with a woman—in a protective mode. Men speak but often reserve their innermost feelings. Heart words leave most men feeling vulnerable, so they become male bilingual. There is a truth for his male friends and a different truth he feels more comfortable relaying to his woman. You may have gotten into the habit of communicating only what you think people can handle, forgetting the original reason for communication.

When we understand that the original purpose for speech is creative, communication takes on a new dimension. Each time we speak, we create. God has given us this ability so we can create bonds of connectivity. Effective communication will create and often rebuild relationship bridges.

Men become highly skilled in the art of verbal contemplation (VC). In other words, while you are processing and contemplating, you are not simply sitting like a bump on a log. Instead, you can use a series of questions to help you sort out the significant points in the conversation and then decide how to articulate in a manner that is beneficial and truly addresses the situation.

The moment you begin to use verbal contemplation and thoughtful responses, you begin to walk into a new level of manhood. If you are going to lead others—be a father, be the rock of the family and the head of household—you must become a master of VC. The first step to VC is being in control of your emotions.

THE ART OF VERBAL CONTEMPLATION

The VC process is the best way to help a person communicate with you and help you determine what the problem or dilemma really is. By asking carefully chosen questions before articulating, you can get to the bottom of the real issue behind the problem and articulate a beneficial solution or conclusion. The Bible offers a simple foundation for initiating the art of verbal contemplation: *"You must all be quick to listen, slow to speak, and slow to get angry"* (James 1:19b, NLT).

Asking two or three simple questions will move you from the surface emotions to the heart of the issue. One of the secrets of effective communication is to ask the person you are speaking with to restate his or her answer in a different way. By using VC, you are an active participant in the conversation, while at the same time fulfilling your need to contemplate before articulating.

The first three questions you need to ask to facilitate VC are:

1. What do you want for you?
2. What are you feeling?
3. What are you doing about it?

Another process is to introduce a clarifying question or statement:

1. Are you saying . . . ?
2. So you are saying . . . ?
3. So you mean . . . ?

I encourage going through these questions two or three times, which is likely to produce somewhat different answers each time. Answering differently helps a person go deeper. Often the presenting problem or communication isn't the real problem—a deeper issue exists that requires contemplation in order to reach the root of the situation.

The answers to these questions will give you a clearer understanding of where the other person is coming from and what, if any, the need for action might be. Once you have discovered the real issue to be discussed, you learn to articulate clearly and in a manner that is beneficial to both parties.

CONTEMPLATION—THE KEY TO SUCCESS

In leadership, the use of VC has been one of my keys to success. The verbal contemplation step is the point at which wisdom is birthed. I've learned that once my words are released I cannot get them back.

When a man moves into leadership, he must quickly learn that he cannot respond in like kind when presented with a crisis. When a person comes to me sharing about a crisis, I must first determine if what he or she is saying is from God's point of view or as a result of a personal, selfish perspective. If this person has not been forthright or balanced in his or her explanation of the situation, the verbal contemplation step keeps me from acting prematurely and making a wrong decision concerning the situation. If I misunderstand something in the contemplation step, the error will be on the side of caution rather than impulsivity.

In going through my own VC process, the questions I ask are designed to separate personal issues from God's purpose:

- What does God want for me?
- What does God feel about me?
- What does God want me to do?

Seeing oneself and the situation from God's perspective radically transforms the nature of human communication.

I have also discovered some simple "C" keys to effective communication. Effective communication includes the following dynamics:

- Clear—all people clearly understand what's being said.
- Consistent—a consistent message is continually communicated.
- Caring—caring commitment to God's best for the other person.
- Clean—pure and nondemeaning words of life to others.
- Confrontational—facing the truth and any need for repentance and forgiveness.

I have found that effectively using the verbal contemplation step also gives me time to deal with my own emotions. Asking questions and contemplating before articulating gives me time to see how much of me is in the decision. When people try to draw me into acting as a hammer for them, I implement the verbal contemplation process to keep me from reacting prematurely or incorrectly. I also find out if they are really asking me to help them or if they just want someone to agree with what they have already decided to do? Once I know the answer to what they really need, I can boldly proclaim the truth of God concerning that situation. A large part of being an effective leader means boldly communicating the truth to those who are called to follow him.

Your voice has been designed to produce a response. Your influence is exercised in your ability to manage outcomes through your voice. Your greatest strength is in your voice.

Dare to communicate effectively. Your relationships will be enhanced and your leadership will be respected!

I dare you to rediscover your God-given voice and determine to become a presence reflecting God's image and embracing God's assignment for you to speak.

- Reverse old negative behaviors and become a positive influence for those around you.
- Learn the voice of God in your life.
- Become skilled in the art of verbal communication. Speak clearly, so you are understood, and listen carefully, so you comprehend what you are hearing.

3

DARE
TO LEAD

*Progress is never deterred by a few steps
backward. True leadership is displayed
during difficult times. It is important
as a leader you correct some things,
overlook others, but see it all.*

MEN, YOU WERE CREATED TO LEAD. Leading means you establish your true self. When you deny the true you, you miss an opportunity to show that you possess strength, character, and ability. Establishing yourself is actually refreshing. Your opinions, points of view on significant issues, and conversational style reveal who you actually are; they reveal the real man. You must dare to lead!

When you conduct yourself as a leader, your leadership ability will be tested in at least two ways. First, the strength of your leadership is partially revealed when you are guiding others through a crisis. More important, the strength and integrity of your leadership ability is more profoundly revealed when you are in personal crisis yet continue to lead others effectively.

If you can lead only when there are no profound challenges in your own life, your credibility as a leader will suffer. Problems never show up when it is convenient. Men and women reveal their maturity when they handle unexpected problems with a calm and balanced approach.

Many men are what I call sweepers. It is a part of their God-given ability to gather and protect. Your development as a man is triggered as you care for others, as you become a man they can depend upon.

It is presumed to be outdated to regard leadership as a principal characteristic of manhood. Sometimes men try to hide their inclination to lead because they think it will be deemed offensive. Then, when a crisis arises, they are unsure if it is appropriate to establish their ability to provide directives.

A man's physical appearance hides a lot of things concerning the inner man. It is assumed because you have muscles and a deep voice, there is a sensitivity void. But many men are very rejection-sensitive. Approval means a lot to you and most men. We seek approval from family, friends, and females. It is the fear of rejection that keeps many men from volunteering to lead. The hesitancy to lead produces a lack of experience and decision-making ability.

Leadership is a characteristic needed in every phase of your life. The reluctance to lead is usually connected to your fear of rejection from a manhood perspective, along with a fear of making a mistake. We often leave the decision to someone else, observing and anticipating failure on the part of another decision maker. Men go to school on another man's experience. Gambling on perception and accountability are often easier to avoid than the vulnerable position you may feel when making decisions from a leadership perspective.

The avoidance of leadership responsibility inhibits your development as a man. Contrary to conventional wisdom, leaders are both born *and* made. There are some qualities that must be present, but they must also be developed. The leader in you requires a risk.

The people and church I lead are my first church. I have led in business, school, sports, and civic organizations, but those decisions were not as personal as the ones I make today, which are often life-and-death in their impact. There is no doubt in my mind that the success of that leadership is directly related to how I serve others. Leading does not prepare you for leadership, serving does.

Eighteen years ago, I took the responsibility of a very small congregation. We had about twenty-nine active members. There was a lot to be done and not many people to do it. I began to serve. Cutting grass, picking up paper, stripping paint, waxing floors, and cleaning bathrooms—whatever it took.

I acted as teacher in addition to all of that. It seemed the more I served the more there was to be done. I coined the phrase "Them that does does more," as I developed an appreciation for those who tried to serve along with me. The serving allowed me to set two standards: one for whoever would serve and a paradigm of sensitive leadership for myself. A man who has never cleaned a house will never fully appreciate what it takes to clean or maintain one. You can't lead effectively and productively when you have no appreciation for what it takes to accomplish the work. I learned how to lead by doing.

When I accepted this responsibility I was full of enthusiasm but had very little practical experience leading in this context. I had been a servant in every other ministry I had ever been a part of, however. I had always led from a practical position. The functions of the people I led were familiar to me because I had held those positions before. When it was my turn to lead, I had an idea of what it took to complete my directives. Serving gives you a better problem-solving perspective.

But you don't know you are a true leader until *you* get into trouble.

Nothing prepared me for the request of a family to make the decision to take a loved one off life support. I was called to a hospital one night. The comatose man's family was present. They wanted me to make the decision for them. I walked into the room. Grim is an understatement. As a spiritual leader I was supposed to know what to do. I considered how I would feel in the exact same situation.

I told the family to give the patient every opportunity to recover. They agreed. After a few days, there was no change. I returned, prayed, called the nurse, and made the decision for the family. They disconnected the man. The hardest thing to do was to bear the responsibility for the decision. The fear of the responsibility was a major issue. But leaders must lead by making very tough, unusual decisions.

FOR WOMEN

EXPECTATIONS

I am amazed by the expectations most women have concerning their need for a man to be a strong leader. Even if this characteristic was not desired during their early dating stages, it becomes evident and intense during the developmental stages of the relationship.

Many times, after a relationship has become intimate, you will assume you can occupy a more assertive position in the relationship. Intimacy often implies permission for both men and women to become more assertive and influential with each other. The confusion arises in intimate relationships when a man or a woman says,

"You don't know me well enough to ask me that," or "That's none your business."

When you say things like that, the value you place on yourself has suffered. Intimacy should be the result of a relationship where trust, communication, and complementary strengths have developed. Experience reveals the longer you are in a relationship, the more a person's character, nature, and tendencies are revealed. The true you was created to be exposed in your relationship. Whether it is with a sibling, relative, or coworker, or in a love relationship, a close or intimate bond will expose you—warts and all.

Intimate relationships reveal some profound differences between men and women. There is nothing wrong with that admission. It's the elephant in the living room of relationship. We are different, and we have a tendency to allow these differences to become negative rather than to serve their original purpose—delivering to each other what we cannot give ourselves.

The Bible is pretty clear on this: God made men and women in His image. There is no inferiority between the sexes, no subordinates or superiors from a value perception, no one sex dominating the other. God's design is one of mutual submission, shared responsibility, caring, and nurturing. We were created to reflect God's image individually. We were given particular roles and responsibilities.

Adam and Eve were given a set of challenges to reveal the abilities each of them possessed. Adam was operating in his assignment to name all of the animals and Eve in her interaction with the serpent. Both challenges were well within their ability to succeed, because both situations were within their God-given authority to influence a positive outcome.

God clearly has given us all an ability to lead, an innate ability to exercise authority that human beings were all created to possess. Both Adam and Eve were given the ability to successfully manage the challenges that each had been presented with. But men and women exercise leadership from remarkably different points of origin; about that there is little dispute. Both men and women were created in the image of God and given the ability and authority to effectively manage their minds and emotions to be leaders in their spheres of life.

HOW TO BEGIN TO LEAD–NOT DOMINATE–AS GOD INTENDED

You must master your emotions. The rule is to think first about what you want to accomplish in the situations you face. Thinking about outcome will give you time to check any disruptive emotion. Always remember: If it is going to go your way, there is no need to get upset.

Don't adopt the emotion of the situation as your own emotion. If it's an angry situation, *you* don't need to be angry. If everyone else is upset, *you* don't need to get upset. A calm and direct approach works in a crisis. This is true leadership.

You must listen well to react appropriately. Gather information to make an informed decision. Remember your power to persuade, not force, is one of your greatest strengths. Use the natural persuasiveness and power of your voice as you reflect the character of God.

Leaders must be patient. Approach a situation with a solution, but those you are leading must be won over to adopt your idea.

These are just a few characteristics of true leadership. You have been created to lead effectively, passionately, and sensitively.

I dare you to discover the leader in you, which means become a positive, consistent, and reliable man.

- Master your emotions.
- Discover the calm inside of you.
- Overcome the fear of rejection when you begin to lead.

4

DARE
TO SUBMIT

*Vision submitted to vision will
become your reality.*

T RUE SUBMISSION IS NOT the negative leader/submission dynamic that we've historically seen between men and women.
Submission was designed by God to yield a synergistic relationship, where the two work together to produce a result greater
than the sum of their individual capabilities. This cooperative action
is to be based on love and unity, so that the two will be greater than
either could be separately.

We learn from the Bible in the book of Ephesians that this syn-
ergism meant submitting to each other and to God (Ephesians
5:21–33). This is probably one of the most misunderstood passages
in the Bible. Somehow Bible readers overlook verse 21: "Submitting
yourselves one to another."

The idea of submission has been misconstrued by many who teach the principle. The Word does not teach that we men are dominant and should bully women, who must obey our every command. All principles in the Bible have been given for one purpose: unity. God gives us all the spiritual gifts to unite us. It is never God's intention to divide one child of God from another. God's ultimate aim is to produce unity.

The concept of Biblical submission is much maligned. To get at the truth, let's take a fresh look at the concept.

The very word "submission" seems to send ripples through a crowd. To many men, female submission is thought to be the birthright of all men and the only acceptable behavior for godly women. To many women, submission has become a profane word that is merely the means by which men seek to dominate women.

Submission can be understood as "loving cooperation between two people." Biblical submission, or loving cooperation, begins with mutual submission. Submission means to bring yourself under. That's why the Bible says to submit yourselves one to another.

Submission is supposed to be mutual between a man and a woman. You are not to be submitted to; you are supposed to first submit yourself. Submission is a sincere, intellectual, heartfelt act based on character rather than gender.

The Bible never teaches women to submit to men solely on the basis of gender.

God's Word says, "Submit yourselves . . . ," clearly defining self-submission for both genders. The misunderstanding of the concept, however, is rooted in Genesis 3:16 (NIV): "Your desire will be for your husband, and he will rule over you." Our understanding of submission has been perverted, mainly by unenlightened teaching and distorted cultural influences.

Scripture has been used to justify a number of human evils—from slavery to the Holocaust. God's Word can never rightly be used to sanction the abuse of another. Many Christians confuse obedience with submission. The traditional wedding ceremony has included the wife's promise to "obey" her husband. Scripture never instructs wives to "obey" their husbands. Rather, a love based on mutual respect is the guiding principle behind all decisions, actions, and plans (read 1 Corinthians 13).

Another misapplication of submission is that it applies only to the woman. In both precept and example, the Bible clearly outlines that submission is the lifestyle required of all Christians and that within committed relationships it is a mutual offering. Both partners are to live in daily, personal, and voluntary submission to Jesus Christ as Lord and Savior. Both partners, aware of their status as "heirs together" in Christ (1 Peter 3:7) and equal members of the Body of Christ (1 Corinthians 12) are uniquely gifted by God's Holy Spirit to build up the body of Christ and their own relationship.

FOR WOMEN

REAL SUBMISSION

Before there is any submission of wife to husband in a marriage, you both must already be submitting to each other in the Lord. You are not expected to put up with every ill-advised idea your spouse has just because he is male. If your family is not being led in a godly direction, it is the man who is first and most accountable to God—as it happened in Genesis 3:9. God holds the man responsible for taking his family in directions pleasing to the Almighty. This is not accomplished by shouting orders, but rather by the man setting an example of godly living and loving service and loving sacrifice.

So what does submission mean for you? It does not mean the man has the right to give orders—any orders—and you simply must comply. Rather, it means you are willing to let the man lead the family in a godly direction. Choose a man you *can* submit to. You can help by encouraging him to take on this God-assigned role.

If you are more qualified for leadership, do not usurp this role. Graciously help him learn to grow into it, if he is willing. Encourage and support him as he moves in that direction. When your man is playing the part he has been assigned, he will not be imposing his agenda on you, but you will grow toward Christ's will together.

Mutual submission invites into the relationship love, respect, honor, and dignity. This is the kind of relationship Adam and Eve were to manifest in the Garden—one of co-regency, rather than that of a superior over a subordinate. They were to rule with specific authorities that, when joined together, would operate successfully within the environment God had placed them.

What does submission look like for the man who dares to submit, not just in relating to women but to God, as a character issue? The crux of what it means for a man to dare to submit is this: Be accountable to others, responsible for your actions, courteous to others, and thoughtful. You are responsible to others as well as having your own authority. If you will be great, you must be a man of submission.

When you submit to those around you, your manhood is not diminished. It is actually cultivated. Productive submission is possible for you when you possess a positive self-image. You are developing a new image as you reflect the image of God.

Submission is not a loss of authority or power. It is an act of your will in the appropriate situation. You must know when to submit and when to lead. So wisdom is extremely important. Strength is not your challenge. Strength is not a man's greatest challenge. Wisdom, the ability to act appropriately, is often a great challenge for a man.

We are created to be refined in relationships, both professional and personal. Mutual submission is the key for you to discover who you are and can be as a man. We, as men, think of submission as a rule for women. But it is key to our personal discovery of our true manhood.

Submission, loving cooperation, is absolutely contrary to what I absorbed growing up, and maybe that is your experience also. But I dare you to discover a man hidden in you that is a sleeping giant of leadership and manhood by daring to submit.

I dare you to submit.

- Discover a deeper sense of caring.
- Lovingly cooperate with others.
- Accept responsibility.
- Reveal your character.

5

DARE
TO OBEY

*Your consistent obedience to God produces
sovereignty that expresses the image of
God working in you, as manifested in
your daily living. The Biblical truths
"by their fruits you shall know them"*
(MATTHEW 7:15–20) *and "faith
without works is dead"* (JAMES 2:14–26)
are important life considerations.

O BEDIENCE IS A key element in the development of your
manhood. It is one of the characteristics that produce a secure relational environment for those you love. Your obedience to God results in consistency, commitment, and what I like to call
a "safe place" to dwell for those we love. It creates a structure for
those we care about to be nourished and encouraged. When you understand and emulate the love of God, you develop consistency.
Obedience and consistency are two sides of the same coin.

Obedience and consistency lay the foundation for manhood and
balanced leadership. In order for you to be respected as an authority
figure, your own life must exhibit a consistent pattern of obedience

that includes a healthy respect for authority. Without that respect, you will have difficulty being in authority in the lives you touch. You see, when you understand the importance of following rules, you develop the steadiness and commitment needed to produce security in the lives of those for whom you care. Therefore, develop constancy in your work ethic, financial stewardship, and relationships. This dependability grows you up as a man and makes you a candidate for effective leadership in your spheres of influence—work, church, community, and family.

Adaptability is a critical component of consistency. It is the ability to adapt to the situations you face—to keep your commitments and meet your objectives—regardless of what changes around you. The most effective men develop a personal style that allows them to alter their approach to a problem depending on its type. Adaptability is essential, because you will face changing landscapes as you navigate your responsibilities.

Life is predictable only in its unpredictability. You may find it difficult to adapt to new situations, but inflexibility will render you ineffective to those you care for as they face challenges that need your support. Meeting problems with traditional methods when situational relevance is needed can sabotage your ability to become a meaningful participant in their lives. For example, your children need firm leadership and a strong father figure in their lives. But if you always approach their dilemmas with rigidity, you only succeed in shutting them out rather than drawing them closer.

The major challenges to adaptability often involve adjusting to new situations in family, financial challenges, and business. Certainly, tradition has its place in life. But locking into tradition can hinder the leader's ability to respond appropriately to new challenges, as the traditionalist attempts to fit contemporary situations into historic solutions.

This kind of inflexibility can cause you to miss important opportunities that can yield life-changing effects in people's lives.

My own adaptability was challenged when I was faced with an opportunity to rescue a young lady in a situation that was completely out of my personal and ministry comfort zone. A young lady who made her living as an exotic dancer—a stripper—had begun a relationship with God and joined our church. She then began to struggle with breaking from that lifestyle and the considerable income that it yielded her. She had a child and other financial obligations that made her feel she needed that level of income to survive.

She had allowed me to counsel her, and I began to understand the financial pressure she was under. Her lifestyle carried heavy financial obligations because she had responsibility for a child and she had acquired possessions that she was in debt to pay. She wanted a different life but was genuinely concerned with supporting herself and her child. As a church, we were modeling a lifestyle that challenged her sense of what was an appropriate livelihood for a godly woman. The members of the church embraced her and took her into their care. She began to see a productive side of the church community, but the pressures of her financial responsibilities were a constant challenge for her. Her involvement in the life of the church increased. She was doing well, but I recognized the pull.

I'd introduced her to a few people who had had similar experiences and were great examples of transformation. The interactions she had with the church in a brief time had given her a sense of security she had not felt in a long time. One of the most difficult transitions for her was getting used to people's concern for her future, rather than her past. They encouraged her, helping her understand that the church would be extremely active and supportive in her search for a new career. She began to have a different outlook, but the pressure of income and the insecurity of the transition lingered.

It was very clear to me that as a leader I had made a very positive impact on her life, showing concern and care without the agenda she had come to expect from all men. As a pastor, I saw a young woman who was intelligent, strong, energetic, and wounded. A person with options who had convinced herself that her present was the only option she had.

Consistency reveals a lot to the people whose lives you touch. As a pastor, I worked hard to improve the lives of the people I served, and she had watched me carefully. As she looked, she was searching for authenticity. She had watched with skepticism, at first, which evolved into admiration.

Then I heard rumors that she was working in the club again. I made a few discreeet inquiries and was not totally surprised to hear she was back at work in the strip joint. She was unresponsive to phone calls and messages sent to her from the church. I realized that because of the uniqueness of the situation, I would have to alter my approach. Leadership must adapt. This unusual situation needed an out-of-the-box solution. I managed to find out her stage name and called the establishment to see when she was working. Understanding my role as a leader and as her pastor, I drove down to the club. It was an extremely unusual place for a pastor to find himself, a nontraditional place for ministry. She was not lost, because I knew where she was, but she definitely was a lost sheep in Jesus' words.

I took some of my men with me as intercessors (believers experienced in conversing with God in prayer) and instructed them to stand outside, praying and watching. Admittedly, it was not the first time I had been to a "gentlemen's club." In my twenties, I had a friend who worked in one of those places. By this time I had reached my mid-fifties, and the sight of a woman partially dressed certainly was not a new experience for me. By then I had visited many women in hospitals and prisons.

I entered the club. It had been a long time since I'd been in such a place, but it seemed as if time had stopped inside. People were still going nowhere fast. I was immediately aware that I didn't fit in, but was not uncomfortable in any way. I was in no danger of being tempted and was not concerned about the opinions of those who recognized my face. I was there on business.

As my eyes adjusted to the darkness, I could see men drinking, laughing, and having a good time as their attention focused on the stage. Unlike them, I did not see a stripper onstage. I saw a daughter, now my spiritual daughter, in a place doing something her Heavenly Father and now her spiritual father could not abide. The sounds of the cheering crowd offended me—someone connected to me felt as though this was the only way she could live. Her nakedness only aroused feelings of anger and extreme disappointment. I was having a father's reaction.

Despite the many bouncers, I walked up to the edge of the stage and looked into her eyes. She froze like a deer caught in the headlights. At that moment, I knew that I was able to exercise the sovereignty God had given me in her life. As a spiritual father, I said, "You had better get down from there now and come with me."

I removed my trench coat and wrapped her in it. And I walked her out of there. The bouncers started toward us, but I cautioned them to step back, and told them, "I am taking her out with me." We walked through the crowd and out the door. The intercessors met us, and as we got into my car, I realized that I was actually getting an opportunity to be what I was calling myself: pastor.

The only thing that gave me the authority to speak into her life was the image that I had exhibited before her. Through my example she saw the love of God, strength, care, and consistency. She felt I was real because I had come to a place she never expected to see me and did what no one had ever done—rescue her from the situation. She needed a father to come and get his daughter. I looked her in the eye and said, "This day in your life is over and you are going on to another way."

She left that place with me and began a new lifestyle under Christian counsel and guidance that focused on God. She is married now, raising her children in a godly home environment and working in a God-honoring profession.

In my many years of pastoring, I have walked into crack houses and pulled ladies out who were having sex to trade for crack. I have gone in obedience to God, and with the authority I have been given as their pastor. (I'll talk about being a man of authority in the very next chapter.) I even took my gun, realizing where I was going. David did not go up to face Goliath with only a prayer! (1 Samuel 17). He picked up a rock and used the weapon God had trained him to use. David was true to his identity and adapted to his situation without compromising his perception of himself. So I took my weapon, appropriate accoutrement for the situation.

Don't get me wrong, brother. I am not telling you to start packing! What I am saying is that I was not operating in an unrealistic faith in an unusual situation. The crack house situation, like David's, required uncustomary preparation. I was prepared to handle the context I was entering, but it did not transform me into someone who felt he belonged there.

In both the crack house and the men's club, I was seen by people who thought it was inappropriate for a preacher to be seen in a strip joint or a dope den. They proceeded to spread rumors, either not knowing or not caring why I was there. But I remained sure who I was and was validated by the success of both situations.

Sometimes doing the right thing and obeying God is difficult because people don't always understand why. You have to know you're doing the right thing and allow that fact to validate your opinion of yourself, even when others doubt you. Sometimes obeying God can cause controversy and cause people to doubt your sincerity and commitment. But you must dare to obey.

LEAVE A POSITIVE LEGACY,
A LEGACY OF LOVE

Love of God, as the focus of your life, is the beginning of a life leading to unselfish love and the creation of a productive relationship legacy. In other words, negative relationship legacies are never changed without the love of God first transforming your heart so the fruit—the reality of your love—can be seen, tasted, and experienced by those for whom you care. This kind of "demonstrated love" helps build a legacy of strong relationship. This love legacy is the type of inheritance every man should leave to those he loves. It must be exhibited and taught if those who depend on you are going to be equipped to succeed where you may have struggled or failed.

God commands us all to love one another in an unselfish and sacrificial way. Your obedience to that command positions you to purposely change the way you love one another. It leaves a positive legacy while providing a safe place where those who love you can dwell. Whether it is in your work, recreation, business, or spiritual pursuits, your obedience will cultivate those around you, creating the type of manhood that is dependable for those who love you. Your obedience sets an example for those whose lives you impact. Imitation is the preschool of life, so when you are an obedient vessel, you express sovereignty into others' lives and teach them to be obedient.

How can your children choose to obey you if they have seen you being disobedient to God? The power of your authority is birthed out of your obedience and your integrity as a man. That obedience gives you leverage to express sovereignty in the lives of those people attached to you. Many men simply don't understand that obedience is the key that connects them to what God wants to do in their lives. It's important we open this concept a little further.

WHOM WILL YOU PLEASE?

God made the Garden of Eden a priority in the book of Genesis, immediately revealing that God is concerned with position. Adam and Eve were placed there and given a working promise called the Garden of Eden—a productive place where both man and woman could live a successful and enjoyable life.

His plan was for them to live perpetually in this prepared place. As long as they obeyed the rules, they enjoyed the grace of the Garden, which was the spontaneous overflow of God's love and provision for them.

Obedience is the positional guarantee of God. While they were obedient, they enjoyed the blessings of God. Their disobedience placed them under the judgment of God. Obedience kept Adam in his position in the Garden. Obedience gave him superiority over the animals. Obedience gave him sovereignty over the Garden itself. Obedience made him a leader to Eve, and obedience would have given him the power to correct and even rescue her.

Adam faced a test every adult must face: Will I ultimately please God or people? Your obedience affects your total environment. You are created to prosper within the three laws of environment/position, relationship/people, and laws/obedience. Instead of remaining at a productive level of obedience, he chose to compromise his relationship with God by going along with the perspective of someone he loved. Consistent obedience secures your position and establishes your commitment. Let's explore this equation in the next chapter.

The Bible teaches that we should leave a legacy of promise and blessings. That means not only does your life leave a positive influence but you leave a positive legacy for those you love. A legacy is a jewel that mature men and women see as one of their chief responsibilities as an adult.

No matter what type of life you decide to live, you will leave a legacy. Each time you speak, you are creating something potentially lasting in the hearer. That is probably why the Bible tells us to "season" our words with grace and be careful of saying thoughtless things to one another. Your words are always creating, but there is another powerful way to create legacy. You establish your legacy when you exhibit a history that is confirmed and validated by your words and actions. Predictable, consistent, obedient behavior lays the foundation for long-lasting positive memory. When you lay this type of foundation for legacy, those you love have confidence—both in you and in the relationship.

One of the keys to consistency is a basic understanding of your failure triggers. There is something you think or do consistently before you break consistency. One thing I've discovered about myself is I hardly ever fail to do something that is meaningless. The important things in my life are the things I don't want to do. Recreation is something I usually feel like doing. Work is something I don't feel like doing (more than I would like to admit!).

I've learned how to overcome a failure trigger. As soon as I don't feel like doing something, I know it must be important. So as I am saying to myself, "I don't feel like it," I am moving myself toward the task at hand. A man cannot allow his feelings to interfere with his consistency. Consistency will assist with adaptability.

When you are open to new ideas, the possibility for new success is possible. Those around you will benefit from their freedom to suggest and from your ability to hear new ideas and apply new solutions. A man with a legacy of openness to new things will most often benefit from perspectives that are different from his own. As I've told you before, consistency produces security. Positive consistency, which actually builds a solid foundation in a man's mind, is rarely threatened by new ideas. Be open to different perspectives to mature and build a strong legacy.

FOR WOMEN

ADAPTING TO HIS CONSISTENCY

A man's consistency can be a two-edged sword. Most consistent men will feel challenged when their reliability is chastised. You know, when you want him to break his pattern but he refuses. You may have chastised him because you wanted him to do something uncharacteristic. This is a trade-off you may have to get used to.

His consistency is not simply what he does, it is who he is. He will feel as though you only want his consistency when it fits your agenda. Don't allow yourself to be frustrated by something you really value in him. Look at the big picture of your relationship. It will minimize your frustration.

Because you are a woman, your consistency will be an inspiration to the significant men in your life. When you dare to obey (roles, structure, authority), that obedience builds the consistency needed for success in your every endeavor.

With obedience comes the development of a personal standard. Be true to that standard. It will produce an expectation in your life.

Don't lower your expectations and standards to please anyone, especially those who have no standards for themselves.

■

I dare you to obey, set the standard for your life, and keep your expectations high.

- Leave a legacy of love. Obey God's command to love one another in an unselfish and sacrificial way.
- Break the cycle of failure by recognizing your own triggers for failure.

- Learn to adapt. Develop a personal style that allows you to alter your approach to a problem depending on its type.
- Commit to consistent obedience that will produce the kind of consistency that leaves a legacy of reliability, accountability, and dependability.

6

DARE TO TAKE
AUTHENTIC AUTHORITY

If you are truly in authority,
don't get upset. Why scream,
if it's going to go your way?

THE EXPERIENCE OF extracting my parishioner from the strip club probably impacted my life as much as hers, because I realized the God-given authority within me to impact the lives of people assigned to me. In that moment I was a man daring to reflect the image of God. By going into that club, refusing to participate in the sin, and literally taking control of the situation, I modeled the example given to us by Jesus.

Jesus, on the cross, teaches us a lesson in the importance of self-perception. He never lost contact with his mission, although He was in a place of apparent isolation. He looked beyond his excruciating physical pain to make sure His mother was taken care of, to guarantee one of the thieves crucified alongside Him a place in heaven, and to ask God to forgive those who orchestrated His unjust conviction. Jesus never lost connection with Himself, His image, or His perception of Himself. His life situation did not alter His identity.

Many people find themselves changing their beliefs, convictions, and perception of themselves with each adverse season they face. A man or woman must be secure in his or her beliefs and self-perception in order to stay true to self during critical seasons in life.

When the apostle Paul says, "I have become all things to all men" (1 Corinthians 9:22), the strong implication is, "But I don't compromise who I am for those people." This is an important Biblical and life principle. Paul's lesson in self-perception is based on another concept discussed previously.

When a man or woman understands he or she is created in the image of God, a new dimension of self-perception occurs. Your lost sense of value is rediscovered as you begin to attain what the Bible calls a renewal of your mind. A renewed mind operates from the context of God and a new destiny rather than a negative past. When self-perception is stable, you will stay true to yourself even when you are in the company of those who may not share your morals and beliefs.

There is a Biblical story of a young man called the prodigal (see Luke 15). He was raised in a good home with a father who presented a consistent example of his beliefs and morals. The son decided he wanted to dissociate from his family structure and leave home. Using the money his father graciously had given him, the young man went as far away from home as he could. He connected with a crowd living a lifestyle that contradicted his upbringing. He was influenced by them to his detriment. He completely detached from who he was raised to be.

He partied with his newfound friends until his money ran out, engaging in a lifestyle he would have never considered at home. When the money was gone, however, he realized that he had gone from being a prince to a slave. He had lost his perception of himself. As he contemplated his fallen position, the Bible says he came to himself. The implication is that he was ready to reconnect with his true identity.

In 1 Corinthians 9:19–23 (NIV), Paul says:

> *Though I am free and belong to no man, I make myself a slave to everyone, to win as many as possible. To the Jews I became like a Jew, to win the Jews. To those under the law I became like one under the law (though I myself am not under the law), so as to win those under the law. To those not having the law I became like one not having the law (though I am not free from God's law but am under Christ's law), so as to win those not having the law. . . . To the weak I became weak, to win the weak. I have become all things to all men so that by all possible means I might save some. I do all this for the sake of the gospel, that I may share in its blessings.*

Although it might seem like he is taking on many roles and molding himself to please others, the truth of the matter is that he *is* being true to his identity. He knows who he is and what his role is—to share the word of God. When he came into contact with people who did not believe as he did or have the kind of life rules he had adopted for his life, he did not compromise his beliefs or his conduct.

A significant part of God's plan for men is for us to realize that whatever environment we are in, we have the ability and the responsibility to be fruitful, multiply, replenish, and subdue if we dare to take authority. That means a life of consistent productivity, the ability to add to that productivity, and the strength to recover from economically challenging times and to regain control when circumstances appear to have gone out of control.

Every man is equipped to bring any situation under control, no matter how chaotic it might appear. Doing so requires the same objectivity you use when you observe your favorite team play a game. As an observer, you can discern what your team has done incorrectly and see clearly what they need to do to recover. This is something you do instinctively.

Most of us men exercise more of this kind of control outside of our relationships rather than within. It is a common mistake.

While watching a game, you are aware of all of the variables—who is performing well, what player is being utilized according to his strength, and who needs to be pulled from the game, as well as the strengths and weaknesses of the opposing team. When you become aware of your instinctive God-given ability to manage any number of variables at the same time, this principle becomes a dominant characteristic in your life. You gain a new understanding of your ability to help those you care for when they are in distress and add to your résumé of strength and respect. You become a calming presence amid confusion. When things are chaotic, your loved ones look to you for a reasonable solution. Others say things like, "As soon as you got here, I felt better." You instill confidence even in the midst of uncertainty.

This control has very little to do with physical strength and everything to do with the authority of God that is reflected in a man's voice. When you know who you are in Christ and speak with your God-given authority, you can successfully take control of a situation. For example, I have a 138-pound dog that is fully capable of physically overpowering me. But I don't use physical power or even shout at him to get him to obey me. I merely speak to him in the authority I have been given and he obeys.

A father can come home, speak with quiet authority, and take control over what the mother has been battling against all day long.

When you reign with God-appointed sovereignty in your environment, there is an authority that God releases in your voice that will command peace and restore order. Jesus, aware of His authority over the environment, spoke peace to the storm and it had to obey Him. When you have been consistently obedient to God within your environment, your voice reflects the authority of your position and you can effectively take control over the storm and the chaos.

When you have been consistently obedient to your Heavenly Father, your authority is no longer questioned. It may be challenged but not questioned. Your influence effectively reduces the degree of explanation you have to offer when making a decision that affects those under your authority. They have become so secure that when you make a judgment call, they know you have done your homework and sought the Father's heart in the situation. There is no need for them to ask a thousand questions. They know it is going to be the right decision and that you are in control of the situation. But this type of security can only come when those around you have witnessed your consistent obedience to God and experienced the good fruit of your decisions. This authority is not given; it must be earned.

Conversely, if you are inconsistent in your obedience, your every decision will be questioned, sometimes unreasonably, because those under your authority feel no sense of security in the relationship. They wonder, "Are we going to have to go through all this again? What if he is making a mistake? How can I know that what he is suggesting is the best way to deal with this situation?" These questions are not necessarily questioning your authority but are the result of fear caused by your inconsistency.

A Man, His Mother, and You

Males often process early experiences with negative authoritative female examples either by becoming overly aggressive or as manly as milk. A man who has had all of the fire taken from him has been convinced by example that nonconfrontation is the only way to get along with the significant women in his life.

If you're involved with such a man, the relationship problem for you is that at some point you will need him to assert himself and he will not be able to.

Or maybe you chose a man who has adopted a legacy of victimization. Feeling his authority is nonexistent, he tries to overpower you in the relationship. Sometimes these feelings are worked out by extreme aggression or predatory sexuality. Sex becomes the only way his masculinity is validated for him to feel dominant and in charge.

You may have met a man who seems to want you to care for him, yet he shows little appreciation, often using aggression or sympathy to get what he wants. At times you've wondered if he was slightly amused by whatever difficulty you faced. It may even have felt as though he derived pleasure from your problems, while offering you little or no support. He may be revealing a benign hostility.

You want a more assertive man but you love this guy. Meanwhile, he desires a woman with whom he is able to be a man, but this relationship feeds his issue. You fear a strong man and the vulnerability you feel from previous relationships, while he can only satisfy his need to feel equal by exploiting your weaknesses and enjoying your struggles.

Neither of you can provide a safe place to be loved until he dares to become a man of authority.

God has given every man the strength and ability to protect those who have been assigned to his responsibility. As a man, you must welcome the challenges of life, because they confirm that strength and ability to protect and your commitment to lead a consistently obedient life. As you meet the challenges of life, you begin to discover the ability God has given you.

The fundamental problem with strength is that you really don't know how strong you are until your capacity is tested. Another issue with strength is what I call the "professional boxer syndrome." That is, you don't really know how much strength the last crisis used until you get into the next challenge. For example, most professional fighters are not aware they should have retired until the lack of ability is revealed in the present battle.

Always remain aware of your ability to handle adversity. A tough situation can leave you with the strength but not the desire to fight again. To take authority, you must be keenly aware of your strength and understand you are wired to increase in strength during adverse times.

STRATEGIES FOR HANDLING ADVERSITY

Never adopt the emotional nature of the adversity as your own. The leader can't panic in front of the troops. Moses couldn't panic with the Red Sea before him and Pharaoh's army behind him. Martin Luther King Jr. couldn't panic facing crowds of hostile protesters while the FBI was constantly peering into his life. As a responsible man, you can't panic when the waves of adversity sweep over your life.

Listen for logic and truth in whatever is being explained to you. Rely on your past experience in handling a similar problem. It may not be the exact same problem, but there will be characteristics similar to other problems you have faced. Always analyze the natural and the spiritual aspects of the situation.

When a problem is presented to me with a lot of emotion, I usually ask a few fundamental questions to figure out if the problem is life-threatening or life-altering. Are you terminally ill or are you in physical danger? That question usually brings the SS *Panic* back down to earth! After the panic has subsided, you can begin to get a more rational explanation of the problem or events that have caused the turmoil. You are now establishing yourself as a calming, rational presence. This is a key for you as a man. You are establishing the strength of your presence and voice. As a man, you will be sought out for your wisdom based on an established track record. Don't fall into the trap of adopting the emotion of the person or the intensity of the situation as your own.

As a man who leads in the lives of those you love, you begin to welcome the challenges you must face. In so doing, you are confirmed as an authentic man and leader.

You discover what kind of man you really are when faced with a problem. You exercise your authority based on how consistently you have chosen to model obedience. The more you tap into God's image, the more you know of divine principles and commands. The more consistent and obedient you become, the easier you make it for those assigned to your life to be connected to you.

The Bible says we know the true identity of trees by the fruit they bear (Matthew 12:33). The tree/fruit example is really about authenticity. It reveals a principle concerning how people will come to believe you are who you profess to be. Your authenticity as a leader is established through consistent behavior that reinforces the words you have spoken. When you model this kind of behavior, confidence and a sense of legitimacy become a part of your persona. Those you love now have a standard of behavior to emulate.

FOR WOMEN

STANDARDS

As a female, you probably established your standard of treatment by watching significant mature males interact with the key women in their lives. You may have watched how your father treated your mother or how your neighbor treated his mother. Basing your conclusions on these interactions with male authority figures, you may have learned and accepted unacceptable behavior in your adult life.

As a girl, you probably dismissed the way your brother or other male relatives treated females. But you were more likely to view treatment from male authority figures with a sense of legitimacy and acceptance.

Until your acceptance of such behavior can be connected to early life examples, you may continue to accept treatment you logically acknowledge is wrong for you. To understand the quality of your relationships with men, begin by looking back at the examples firmly rooted in your psyche during your developmental years.

One of the first things a man must accept in order to develop authentic authority is the absolute necessity for time, patience, and consistency. The consistency time factor is essential to the development of authority. It takes time for you to develop a reputation for reliability.

Reliability is one of the foundations for the acceptance of your authority as a man. When your word can be depended on, you will develop the influence you need in order to exercise authority. As your words and actions become more consistent, those who depend on you will develop greater respect. The number one reason for authority rejection is inconsistency and demanding from others what you do not demand of yourself.

Be an example of what you stand for. It does not mean you won't occasionally make a mistake. But the mistakes must be occasional in order for those you lead to trust your leadership. If you want to be a leader, the standard set for you by others will be higher than the one they set for themselves. It goes with the territory.

You will ultimately gain more respect with an authoritative style that is loving, firm, and flexible without diminishing your ability to appear consistent. Influence, not force, is the style that develops authentic authority.

I dare you to decide to demonstrate authentic authority.

- See yourself as created in God's image and be secure in your self-perception.
- Shift from the power of your voice to the influence of your voice.
- Recognize that time, patience, and consistency are essential in order to develop authentic authority.
- Be consistently obedient to God and your authority will not be questioned.

7

DARE TO HAVE A STRONG SENSE OF SELF

Discover the thing that makes you special.
Admit what you don't do well,
then change it.

I WAS IN A board meeting at a nationally known university when one of the board members, a lawyer, began to question my position as a political and religious leader. After a few moments of conversation, it became very clear his problem was not with my politics but my vocation as a pastor and the success of my work. The conversation had a very subtly unpleasant tone, based on his view of religious leaders. He finally stopped talking in general terms and began to question my motives for being in ministry. He started by assuming I was not doing anything to benefit the community—taking care of the seniors and children—and finally moved on to my political involvement. He indicted my political involvement as ungodly. According to him, I had no place in politics. I explained to him the Biblical basis for influencing the political process. Every Biblical king (political figure) has a prophet or priest (religious figure). Doing the work of God set me at odds with this person. The straw that broke the camel's back was his assumption that I could not be believed!

I asked him who in the business world was known for lying more than lawyers. The conversation stopped. I did not defend or doubt myself because I know who I am.

At some time or another we all have faced making a decision that placed pleasing a person at odds with God's will. Most people will tell you they want a relationship with someone who seeks to do the right or the godly thing when making decisions, but we find ourselves facing the challenges of pressure from peers, family, friends, and loved ones.

There have been times in my life when trying to do the right thing has caused people to develop feelings of resentment toward me. I have been accused of trying to act perfect. "Not-everyone-is-as-perfect-as-you" resentments have taught me that trying to do the correct thing is not always appreciated. You would think most people would welcome a person trying to live a consistent, godly lifestyle, but instead many feel negative pressure from it. By negative pressure I mean a person who feels that you have a standard too high to live up to. The person feels unqualified to be in a relationship with you.

I was in a very serious relationship for a number of years with a woman. We got along pretty well, and had aspirations and many likes and dislikes in common. We did have a few upbringing issues and differences, but nothing severe enough to compromise the strength of the relationship. Both of us tried to adjust these minor differences— at least we thought they were minor until the relationship became more committed and the expectations began to deepen.

Even when I was unsaved I was not a bad man. I was considered a good catch in the context of my life at the time. As the relationship progressed, I began to act in accordance with what I thought was a man putting away childish things.

Then I got saved.

I began to change for the better, and she acknowledged there was a positive transformation. She liked the change and its benefits to her in the relationship. I never pressured her to take the same steps or adopt my beliefs. I assumed the changes she saw in me would be enough motivation to inspire change in her.

Then hell came to visit.

She explained she thought I was a much better man now that I was saved. I treated her better, and was more committed, consistent, considerate, and understanding—a better communicator and all-around better to be with. I had begun to obey the principles in the Bible, especially those concerning a man's role and the type of image that should be presented. She said I had always been a good man and was growing into a better person each day. So what was the problem? I was no longer the person she had fallen in love with.

So let me get this straight. I am better but it's a problem? We talked until I understood. She felt pressured to, in her words, measure up. She was not inspired by my change for the better. She had some habits she felt I would not want to deal with. I was willing to try to work through them. That's not what she wanted. She began to test the limits of the relationship, doing all the things my life did not represent. She finally asked me to make a choice between her and God. She lost.

When I talked to her a few years later, she had gotten hooked up with a guy whose life was really different from mine but who left her room to continue to do the things she felt our relationship didn't. Her life had stopped cold. She regretted her decision to take offense at the change in my life rather than being inspired by it. It was a change she said she really needed.

I had been fairly consistent before my conversion, but the reason was entirely *self*-motivated. My radical change began with an ever-increasing commitment to God. I had relinquished trying to conform to the image of a woman and started to be a man pleasing in the sight of God. It helped me understand the spiritual challenge of trying to conform to an image pleasing to God rather than a woman. (Both men and women share this difficulty.)

The average man spends his life cultivating an image that will please a woman. You buy the kind of car and wear the kind of cologne that you think will attract a woman. You rehearse the lines and dress in a way that you think will appeal to that special woman. In so doing, you are, in fact, presenting yourself as bait. As a general rule, a man is not cultivating godly characteristics to attract that special lady he believes is important to his personal happiness. Instead of asking God what he should do, he thinks, "What would that special *she* like me to be?"

As a result of this kind of thinking, the image you project appeals only to the carnal side of a woman. You aim to please her fallen nature rather than attract her via the divine nature. When there is no spiritual side fed in this relationship, the woman will never be fully satisfied. You have succeeded only in attracting the deceitful lusts in that woman. Eventually, she will need the commitment and security that only a godly man can provide. (Women fall into the same trap.)

FOR WOMEN

JEKYLL AND HYDE

I have talked to many men and women who feel as though being reliable, conservative, and consistent are not the preferred characteristics in male-female relationships. Many conservative men feel that women want a good man who is also a bad boy. Those same women, however, don't want to be asked to represent anything other than their true personality themselves. Many attractive women with great personality and mobility feel they are not appreciated because they do not represent the classic standard of beauty and are overlooked for someone who has the look but very little else to offer.

Both men and women feel that the standards for relationship and attraction change too rapidly and they have become insecure regarding their ability to compete in what should be a much less stressful situation. I believe I may be able to shed some light on this subject. Men and women alike are attempting to appeal to the fallen side of one another rather than the God side. The appeal is usually to the flesh first—the visual. But after time passes and there is a need for other qualities, many men and women find themselves disappointed in the person they once found irresistible.

Often women have been raised to think the priority in life is to get a man. You are supposedly incomplete without one. It has become almost instinctive rather than choice. In this quest, you learn how to appeal to a man's flesh. It's a "Look at this! Mine is better than hers, bigger than hers, or nicer than hers."

The fleshly appeal has become an accepted part of the dating process. The accentuation of body parts is almost primal in its purpose; highlighting those "assets" that lead to a mating ritual is all too common.

For both sexes it is proof of the insecurity we feel regarding whether we can compete with others of the same sex. Substance has become a secondary concern. Realize there is a consistency between what you offer as the attracting factor and the reason a man is initially attracted to you. First impressions will often set a tone for the rest of the relationship. You may get a man's attention with your looks and dress, but that cannot sustain a meaningful relationship. If the relationship does not develop past an immature external appeal, there is likely to be a problem of perception and expectation in the immediate future. Relationships built solely on flesh appeal rarely develop into a lifetime commitment.

Your sense of self will begin to develop when you decide on a life goal. A strong sense of self does not mean you develop insensitivity to the opinions and perceptions of others. You still must get along well with people to be successful in life, but the idea is to mold yourself into an image that pleases God first, and you will ultimately please the balanced, rational people you interact with.

The key is choosing the consistent expectation of God versus the rapidly changing expectation of the opposite sex or the latest media-driven perception of who you should be and what should be important to you. It is difficult to develop a consistent secure sense of self if your life priorities are constantly changing.

You must discover your created, God-given purpose. That becomes your goal for self-development. That discovery gives you a solid foundation on which to build. Then begin to surround yourself with people to whom you give an influential voice who have the same goal principles.

Remember, the expectation of people cannot become the foundation for your sense of self. The opinions of others can help you identify the correctness of your path, as well as help to correct your perceptions when you stray from well-accepted positive character traits. You will never become a consistent individual with a strong sense of self if your sole desire is to mold yourself in the image of a person whose priorities, likes, and dislikes change every thirty days.

Last, be honest with yourself about yourself. Lying to yourself about your accomplishments and failures will damage your ability to build a strong, responsible, consistent you.

I dare you to discover who you really are.

- Look at who you are and recognize whom you have spent your life trying to please.
- Mold yourself in an image that is primarily and ultimately pleasing to God.
- Have confidence in your accomplishments. Let your accomplishments defend you.

8

DARE
TO COMMIT

*Wisdom demands commitment. Don't ever
underestimate the power of the process.*

ISTORICALLY, commitment has been perceived as something
that is validated and generated from outside of us. Real commitment requires deep inner resolve. It is based on something inside of you. It has little to do with the other person's
behavior. We all operate on a level of *real* commitment at times, even
if we don't realize it. For example, you are very consistent in some
things you do. Going to work when you don't feel well, meeting a
friend who is always in a crisis, keeping a friendship for years with
someone who is difficult to like, or simply making your bed each
day—all reveal a level of real commitment. In all of these examples,
you say something to yourself concerning the activity that is not nec-

essarily based on the behavior of the other person or the nature of the circumstance. We normally don't call this type of behavior commitment, but it really is. You have already demonstrated the ability to be committed to things, places, and people where there is not much guarantee of reciprocity.

Love and family relationships test commitment in a more intense way because relationships require you to overcome behavior in others that appears designed to break your commitment. You probably have experienced some people and situations that are extremely difficult to navigate, yet they have revealed the strength of your attachment.

Commitment also has a negative side. This kind of commitment is reflected, for example, by staying in the wrong job for all the *wrong* reasons, or remaining loyal to an ungodly boss. This kind of commitment is a silent inner pact that one has made with oneself that one will stick this out no matter what. Often we allow this type of commitment to overrule common sense. The problem is, we forget that we are made in the image of God, not in the image of the world. We gauge our level of success more on our record of loyalty than we do on what we have accomplished within God's plans for us.

Real commitment is essential in your relationship with a woman. But this commitment must be built on recognizing and responding to the image of God within you. A healthy relationship can happen only when you as the man set the standard through consistent obedience to God, which leads to a commitment to righteousness, a lifestyle of faithfulness, and a woman who matches that commitment and lifestyle.

As previously discussed, obedience and consistency go together. They have to be together. These two traits express God's image in you and bring security to everyone connected to you. Mystery in a relationship breeds uncertainty and insecurity, while predictability produces security. There probably have been situations and relationships in your life when reliability did not exist. Not knowing what to expect from a person makes it difficult to commit and damages confidence in that person.

In order to commit, you need to know you can be dependable. Dependability is a characteristic of love. Being involved with someone who is physically present but emotionally unpredictable is a very anxious way to live. Those you care for need to know by your actions they can depend on you.

Commitment is also reflected in openness. There are enough unknowns in life. Keeping someone on a need-to-know basis does not foster confidence in you or the relationship. It only teaches those who love you to protect their feelings from you. Mystery and unaccountability will always contribute to insecurity. Positive predictability, birthed out of consistency and obedience to God, will always produce security. This kind of security is established in a home where the man diligently seeks to know God's will and God's heart. He desires to reflect the image of God in his family unit.

Many men ask me how they can know God's will. There is no real mystery to knowing the will of God. The will of the Almighty is always connected to acceptance of the Word—the Bible. God's mind and heart are completely revealed in the Bible. So if you desire to know the will, heart, and mind of God, you can find it there. All it requires is a decision to come into agreement with the eternal wisdom provided there. A sincere belief in the reality of God has to precede acceptance of the Bible as God's way of speaking to you. "But without faith *it is* impossible to please *Him,* for he who comes to God must believe that He is, and *that* He is a rewarder of those who diligently seek Him" (Hebrews 11:6, NKJV).

Commitment has four key components: diligence, patience, obedience, and consistency. They are the four parts of the same key that opens the door to truly accomplishing God's plans for you as a man of commitment. We've discussed obedience and consistency in Chapter 5. Let's look at the former two components.

"Diligence" is a word the Bible uses for stamina and patience. Diligence is never seasonal. It has to become a part of your character in order for you to accomplish it. Diligence means you focus on the mission at hand despite the things that come to distract you from your goals and commitments. Every man faces three challenges when he leaves his home each day: the intoxication of wine, the lure of money, and the temptation of the opposite sex. I call them booze, bucks, and booty. You probably recognize that you face at least one of these challenges each day when you venture out. To stand strong against these influences, you must be focused on the importance of your assignment and stay connected to the will of God. Diligence makes you stormproof.

You become stormproof when you overcome previous challenges. If you respond with persistence and diligence, the experience gives you greater strength for the next challenge. A new code is established within you. Diligence causes you to model responsibility.

A MODEL OF RESPONSIBILITY

As a model of responsibility, you accept principles as rules of conduct and engagement for your life. You adopt standards. The affection you have for your life assignments impacts how you approach your responsibilities as well as your destiny. When you accept your role of responsibility and accountability, especially in unfavorable circumstances, you emerge stronger and wiser with a greater sense of who you are.

Your model of responsibility reveals your ability as a true leader who can be depended on in a time of crisis. You birth confidence and security in those you love and become the go-to man in your family and among your friends and coworkers. You establish a presence that exudes confidence and safety.

My grandfather was a tower of strength to me. I still find comfort in his memory even though he has been dead for almost forty years. A man who is faithful to his life assignment with excellence and consistency will speak to those he loves through the life he lives. It should be the hope and goal of every man to leave a legacy that perpetually speaks to those he loves.

When you dare to model responsibility, and do so diligently, according to the principles of God, the woman in your life begins to have a different relationship with and expectation from you. She begins to have confidence, feel confident, because she knows you. This is a place many men desire to occupy in the mind of a woman, but they are excluded because they have settled for acting macho rather than being a man.

You have to decide responsibility and commitment are your friends. They are inseparable. You must develop a working relationship with them. Unfortunately, "commitment" has become a controversial word that many women feel men fear or don't know how to define.

You have to mean what you say. The seriousness of what you say is confirmed by what you do. Commitment must be consistent or a man will develop a reputation for unreliability. A loss of respect will not be far behind. Constantly keep in mind that your daily behavior is creating a perception at home, at work, or in the community. A reputation for responsibility is built on consistency.

One of the things I remember most about my grandfather was his reliability and consistency. These two qualities were so strong in him that I never expected him to fail in his commitments. I had confidence he could do whatever he said he could. That consistency made him the willing rock of our entire family. As a man, you must build a legacy of reliability.

FOR WOMEN

LOVE: IN SPITE OF OR BECAUSE OF

One of the hardest things to do is love someone in spite of himself. We have been instructed in the Bible to love one another with the love of God. That kind of love is based on the value the giver places on the object. It has little to do with the value the object places on the giver. This kind of love is sacrificial by nature, not usually looking for love, loyalty, or demonstrated appreciation in return. It is a love like that of God, who felt a sacrifice was not too high a price to pay for the salvation of the world. Its foundation is not in anticipation of a return but rather finds its bedrock in that love developing the beloved. It is a difficult love to give, but it can be done in the right context.

We can never love as completely as God, because we need to feel we are appreciated to feel fulfilled. But when love based on the model of God is shared by two people in a relationship, it brings a sense of fulfillment to both. When both are committed, a safe place to dwell called love is created, and God's design for the man-woman relationship is experienced.

A man or woman must become easy to love by fostering a relationship atmosphere that nourishes and cherishes the one loved. Each adult has to act with a sense of maturity when the usual challenges of life occur. You can never be quite sure how trustworthy an individual will be in a crisis unless you allow enough time for life to present enough challenges to reveal how the person you love reacts to the unexpected and troublesome aspects of life.

Love can be an adventure full of mountains and valleys, pleasant and stormy days. A relationship with the wrong individual will develop either commitment or stubbornness. Sometimes I am not sure which one.

I was in a relationship with a very challenging woman. She was a train wreck and a tornado wrapped in a very attractive casing. Her frailty and instability, in hindsight, fed into my need to be needed. I liked fixing things, turning things around for her. She became a major project.

The problem was she did not see anything negative about herself. Her family had given up and then I showed up. At first I was committed, then I became stubborn. Finally I realized stubborn commitment is insane.

PATIENT ENDURANCE WITH PRACTICALITY

Patient endurance is wise, realistic, and practical. Patience is the ability to stand in wait without panic because of your faith in God. It represents stamina even while you feel stuck in a holding pattern waiting for God to intervene. Patient endurance means possessing a calm persona while time and circumstance converge to bring about change. This characteristic in a man is a product of consistent obedience. Consistent obedience builds your ability to stand firm in unfavorable situations while you work through your problems and the problems of others. It is your faith revealed in your God-given abilities and the power of God in your life.

Sincerely walking in the image of God empowers you to patiently endure the process others may go through in finding victory in their own lives, and to remain committed to them. You can work through personal disappointments while fighting personal and relational battles that others deem lost causes. You may have a child who appears to be beyond hope, but like Michelangelo, you see something in the stone no one else does. Or you see a tedious project to completion because you understand it will have value in the future. This strength is fortified in you as you go to work each day, seemingly fighting an uphill battle because you understand that your family's welfare hangs in the balance. When you live in God's image and understand your own sovereignty, you can tirelessly fight on, knowing God has equipped you to prevail. You know victory is at hand.

A little earlier, I talked to you about patience. In most of your minds, patience may have a weak connotation. In our society patience can be synonymous with weakness or with missing an opportunity, or can be seen as a characteristic of senior citizens. It is actually a vital tool of observation and success. A vital tool, because patience is endurance.

Patience has an observation component. While one is exercising commitment to anything, patience is absolutely necessary. It will be easier for you to exercise patience and commitment if you have thoroughly thought through the process of what it is you are waiting for. Most men and women become impatient when the process of reaching a goal has not been a part of their thought process.

So patience is developed by thinking through the process of achieving a thing and reflecting on similar circumstances you and others have faced. Experience is a key element in developing patience because experience gives you hope when facing new situations.

I dare you to become consistent by becoming a man of your word, so positively consistent that your reputation and legacy are radically changed and your diligence becomes a source of inspiration to others.

- Be open in relationships to foster security and confidence.
- Respond to challenges with persistence and diligence.
- Remember that we are made in the image of God, not in the image of the world.

9

Dare
to Forgive

*Force and physical strength should
never be a man's signature,
but rather forgiveness.*

W HEN YOU AS A MAN in Christ consistently exhibit the character or fruit of the Spirit of God, mercy and grace become
a natural overflow of your desire to reflect the image of
God. When you are secure in your role, you can easily extend mercy
and grace to those in your sphere of influence. The man who desires
to walk in God's image must also interact with others with in-depth
understanding of people in their life struggles.

We learn of the inextricable connection between mercy and the
grace of God in the Garden of Eden. God walked with Adam and
Eve to get a close-up view of fallen creation. God came from heaven

to understand them, and instead of destroying them for the choices they'd made, God extended grace and mercy. God forgave them both for what they had chosen to do and provided life for them anyway. When Adam and Eve fell in the Garden, justice was appropriate, but grace was dispensed. They deserved justice, judgment, and condemnation, but grace tempered God's reaction to their sin. This concept is consistent throughout scripture. God's mercy and grace are always in place before judgment. God's mercy and grace allow love to prevail in our lives when justice is exactly what we deserve.

The law of the Old Testament finds its spiritual fruition in the grace of the New Testament. Grace is only mentioned once or twice in the Old Testament, but it exists as a principle in God's interaction with humanity. Grace adds a new dimension to the law, largely unidentified in the Old Testament but experienced by God's people. Grace precedes judgment. So instead of justice—destruction or punishment—God chastises us. God's love overrides His anger.

The leadership a man brings to those he loves must always be tempered with mercy and grace. When you remember the grace God freely gave you, you will lead with love as a primary characteristic. Force and physical strength should never be the central features of your leadership style. Grace and love are the foundations of God's relationship with us.

Grace reflects the love of God. As you reflect the character of God in your daily living, you will extend grace to those in your life. By operating in consistent obedience to God, you develop an understanding for the trials of your significant others. This understanding produces an overriding sense of forgiveness or grace. You must possess the ability to forgive, which can only be birthed out of building your capacity for patient endurance.

Being called to impart the truth of God into a relationship requires the capacity to forgive. You have to give people room to make mistakes. Sincerely walking in the image of God empowers you to forgive the gravest offenses while patiently enduring the process others may go through to be victorious in their own lives.

FOR WOMEN

STRENGTH TO FORGIVE

Many women are not used to a consistent, obedient man who is forgiving. If you are accustomed to relationships with inconsistent, unforgiving men, you may have an adjustment problem. This new kind of relationship may be what you've always wanted, but you continue to react according to expectations from the past.

There is a period in a new relationship like this when your man will feel underappreciated. When old negative feelings surface, your man should try not to react emotionally, but rather consider the relationship experiences you've had.

Even though your man should be patient, remember that he is not God, and as the woman in his life, you must have some accountability. Your adjustment period is not a license to be inconsiderate to him or think he should forgive everything. You must be both responsible and accountable. Don't allow baggage from past relationships to overshadow your potential to enjoy your relationship with this man, who has demonstrated himself to be both consistent and obedient to God, and don't see his forgiveness as weakness.

Understanding and Forgiving

Sometimes a man can be committed to the wrong woman. She's the kind who sees a forgiving, understanding man as someone to be taken advantage of. Try though you may, she does not respond appreciatively to good treatment. You may have encountered a woman who has been hurt many times before, but upon meeting you, she's decided that it is her turn to take advantage. Only after the relationship is irreparably damaged does she understand you were a blessing in her life.

The common solution for these types of people, whether male or female, is to lay the responsibility for repairing the relationship on the offended party. They need you to believe they did not know what they were doing or have finally realized (after being told numerous times) they were doing something hurtful to the relationship.

Maybe you've been in a relationship with a woman who feels you should continue to treat her well, yet be content with being unappreciated. Her words cannot be depended on, because she claims to understand what you need but her actions prove she is unwilling or incapable of delivering. Because of her history of abuse, she actually responds better to negative treatment.

In order to stay in a committed relationship with this type of woman, you would certainly have to change some of your positive attributes, become less forgiving. You would possibly have to become callous in your interaction with her, because your kindness is interpreted as weakness.

By now you're probably asking, "Why would I want to change my character just to be in a relationship with someone like that?" That's precisely the point. There are some things you should never have to understand or forgive, because if a person truly loves and cares for you, such behaviors should never surface. Fiscal irresponsibility, emotional and relational dishonesty, gross selfishness, a consistent lack of accountability and responsibility, violence, and disregard for your needs are examples of conduct that does not characterize a genuinely loving relationship.

Over the years I have met countless men who think being mistreated is the norm in relationships. It's not only women who are abused! Such people are usually damaged emotionally and think it is normal to feel as they do. No matter how hard you try, you will have an extremely difficult time trying to relate to this type of adult.

Many people will defend their selfishness, saying, "I should be loved for who I am and not be expected to change." Real love cannot bear to see its object behaving in a way that is damaging to the giver and not try to teach another way. When you are struggling in a relationship with a woman who thinks her chief contribution is her presence—her beauty, her sexuality—you are wasting your time. People who contribute little more to the relationship than their presence usually think the world revolves around them and are insensitive to how their actions affect you.

Patient endurance gives you the capacity to forgive and extend grace to those God has given you to love and has put under your authority, but it is practical, as discussed in the previous chapter.

A man and forgiveness is not the same thing as a man and weakness. You must know from the beginning that forgiveness includes structure and expectation. Just because you are a forgiving man does not mean you are a weak man. As you develop forgiveness, I don't want you to become a chump. A forgiving man is an understanding man. But there are some things you should not have to understand because they should never happen. Forgiving a person does not eliminate your internal standard for what is acceptable.

So a forgiving man is not an individual who allows himself to be taken advantage of. You have an obligation to let those around you know, in conversational ways, what your personal boundaries are.

Now, what do you do when the boundaries are crossed?

You have an obligation to let those around you, especially the woman in your life, know when she has crossed the line. If you don't, she may continue a behavior that will eventually hurt the relationship. If someone, male or female, continues behavior that is hurting and inconsiderate, he or she is demonstrating a significant lack of caring for you. It's time to forgive, but it is probably time for you to make a relationship decision.

Those of us who have issues with our fathers especially need to remember that forgiveness is more for the forgiver than the forgiven. When you hold on to unforgiveness, the person who offended you has a lot of control, too much control over you. You have given that person too much control of your mind and emotions. Forgiveness removes this control.

A restored relationship may never develop, but you must forgive those who don't deserve it in order to truly free yourself from the incident that caused the hard feelings. I often forgive to get a person out of my mind and emotions. It's not always for them; many times it's for me.

As you consistently forgive, modeling this lifestyle before others, you instill confidence and trust in those you are called as a man to lead and can exercise your God-given responsibility to love and participate in their lives.

I dare you to forgive those who have offended you.

- Remember the grace God freely gave you and lead with love as a primary characteristic.
- Establish your personal boundaries and communicate them to those around you.

- Let people know when they have overstepped your boundaries.
- If people continue to hurt you, forgive them, but know it is time to decide if you still want that person in your life.
- Let go of unforgiveness and free yourself from negative situations and offenses in your past.

10

Dare
to Praise

*God has given you the ability to connect
to the Almighty through faith, prayer,
the Bible, and praise.*

W E MEN HAVE AN ABILITY to connect to God, but there are
times when our gender gets in the way. Prayer is a discipline many men gravitate to, because it can be done
silently and privately. Faith is also another part of a man's spiritual life
he can exercise without much overt exposure. Praise is another matter. The Bible is clear that praise is an articulation that often requires
public expression. Many men have difficulty when it comes to this
form of spiritual expression. As a result, they are not availing themselves of this powerful spiritual weapon. Men who have not had a
revelation of the power of masculine praise are lacking a powerful
tactical weapon that God has given every man.

Many men seem to feel praise is a feminine expression, yet consider it manly to be extremely vocal at a sporting event. A man's comfort level at being expressive depends on the context. Many houses of worship are occupied by silent men, while nearby stadiums are filled with the roar of male voices.

I used to wonder why we men are extremely outspoken at sporting events but have a problem with spiritual expression through praise. As I thought this thing through, I realized that men may not be fully aware of the strategic nature of praise and our key position and role in the tactical plan of God. And praise traditionally has been the arena where women participate and men spectate. Praise and females are almost synonymous.

The problem with praise and the average man is a matter of assumption and perception. At a football game, the context is decidedly male, with just about any outward expression deemed appropriate. Silence would be considered as unusual and indicate the possibility of a man having a bad time at the game. What's interesting is that a man is apt to be vocal at a bad game to voice his dissatisfaction with the poor performance of his chosen team. So good or bad, most men will be very vocal at a game.

So it is safe to say the historical context of an event, especially if it is perceived to be a male- or female-dominated context, often plays into a man's comfort with outward expression. Another factor is familiarity with the nuances of the event.

At a game, a man is probably familiar with the specifics of the particular game. At church with God, he may be unfamiliar with what to say and where to say it. At a game with his peers, he knows when to respond and what to respond to. His masculinity is never in question, because of the male context of the game. His praise at a game for the performance of an individual player or team never diminishes his masculinity. Church is another matter altogether.

Church is a female-dominated context. So a man will hesitate to emulate the behavior and the gestures of the majority. Many men feel praise is effeminate or soft. The more a man learns about God and the appropriateness of a praise response, the more emotive he will become.

Most men understand military principles and terminologies— soldiers, combat, front lines, victory, and defeat. When you consider the Biblical principle of military warfare, your understanding of the spiritual will change dramatically. When the armies of Israel were about to go into battle, God's military strategy was to send the praise unit onto the battlefield first. In 2 Chronicles 20:20–30, the choir/praise unit marched into battle before the troops. So in a full-scale battle, the first warriors on the battlefield were the men praising God. It is a parallel for the spiritual life of a man.

When the armies of God used praise as a frontline weapon, the enemy actually was being engaged spiritually prior to the physical attack. The choir full of men would sing of the greatness of God, giving the enemy the opportunity to decide it was useless to resist the armies of the Lord. Their praise predicted the victory that was soon to follow. The victory was first spoken in praise, then manifested on earth.

When your praise is silent, whether at church or home, you are strategically out of position in the defense of those around you. Your praise positions you at the front line of offense and defense in the warfare of your life, your loved ones, and the life of your church. When you do not lead in praise, you leave your church without the benefit of your spiritual strength.

Understand that when a church comes together in worship, a spiritual battle for souls is under way. If you desire to see the Word and will of God work against a very active spiritual enemy, you will become very active in praise.

So as a godly man, you must enter the worship experience understanding a battle for souls and the blessings of God is about to begin. Believing this, begin to give God praise before you leave the house for the battlefield called work, by thanking God in advance for the victories you anticipate during the day.

I began to teach the men of our church and men's groups around the country how the men in a house of worship can tip the scales in the spiritual battles of those with whom they share a worship experience and life. Men have the responsibility to get off the sidelines and enter a strategic part of spiritual warfare women have been occupying without them. It's time for every man to take his proper position as leader in the lives of those he loves as well as in God's plan for spiritual victory in his life and the life of his church. Praise is a spiritual weapon that causes things to happen in the spirit first, then in the natural world. God responds to praise! It is a powerful connection and an effective way of communicating with God.

To demonstrate this point, let's look at Joshua's battle at Jericho (Joshua 5:14–6:27). Joshua and the priests obeyed God's instructions to praise Him and brought the walls of Jericho down. This miracle was far beyond human ability and strength. *The battle had to be won in the spiritual realm before victory could be achieved on earth.* Our chief weapons are not natural but spiritual. There was a victory in the spirit as well as in the natural, because of men praising the Lord. Praise makes a man a more powerful force in the Kingdom of God. The Lord empowers the man who gives him praise.

God had already secured victory in the spiritual realm before Joshua achieved victory on earth. Before Joshua's men even marched around Jericho, God told him, "See, I have delivered Jericho into your hands, along with its king and its fighting men" (Joshua 6:2, NIV).

God revealed to Joshua that *the battle had already been won* in the spirit realm. All he had to do was faithfully obey God in the natural realm. His obedience to God's instructions and the praises rendered by his men transferred God's victory from heaven to the earthly realm.

Jericho represents any thing or person blocking your entry into

God's promises. You cannot remove these obstacles without praise. If there is something standing between you and the fulfilled promise of God in your life—whether it's in your home, your family, or your business—praise God for a victory in heaven that will be experienced on earth.

Once the truth of a spiritual victory has been established in your life, it is time to conduct yourself as though the victory was already yours. Believe, and react to old challenges in a new way. The victory can only be achieved once you begin to approach your Jericho with a new perspective and perception. When you walk in spiritual victory you will have a new perception of yourself and your ability to handle your challenges. At the same time, your perspective on those same challenges will be radically altered, because your self-perception will have changed. You will see your Jericho differently because you will see yourself differently. The thing that once appeared insurmountable now becomes manageable.

Consider the Biblical example of the man at the Bethesda pool (John 5:1–16). After Jesus instructed him to take up his bed and walk, his perception of his ability changed radically. He had been given the spiritual ability to overcome his years of physical dysfunction. The key to his deliverance was to get up from the place that symbolized his inability. His ability to rise had already been accomplished in the command of Jesus. The lame man responded positively to the spiritual change by physically reflecting what had happened in his spirit. It was up to the man to reflect a reality already completed in the spirit.

Praise can make the walls of isolation, failure, and hopelessness fall down. By faith you must reflect your belief in this spiritual truth. Then you walk in consistency, strength, and victory. You are a conqueror because the victory already is won by God. It is your responsibility to live a spiritually directed life as a reflection of that victory. So praise God and let the victory be yours to share! Walk in the knowledge that your Jericho is already defeated, because God has already secured victory.

When I preached this spiritual principle at our church, over two thousand men came forward that day. I told them, "I want you to lift up a *shabach* in this place." *Shabach* is Hebrew for a type of praise. It is a war cry. King David said, "Because thy lovingkindness is better than life, my lips shall praise [*shabach*] thee" (Psalm 63:3, KJV).

At first, many men in the congregation were uncomfortable demonstrating their praise to God. But that day, after teaching about an audible praise, the men came to the altar like the men who marched around Jericho on the seventh day. A new confidence arose within them in corporate camaraderie, each man strengthened in the knowledge that he was not alone in his praise of God. They began to harness the same type of energy used at a football game but for an entirely different reason. As they were not reluctant to shout for victory for their favorite team, they realized they should not be reticent to shout God's victory over their Jericho battles.

As the men poured forward that Sunday, I realized this was the first time most of them had ever been given specific permission to praise God publicly. At that moment, I had given men a safe place to release the praise within them. I encouraged the men of our congregation to shout first, just as the men of Joshua's army led in praise.

The men of Israel set the tone for warfare and praise. At Jericho the men had led the people of God in the march around the walls of the city. They exercised their leadership by facing the enemy first, but they also were the first to lead in praise. The Bible says the men lifted up a shout, then the rest of the nation joined in.

After the men offered their uninhibited praise, I instructed the women how to join in and support them. On my signal, the women shouted with the men and the entire sanctuary erupted in praise.

This is where the men are to be in the church concerning praise. This is the position you are supposed to take. You cannot overcome an unseen enemy in the spirit realm unless you are in your proper position. Are you willing to step to the front lines and engage in this warfare? Perhaps you have never felt free to give God audible, uninhibited praise. Shout and feel the reverberations of Psalm 47 shake within you and around you!

Oh, clap your hands, all you peoples!
Shout to God with the voice of triumph!
For the LORD Most High is awesome;
He is a great King over all the earth.
He will subdue the peoples under us,
And the nations under our feet.

PSALM 47:1–3, NKJV

The experience at my church helped me to realize that men need to be in the company of others where they feel safe, where they can be instructed to do what most women do naturally. Once men receive proper instruction and confirmation of their behavior, they will openly and freely praise God. They will dare to praise. This truth has revolutionized my church. The men are no longer out of their proper position in the Kingdom.

Before this experience, if I asked for volunteers to cut the grass or to shovel snow or to unload turkeys for a giveaway, the men would do so, believing they were rightly fulfilling their position. I had to teach our men that their position extended not only into leading the church in strength but also into worship and praise. Men must dare to praise God in their own right, setting the tone for spiritual warfare.

Once our men were aligned in the proper position, we began to see victories over struggles men had been fighting for years. Many men overcame smoking, drinking, and inappropriate behaviors of all kinds. There were even greater victories in the surrounding neighborhoods. Gang violence decreased suddenly. Former gang members got saved in record numbers.

We had been laying the foundation for changing the neighborhood through our neighborhood walks and door-to-door evangelism. But after our men became rightly positioned in their praise, results started to happen. There was an elevation in our neighborhood, if you will, of spiritual authority accompanying the release of praise in these men. A liberty arose in our church as the men became more and more comfortable expressing praise in whatever way they saw fit. This unleashed praise power extended beyond the walls of the church and became the spiritual instrument that God used to level the Jerichos in our community.

LIBERATED BY PRAISE

The men in our congregation now have no trouble coming to the altar, kneeling, weeping, shouting, jumping up and down, giving loud praise, or clapping their hands. They have been given a safe environment in which to appear vulnerable through their praise. I say vulnerability because when a man begins to express himself in ways he and others he cares about are unaccustomed to, he risks rejection. But the men felt safe. The ground for acceptance had been prepared by teaching the entire body that a man's praise was not an imitation of a woman's praise. His praise would be distinct, based on his experience and an expression of his masculinity. His praise would be understood as strength and not weakness.

What a difference in the atmosphere of the church from when I had taken over as pastor of Bethany Church nearly two decades before. It was a lifeless, traditional church in those days, but men daring to praise God has freed us from stifling traditions.

One particular incident helped me realize what had been going on to cause this deadness to permeate this church. One of the church leaders had been trying to inflict his own inhibitions regarding praise on the entire congregation. Whenever this leader was responsible for oversight of the congregation, he set the standard for praise. Every time someone would begin to express outward praise to God, he would instruct the ushers to sit the person down. He could not understand or tolerate such expressive praise, and as a result, stifled it in everyone else. I then realized praise had to be taught to the people of God, especially to men. The women were also waiting to be released to participate in an environment of true praise. They had been stifled in this one area, resulting in a deadness that permeated everything else they tried to accomplish.

As I continued to teach on praise, the congregation doubled in size after only one month. Then it doubled again after two months. Even though this church officer continued to resist, the men in the church matured and grew as I led the way. This convinced me that whoever is leading the church can influence both the intensity and the development of praise in that house. Church leaders must dare to be men of praise, setting the example for the rest of the body of believers. They must set the tone for leadership and praise in the home as well.

My experience with worship was like that of most men. I did not know enough about God to give Him appropriate praise. Most of my worship and praise was a reaction to the others in worship. I did not want to be inappropriate, so I watched others. Little did I know, learning by example as it relates to praise and worship was the correct thing to do. Many great lessons are learned by watching others.

As I grew in understanding and knowledge, my worship and praise became personal. Both began to reflect my experience with God. With a new maturity I expressed what had been impossible to reflect at the beginning of my relationship with God. The depth of your relationship will usually be revealed in your worship and praise.

I remember the first time I was in a church service. It was my grandmom's church in Chester, Pennsylvania. There were a lot of older people. I was a little uncomfortable in this new place—I had a lot of preconceptions and went in a little skeptical. Everyone looked so serious. The ushers were wearing white; the women were wearing their Sunday best. The windows were tinted yellow, giving the room a glow that seemed appropriate for the setting.

People were scattered throughout the sanctuary. There seemed to be no consistency in the music. One minute the people were singing a toe-tapper and the next something that felt like funeral music. The preacher began. He held my attention, and the entire room was soon in the grips of the tension and the story that birthed the message.

When he hesitated, I would hear some people respond as if answering the preacher. Stuff like, "Well, well, that's true, that's true" or "Amen, brother" as well as "Preach!" Everyone seemed to know what and when to say something.

But something else happened.

The choir sang another song. Before the song ended, a lady yelled so loudly I thought she was having a psychotic episode. Before I could ask, my grandmom explained to me the lady had just gotten "happy." I later learned that "happy" meant she was in the Spirit and giving God praise.

I had never seen anything like that in my life. Other women began to join in, but the men stayed very quiet. They simply observed with no emotional reaction. Every week, the women continued to give God praise while the men sat looking. Sometimes it seemed like no more than a woman's emotionalism. But one day one of the men hollered. He kept saying "Thank you!" I had never seen that before.

He made excuses for his behavior later in the week. He said God had been good to him and he just could not help himself. I wondered why he needed to make an excuse and why he had to be able to help himself. I saw nothing wrong. I was hooked.

One day while singing in the choir, all of the expression I had been repressing came flying out. I cried like a baby and did not care what people thought. I was very thankful for the Lord's provision. I'd felt this emotion before, but I did not want the deacon's fixed stare and unspoken disapproval.

The more I learned about God, the more appropriate my feelings of thanks grew. The more my thanks grew, the more intense my worship became. I had developed from an observer into a worshipper. I was ready to be the chief worshipper in every context of my life, as a man should be. I was better equipped with one of my chief spiritual weapons.

The home is a battlefield where you as a man must be equipped to wage war. There is a battle for the future of our children, the safety our neighborhoods, and the leadership of the community. You cannot be content to simply lead because you are a man; you must be the priest of your home and to the family in general. That means you must lead in faith, stewardship, prayer, and praise. As you set the tone by example, praise becomes a welcome and necessary part of family life. As in other situations, those you love begin to imitate your actions.

A man of praise is vigilant concerning the future of his family and friends. He praises God in an intercessory way—praising and thanking God for victory in the lives of his family as well as the overall security of his home. A man must be the standard for praise in his home and invite those he touches to join him.

FOR WOMEN

DO YOU REALLY WANT A MAN OF PRAISE?

You may have lamented the seeming lack of available godly men. You probably have prayed many times for God to send you that kind of man or to transform the man in your life into that kind of man. But are you ready to accept the full implications of your request?

The blessing of a relationship with a man who truly loves and reveres God in total obedience requires something of you as well. A man needs your affirmation and support as he steps out of his level of comfort and into praise.

He will grow spiritually from an environment of praise that is encouraged by you, as you affirm his desire to praise and the ways that he praises God as a man. Encourage his praise as an expression of his manhood, not a hindrance to it.

PRAISE FLOWS FROM OBEDIENCE

A fan's response at a ball game does not begin with the fan but rather as a response to the activity of the team. Praise works the same way. You do not initiate your praise. It is a response to the reality of God in your life. It is actually the articulation of your relationship with God. If worship is based on relationship, then praise is the articulation of that relationship.

Praise is birthed out of an obedient relationship with God. Worship is a natural product of humanity's relationship with God. Worship glorifies God, as the psalmist declared:

All nations whom You have made
Shall come and worship before You, O Lord,
And shall glorify Your name.
For You are great, and do wondrous things;
You alone are God.

PSALM 86:9–10, NKJV

An understanding that your work and your obedience is your worship produces "worship behavior." Anytime God equips you to do a thing, and you do it within the realm of obedience to God, it becomes a form of worship. Praise then becomes the articulation of that obedient, worshipful relationship.

Praise evolves from your obedience to complete the work God has called you to do. You begin to understand that God has created you to worship and praise in everything you do. You begin to understand the power of that praise in your everyday life.

Praise, like prayer, is as much a posture as it is an activity. It is a way of life that becomes a consistent part of your life and character. Like prayer, praise becomes part of your spiritual résumé, a part of your arsenal in spiritual warfare. Praise is the weapon God gives you to leverage the negative circumstances of your life.

Praise is the positive in your life that leverages the negatives. The balance of a positive and negative charge produce power in a battery; the negative charge is leveraged by the positive. Your praise must be an act of your will, a determination. David said in Psalm 34:1 (NKJV): "I will bless the LORD at all times; His praise shall continually be in my mouth." A great leader, David was determined to react to life situations with the power of praise.

Responding to challenging, sorrowful, even defeating life situations through the power of praise is not a denial of the circumstances. It is your decision to react with positive energy rather than the negative, which has no power to move the problem toward a solution.

Praise God for the wisdom to handle tough situations. Praise Him for the opportunity the problem presents, and then praise Him for the solution. Praise is positive and leverages any situation. It provides a benefit to all involved. It is both therapeutic and inspirational. Your praise is therapeutic for you, and inspiring to the woman in your life who witnesses it.

Like your faith, your praise allows you to step outside of yourself, express your emotions, and unleash them away from yourself, constructively giving them to God. Praise is a healthy, positive means of expressing the frustration you feel. But there is a deeper revelation.

Praise is a spiritual method of moving the problem you face out of your way so you reconnect with God. The problem is removed as the focus of attention and God is put in His proper place. When you come out of praise mode, the answer to your problem is usually evident and your perception of the difficulty is now in its proper perspective. First Peter 5:7 says cast your cares upon Him because He cares for you. When you give God praise in difficult times, you are putting the battle in His hands. As David learned in his battle against the Philistines (1 Samuel 17) and Jehoshaphat learned when faced with a formidable enemy (2 Chronicles 20:1–29), the battle belongs to the Lord. God will give victory to the man who obeys Him.

Men, praising God is healthy for you. Praise is beneficial to your church, a part of your priestly role to your family, and an inspiration to the women in your life.

A man praising God joins the women in his life in a powerful spiritual practice women have always enjoyed. Men and women have long prayed together and agreed in faith together, but now a man and a woman can discover the power of praising God together. They will agree for victory in the battles they face together. As the Bible says, they will touch and agree on the outcome of the challenging situations in life, as well as interceding for each other with praise. It rallies a man and a woman together, producing peace, power, and unity.

I dare you to praise God freely.

- Learn more about God. The more you know, the more you will appreciate Him.

- Remember, praise is demonstrated as a masculine thing to do in the Bible. David is the example of an individual, male or female, involved in praise.
- Praise is the expression of your appreciation for God, just as you appreciate an athlete at a game.
- It really is okay to clap your hands enthusiastically, and shout when you remember or hear something that makes you think of the goodness of God.

11

DARE TO GO DEEPER WITH GOD

There is only one permanent relationship.

WORSHIP IS THE PRODUCT of relationship, and praise is the articulation of that relationship. That relationship is exhibited with praise. The language of praise and the language of worship are identical. Phrases like "Thank you," "Bless the Lord," and "I magnify your name" are common to both worship and praise. Worship acknowledges who God is, praise is the response to what God does. Worship is knowing God, praise is appreciating God. Worship is relating to God, praise is the demonstration of that relationship.

The depth of a man's worship is directly related to the maturity of his relationship with God, while the intensity of a man's appreciation produces praise for all God has done. This maturity and intensity is well illustrated by a Biblical example from the book of Romans.

There is a dual cry addressed in Romans 8, which details the adoptive aspect of God's relationship with believers. This adoption is explained within the Roman context: the adopted heir is a full son or daughter. The adoptee's position is not like Cinderella—a stepchild held in low regard. The adopted child of a Roman leader became an heir to all the new father owned. Romans 8:15 speaks of the spirit of adoption producing a dual cry, "Abba, Father."

This dual cry—which actually means "Daddy, Father"—speaks of a believer's infantile dependence on God while having an adult understanding and relationship with Him. An infant-parent relationship is lopsided until the child begins to mature and appreciate the care of a loving, committed father. The "Abba" cry reveals the infant's need and single-minded devotion to having that need satisfied. It is a relationship that is totally dependent on the father's ability to care for the child, as the child can offer little more than its presence. The child does know to turn to the father in a time of need. But the relationship is one-sided for years.

As the child matures, there should be a shift from infancy to relationship built upon experience. The title "Father" reveals a mature understanding of the reality of His care. It is a title uttered by a child who has come to appreciate all the father does. The child begins to participate in the relationship in ways that indicate an appreciation for the father.

Praise and worship develop in the same way. Early in our relationship with God, we conduct ourselves like infants knowing two things—our need and God's ability to provide for it. As the relationship develops, we begin to have a greater appreciation for who God is. Worship develops.

As worship develops, you begin to show appreciation for who God is as well as what God does. Praise develops. Now the worship, based on relationship, becomes a lifestyle, and your growing appreciation for what God does for you becomes a lifestyle of praise. Everything you do honors God, and your actions reflect appreciation for what God does.

Worship and work are to be integrated into your total life as a reflection of your relationship to God. *Avodah* is a Hebrew word translated as both "work" and "worship" in various places in the Old Testament. "The LORD God took the man and put him in the Garden of Eden to work [*avodah*] it and take care of it" (Genesis 2:15, NIV; see also Exodus 34:21 and Psalm 104:23). In other places, *avodah* denotes worship: "Then the LORD said to Moses, 'Go to Pharaoh and say to him, "This is what the LORD says: Let my people go, so that they may worship [*avodah*] me"'" (Exodus 8:1, NIV; see also Joshua 24:15).

What a powerful image—our work and our worship are parallels in our relationship to God! You cannot strive to bring worship into your work, because your work *is* worship. Work and worship are threads used to weave the fabric of faith.

The Israelites understood their work as a means of bringing honor to God. You worship as you do your work and serve your neighbor. Worship God; serve neighbor.

Work is an expression of your God-given ability and creativity, because you are made in God's image. Our work is a testimony to our worship, and therefore to our relationship with God. Work and worship are integrated. Whatever your life's work is, once you accept that everything you have is given to you by God, you understand the principle of stewardship.

Stewardship is taking care of the things someone else gives you. Our parents tried to teach us this valuable lesson. I remember statements like "Clean your room," "Pick up your clothing," and "Do your chores." I didn't realize at the time my mom was teaching me two vital things:

taking care of the things I had been given and appreciation for the person who gave them to me. The chores were my work, and the performance of that work was my way to appreciate her. It's like that with God. Whatever He gives you as work, your performance of it is a form of worship. The higher the standard you have for performing your occupation, the more appreciation or worship you give God.

As a your heart gets more and more deeply involved in relationship with God, your worship intensifies, and praise becomes a natural expression of that relationship. You develop a right attitude toward God. When this happens, God will look upon your praise with favor, and the work of your hands will be blessed.

Worship is not confined to the church, and work is not limited to the business arena. Obviously there are people who believe this, though, because deacons have been known to go to jail for embezzlement of company funds, and Sunday school teachers have been known to cheat their customers to gain extra profit. Many people separate their Sunday worship from their Monday employment, but this is not what the Bible says should occur.

GO DEEPER THROUGH PRAISE

We previously discussed the barriers to praise most men face, perceiving it as the historic province of women and holding the misconception that it is feminine. Going deeper with God through praise is a challenge for us men to break out of the paradigm that has restricted us. For generations, men have missed out on this great weapon of power, believing that audible or overexpressions of praise would feminize them or cause others to see them as weak or vulnerable.

Thankfully, men are beginning to discover the truth that rather than weaken or feminize them, praise actually strengthens them and brings down the walls of tradition that have held them back. They have liberation and new empowerment in their lives through the release of their praise. Think of the generational blessing you can pass down to your children if you teach them to seek God's favor through praise offered in the proper attitude of the heart, rooted in the foundation of a strong relationship with God.

The enemy is well aware that the power of praise can silence him. "From the lips of children and infants you have ordained praise because of your enemies, to silence the foe and the avenger" (Psalm 8:2, NIV). Jesus rebuked the chief priests and scribes when they complained about the children praising Him in the temple area, reminding them of this very scripture. What the enemy has done quite ingeniously is to handcuff men so they never discover the power available in their praise. As long as a man is shackled in this vital tool in the arsenal God has given him, he is limited in his ability to live victoriously.

God wants to remove the shackles of tradition and release you to experience the freedom and awesome power produced through your praise. But once set free, you must never again be ashamed of or hold back your praise to the Father.

Daring to go deeper through praise means moving out of the non-productive, traditional box and into the dimension of expressing your praise from the correct motives of the heart. Determine that you will praise God freely and openly so it does not limit your ability to move victoriously in the spiritual realm. As a man desiring to encompass all that has been made available to you, commit to bringing that same level of praise to Almighty God. Ask yourself:

- Who does more for me than God?
- Who has encouraged me to be all that I can be more than my Heavenly Father?
- Who deserves my praise more than my Creator?

When you dare to praise, you are daring to move from a binding and inarticulate relationship with your Creator to a place in the Spirit where power and breakthrough can flow readily into your life. That dimension of victory can only be entered by releasing true praise—mastering the sin crouching at the door and effectively silencing the enemy.

Praise is such a powerful weapon that God instructed Joshua to use it to bring down the seemingly indestructible walls of Jericho. And praise brought them down!

SAME DANCE, DIFFERENT EXPRESSIONS

If we look at all the stellar praise-givers in the Bible, the majority of them were men—Abel, Noah, Abraham, Isaac, Jacob, Moses, David, Zadok, Korah, Isaiah, Jehoshaphat, and Hezekiah. King David, of the tribe of Judah (which literally means "praise"), was known as a worshipper, a man of praise, the sweet psalmist of Israel. Two of the most effective men of praise in the New Testament were Paul and Silas. Locked in a jail cell (Acts 16) in the middle of the night, they began to lift praises to Yahweh while incarcerated. As a result of their praise, other prisoners were released from bondage, chains fell off, and cell doors popped open. These two powerful men of praise led what I call an "intercessory praise."

One of the problems men have faced in releasing their praise is determining what true praise is supposed to resemble. With many church congregations being predominantly female, they have established the pattern for praise, leaving men who dare to praise with a feminine paradigm to imitate. The problem is that men and women look at the same function through very different perspectives. God made us this way, and it's time we came to understand and utilize those differences to maximize our destinies as male and female.

This principle can be understood more clearly by observing a man and a woman out on the dance floor, dancing to the same song. A man approaches the dance out of his masculinity, while the woman comes forth out of her femininity. They are hearing the same music, doing the same dance, but their expression of it is quite different.

Let's apply this principle to a man who comes to church and desires to praise God. He hears the music and it touches his spirit. He listens to the Word of God and it reaches into his heart. All that is within him desires to tell God of his love and appreciation. He does not need to look to a female for a means to express his praise or to imitate the way the woman offers her praise. He needs to interpret his expression of praise out of the strength of his masculinity and express it, just as he would in his dance.

THE POWER OF INTERCESSORY PRAISE

Once you know that you are to be the first on the battlefield and you are to lift up the *shabach*, you can bring down the walls of your Jericho through the power of praise. Once you see that you can be like Paul and Silas, two men who praised God, you too can open jail cells and set the captives free. Once you discover and manifest the power of masculine praise, you have picked up a mighty weapon that had been hidden from you and you can move into a victorious life.

If you can be kept from praising God, you are basically muted and handcuffed—powerless against the enemy. You are not articulating your relationship in a manner that finds favor with God. Sin then can begin to open the door to your heart and mind. How much victory can there be in your life if you are not pleasing your Creator? You already know that God will not bless a man's disobedience. God does not respond to praise delivered out of an incorrect motive. Dare to go deeper with God—your provider, your banner, and your peace. Then you can have the victory over your personal walls of Jericho.

Have you ever had a person tell you they love you without really getting to know you? Flattered and confused is the appropriate reaction. I see people in my office who meet at the beginning of the month and believe they should be married in thirty days—a lifetime decision made on the basis of very little time together. They are professing love but have not been through time and circumstance together.

My first question to the couple is "Why are you in such a hurry? What's the rush?" Then I suggest they wait, date for a few years in order to get past the initial enthusiasm, really get to know each other and consider premarital counseling before they get married.

I ask the couple how they feel about each other. Comments like "I think he or she is great, a good family person with a great work ethic" are pretty common. The big one is "I want to spend my life with him or her." My response is always "How do you know?" The praise is based on very little real experience and understanding.

There is an emotion/experience equation that must be understood by a man or a woman. That equation looks like this: In the beginning of a relationship, emotion is the primary component, while experience requires time. As the couple gains experience with each other, a balance should occur between emotion and experience.

When the correct balance occurs, it does not feel as if the world has come to an end when disagreement and disappointments occur. The amazing thing is this: Many people don't see the need or the wisdom of a deeper relationship with each other.

It's the same with God. As you build a relationship with Him, as you go deeper with him as a man, you will not think God does not love and care for you because He does not do what you want Him to do exactly as you think He should. This understanding and experience is what builds relationship. It's the foundation for worship.

THE DEPTH OF YOUR RELATIONSHIP TO GOD

The depth of your relationship dictates the intensity of your praise. So how do you cultivate your relationship with God so your praise pleases your Abba Father, the God with whom you have a personal relationship? Prayer, of course is at the top of your to-do list. There are, however, a series of understandings you need in order to effectively deepen that relationship and intensify your praise. The Word of God reveals three of God's perspectives on relationships with us:

- the perspective of environment
- the perspective of relationship
- the perspective of influence

The Perspective of Environment

What are we allowing to become the dominant force in our lives? We need to understand the direct correlation between our obedience to God and the environment we live in—the relationships we engage in and the influence we permit to dominate us.

God explains this concept to Abraham: "Go for yourself [for your own advantage] away from your country, from your relatives and your father's house, to the land that I will show you" (Genesis 12:1, AMP). In other words, God was saying, "There is a problem where you are, and I need you to get away from this environment, apart from these relationships, and out from under the influences around you." God told Abraham to go away from his father's house, which represented the authority being exercised over his life, and away from the influences of his culture and family relationships.

In God's plan, time is always a backdrop for location. God will eventually get you to a place, but the time it takes you to get there is dependent on you and is irrelevant to God. When you've gotten to a place where God needs you, that's when the Almighty begins to do a work in you. Here's a practical example. A wilderness experience can last you three days or forty years, as in the case of the Hebrews leaving Egypt. (Read the Bible book of Exodus.) You will eventually get to the place and receive the promise, whether it takes you three days or forty years. The length of time does not negatively affect what God is trying to accomplish. The key is how long it will take for you to realize what God desires to accomplish in you and learn the lesson that the place is designed to teach you. You choose whether it takes three days or forty years.

Is the environment you live in fostering obedience to God? Is your relationship with God determining the environment you choose, or is your environment determining your relationship with God?

The Perspective of Relationship

Relationships with others in your environment will, in turn, exert a degree of influence over the choices you make. Environment—where you are—is crucial to your advancement in God's plan for your life, and the influence of those around you directly affects the depth of your character development and your relationship with God.

For example, if you are in a place where praise is not encouraged, then that environment and the relationships around you will negatively influence your level of praise. You need to be in a place where your relationships will inspire you to move out of your comfort zone and reach for a higher dimension of praise. If your environment and your relationships do not inspire you to move up and out of a rut, then you will never access the power that God has made available to you through releasing your praise. Your level of praise is directly related to where you are and with whom you relate.

FOR WOMEN

INFLUENCING HIM TO BE BETTER

You can become a positive or a negative influence in the lives of the men who are important to your life. When you support and encourage a man who has already embraced his purpose, he feels an even greater sense of empowerment. It makes him want to do more for the Kingdom of God, and more for you.

The influence of negativity can pull down even the most determined man, just as Samson allowed the negative influence of Delilah to guide his life decisions. Critical voices, unsupportive, unbelieving voices, especially coming from those he most needs to trust and believe in him, can push your man and your relationship into a flow of negativity.

As the important men in your life fight to bring down the Jerichos in their lives, they need you to be a cheering squad and a praying partner, which will inspire them to continue moving in a positive direction.

Many of you may be uncomfortable with men expressing themselves emotionally. Women, you often contradict yourselves. Some women want him to be expressive, but then some may look at his tears during a worship service as weak or effeminate. I have heard women say, "He must have done something wrong. Why is he at the altar?"

The public display is actually a breakthrough for him spiritually and personally. A barrier has been broken. He needs your support. A man who has been liberated in praise will actually be a better man. The person he wants to approve of him is you. It's a bad time for a joke. He will retreat, with a reluctance to emerge again.

The Perspective of Influence

Men must be around other men who openly praise God so that they can learn through imitation. Paul told his disciples, "Even though you have ten thousand guardians in Christ, you do not have many fathers, for in Christ Jesus, I became your father through the gospel. Therefore I urge you to imitate me" (1 Corinthians 4:15–16, NIV). Paul encourages, "Join with others in following my example, brothers, and take note of those who live according to the pattern we gave you" (Philippians 3:17, NIV). People tend to learn best by example; therefore, your relationships strongly influence your behavior.

Once you make sure that your environment and relationships will cultivate and encourage praise, then the influences over you will articulate praise in a manner pleasing to God. The influence of others dictates how successful you are in fulfilling your purpose in life. That is why God told Abram to get out of the country and away from certain influences. All three of those factors—environment, relationships, influences—generated dominating voices in Abram's life. They had to be silenced in order for Abram to move into his rightful position as Father Abraham.

Start thinking about how much environment, relationships, and influences personally impact you. Without the proper environment, right relationships, and godly influences, you will not become a man of praise. If you do not see other men daring to praise, if your environment is anti-praise, then you will not feel free to release and express praise. Environment and relationships result in an influence that will directly affect the level of praise you strive to enter into. Carefully assess the type of environment you will enter and the quality of the relationships you will allow to influence your life.

BECOMING A PSALM 1 MAN

Blessed (happy, fortunate, prosperous, and enviable) is the man who walks and lives not in the counsel of the ungodly [following their advice, their plans and purposes], nor stands [submissive and inactive] in the path where sinners walk, nor sits down [to relax and rest] where the scornful [and the mockers] gather.

PSALM 1:1, AMP

If you want to find favor with God, you must strive to become a Psalm 1 man. This man avoids the scornful and the mockers and all others who are opponents of praise. Just like anything else in life, you are taught how to be a man of praise. The problem with instruction for most men is effectively positioning themselves to receive it. If you will properly align yourself by carefully considering the laws of environment, relationship, and influence, the instruction you receive will allow you to break out of the tradition paradigm and overcome errant teaching you may have received in the past.

Most of the lessons you need to learn, especially concerning praise, are the opposite of what the world teaches and models. The world's ungodly counsel to men encourages you to be cool by being nonreactive and unaffected by what is going on around you. Men, in general, we have been misdirected into conducting ourselves in rather prepubescent and immature ways. What do I mean by that?

Have you ever gone into a church and seen the whole congregation up in praise except for one or two people? They are behaving in a prepubescent manner. They look like teenagers do when they are sitting in a room full of adults. They act as though they are oblivious to the entire atmosphere around them. In their immaturity, they believe they are being cool.

As we have grown into adulthood, men especially continue with this adolescent perception of ourselves as it relates to our environment. We believe it is proper to be nonreactive and noninteractive. So we sit quietly and unresponsively, even in a full-blown worship service, unaware of how our "teenage behavior" is limiting our ability to mature and develop spiritually. It is not healthy for any person striving toward maturity to remain in a teenage mind-set.

I believe praise is contagious. It's vital that we strive to be around and then become that Psalm 1 man. Scripture tells us that to be happy and prosperous we need to carefully select who we allow to influence our lives. Intentional maturity means putting away childish ways (1 Corinthians 13:11).We need to mature and dare to break traditional mind-sets and release our praise!

BREAKING TRADITIONAL MIND-SETS

Daring to break the traditional mind-sets you own concerning men and praise means, first of all, going for a deeper relationship with God. The deeper your personal relationship with the Father, the more can be revealed to you. Your ability to be intimate with the Almighty may be influenced by who is teaching you God's Word. Your level of obedience and how you manifest what you have been taught can be encouraged or stifled depending on whom you spend time with and whom you are trying to impress. Whom are you really trying to please? God or another human being?

Generally speaking, we seek to impress those we respect, and we only respect those we know something about. The more you know about your Abba Father, the easier it is for you to articulate that knowledge in the form of zealous and passionate praise. Proverbs 19:2 (NIV) declares, "It is not good to have zeal without knowledge, nor to be hasty and miss the way." The depth of your understanding of God determines your ability to offer sincere, heartfelt praise. This means getting to the place where your praise is not born out of external circumstances but rather out of the intimate relationship you have with the Father.

For example, if you see a man exhibiting zealous, passionate praise at a football game, it's obviously because he knows something about that team, the players, and the sport. On the other hand, if a European visitor who knows nothing about American football sits next to you at the game, he is likely to ask, "What's going on? Why are you cheering?" Since he has no knowledge of what's going on, he cannot participate in the excitement and praise the players or the game.

You will only dare to praise God when you know God personally. Ignorance of God results in boredom with the things of God. Do worship, praise, and serving God bore you? If they do, you have never learned to praise God!

DARING TO PRAISE IN ALL OF LIFE

What does the expression of praise look like for the man of praise in the church, in the home, and in the workplace?

Praise in the workplace means being a good steward and being invested with the authority, relationships, and positions that God has given you. It is exhibiting an attitude of submission to those in authority over you. Further, you are to be honest in your time and follow the rules of the situation. You are to be regarded as a good employee—responsible, participating, and praiseworthy on the job.

> *Submit yourselves for the Lord's sake to every authority instituted among men: whether to the king, as the supreme authority, or to governors, who are sent by him to punish those who do wrong and to commend those who do right. For it is God's will that by doing good you should silence the ignorant talk of foolish men. Live as free men, but do not use your freedom as a cover-up for evil; live as*

servants of God. Show proper respect to everyone: Love the
brotherhood of believers, fear God, honor the king.

1 PETER 2:13–17, NIV

When you understand that you are always in God's presence—
whether it's on the job, at home, or in church—you will approach
your work differently. So if you are a dishwasher, even though you are
working at a job most people consider menial, you can find peace by
doing it as unto the Lord (Colossians 3:23–24). When you do your job
as unto the Lord, you change what appears to be a menial task into a
praise situation. No matter where you are employed, strive to become
the best employee possible, obeying the rules as a righteous employee, thereby manifesting praise to our God.

The other vital piece often missed, however, is moving from
merely going through the motions of outward praise to that deeper
level where praise is freely flowing from a spiritual motivation. When
a man is at a football game, shouting praise to the players, he exhibits
physical expression without spiritual motivation. When a man of
praise is at work, understanding that his job is God's means of provision, his praise is based on a spiritual principle operating in his life.

Praise in the Community

Within his community, a man should be an interactive part of the
solution, part of the problem-solving leadership in his community. By
becoming part of the leadership, you can help bring righteousness
and godly principles into that community. This also becomes a manifestation of praise as you serve *(avodah)* your community.

Paul gave instruction to Titus as a leader in his community:

In everything set them an example by doing what is good. In your
teaching show integrity, seriousness and soundness of speech that

cannot be condemned, so those who oppose you may be ashamed because they have nothing bad to say about us.
TITUS 2:7–8, NIV

Praise without integrity brings shame to a man's reputation and to his business.

Praise in the Church

A man daring to praise in the church house is consistent in expressing the language of worship unto the Lord. It also means being interactive and actively involved in that praise (read Hebrews 12:28).

When you possess an attitude of worship, your physical expression of praise will have a spiritual element. Your entire being will want to give God praise and express gratitude for what your Abba Father has given you. As you agree with what is being sung about God and feel gratitude for what is being revealed through God's Word, the Bible, your spirit will outwardly need to confirm, via your physical actions, what is being manifested inside you. You express your affirmation and agreement through your praise. Perhaps you will lift your hands. Maybe you will shout a "Hallelujah!"

The expression is personal. It comes from inside of you. It builds on a thought or feeling that is expressed in a way unique to you. It could be tears, clapping your hands, head lifted toward the sky. But above all, it is a product of your personality. You may have historically reserved praise for private times, but it is real and heartfelt, and absolutely begins with your relationship with God.

Praise in the Family

This is the area where the man of praise fulfills his responsibility as the leader, counselor, guide, provider, and protector of those in his care. This principle goes back to Genesis, when Adam tended and tilled the garden that was assigned to him by God. The reason we men need to exercise this authority that God has given us is that the garden has a will of its own, just as your front lawn requires you to exercise your will and sovereignty over it by cutting it regularly. If not, it will exercise its will and grow out of control, creating a chaotic eyesore instead of beauty and order.

In your home, you are surrounded by people who have their own wills, and those lives must be tended and tilled by you as the man God has placed there as the head of household. When you dare to praise at home, your praise brings peace and security to all that abide there. A man leading in praise at home creates an atmosphere, exemplifies an attitude, as much as he makes a demonstration. An attitude of praise is important for you because you have the ability to set the tone in any home you occupy. A man must develop a spirit that lifts and brings security to any room he enters. You have been created to influence.

When I think of my father, I remember two men. One was very intellectual, bright, positive, well-read, calm, quiet, and always ready for conversation on any subject. Then there is the other dad. The alcoholic, brooding, complaining, sullen, critical, and non-conversive man he became. He had the ability to transform a room positively or negatively, but he was not a man of praise.

A man of praise has the ability to lift his own mood. His total point of reference is not himself or his problems. A man of praise always has his relationship with God as a reference and a foundation.

An attitude of praise has its spiritual foundations in the New Testament admonition to "pray without ceasing." This command is not limited to physical posture but urges everyone reading this to maintain an attitude of prayer. So to pray constantly cannot be limited to physical posturing. It is a mind-set, an attitude. This mind-set or attitude is accomplished by an awareness of the presence of God. God is present in all places. He is spiritual, so there are no geographic limitations. The prayerful attitude is an awareness of His constant presence. It is the same with praise.

When you as a man are constantly aware that God is always present, there will be a consciousness that produces not only an attitude of prayer but an appropriate attitude of adoration for the God you now know is always with you. This awareness will produce a change in perspective and perception of your environment, because you have become keenly aware that God is with you.

Once this discovery is made, your approach to life takes on a positive, victorious approach. A man's attitude is like the scenery on a stage in which an actor is working. It is the backdrop for the performance. It sets the tone and mood for the actor's portrayal.

When praise becomes the backdrop for a man's life, his daily demeanor is radically changed. Your conversation, attitude, thankfulness, and appreciation for others begins to influence those who come into contact with you. The home you live in takes on a more positive tone, and the expectations of those you care for change to match your own.

Man, you are wired to positively impact your surroundings and produce an encouraging expectation in others.

I have decided, whenever possible, to harness my innate ability to bring a positive influence into the lives of those I come into contact with. I work hard to produce a positive expectation based on substance and consistency. It started with an attitude based on praise. If you change your backdrop, you will change your impact.

Praise brings us face-to-face with God. Praise ushers you into the outer court of worship, and in the inner court—a deep relationship with your Daddy God—you become comfortable with praise. You must move into how you dare to face God. In daring to praise, you step out of tradition and into a victorious lifestyle with God. Daring to praise brings you into the presence of the Almighty.

■

Dare to go deeper with God.

- Allow your praise to usher you into the presence of God.
- Come face-to-face with God.
- Become an example to others of a praise-filled life.
- Break with the traditions of men so that you can seize a breakthrough with God.

If you dare to go deeper with God, you are then ready to take the next step—daring to face God.

12

DARE TO
FACE GOD

*Discover who you are by looking into the
reflective face of God. You will discover
your limitations, then breach the barrier.*

TOWARD THE CONCLUSION of the first Indiana Jones movie, *Raiders of the Lost Ark*, the Nazis have acquired the Ark of the Covenant and attempt to replicate an ancient Jewish ceremony to invoke the power of God. As the ark opens, Indy tells his traveling companion Marion to keep her eyes closed. Neither of them witnessed the powerful and horrific events that occurred after the ark was opened, but when it was all over, they were the only two spared from the wrath of God. The implication was that they were spared because of an ancient Hebrew belief that a look in the face of God was so powerful that it would strike one dead.

Looking upon the face of God was a big deal in Hebrew scripture. Jacob praised God after wrestling with the angel because he knew that he had looked into the face of God and his life had been spared (Genesis 32:30). God spoke to Moses in a face-to-face encounter, as if they were two friends, yet Moses did not die as a result (Exodus 33:11).

As Christians we believe that we will see God face-to-face at the great day of judgment. But what about the here and now? What would it be like to stand face-to-face with Almighty God? How would you feel? What would you say?

The Bible instructs us in 1 Chronicles 16:11, "Look to the LORD and his strength; *seek his face always*" (NIV, emphasis added). God promises us in 2 Chronicles 7:14, "If my people, who are called by my name, will humble themselves and pray and *seek my face* and turn from their wicked ways, then I will hear from heaven and will forgive their sin and will heal their land" (NIV, emphasis added). The psalmist, apparently desperate for an encounter with his Creator, asked, "When shall I come and behold the face of God?" (Psalm 42:2, AMP). Have you ever cried out like this psalmist for a face-to-face encounter with God, or are you afraid of what God will see if you show who you really are?

Why do we earnestly seek God's face yet at the same time draw back, fearful of actually experiencing such an encounter? Our hesitation to come into God's presence is rooted in the fact that we feel much of what we do is not pleasing to God, especially when exposed to the spotlight of God's holiness. The Old Testament prophet Isaiah understood this all too well when he declared, "Woe is me! For I am undone; because I am a man of unclean lips" (Isaiah 6:5, KJV). Even though we have a heartfelt desire to come face-to-face with our Abba Father, our minds fear God will see how unworthy we are and reject us.

The truth is, the moment you have a personal encounter with God, you begin seeing yourself in a way that is both disappointing and hopeful. You must face your sin and failures, acknowledging that you have disappointed God and others. But in seeing yourself as you truly are, you also must accept God's grace and love. To overcome your fear of rejection, first realize the One who created you loves you unconditionally.

I have to admit this whole face-to-face-with-God thing was a little confusing to me at first. I mean, how do you come face-to-face with someone who does not have a physical face? And some of the people who said they represented God seemed ignorant of life, narrow-minded, and really out of touch with reality. To be quite honest, I did not want to meet God at all, much less face-to-face, based on how most Christians represented Him.

But that is the beauty of God. You have to have a personal interaction with him through what He says He stands for. If you know Him based on how He describes Himself, you will have a very up-close and personal meeting with God.

Have you ever read an autobiography of some person you found interesting? The purpose in reading it is actually to get to know the person better. You may have read biographies. You walked away feeling as though you have personal insight into the individual's life, mind, and heart. None of those writers claim divine inspiration, just their interpretation of the facts, general and specific, as they related to the subject's life. The Bible is the autobiography and the biography of God. When you read it, you are coming face-to-face with Him. God is a mirror reflecting what we should be. Looking into His face reveals who you really are.

As the father in the story of the prodigal son stood and gazed longingly down the road, awaiting his son's return (Luke 15), so our Abba Father is waiting for us to turn around and face Him. Before this moment of "repentance" or change—turning away from selfish mindlessness and toward the loving Father—we don't really know who we are.

A son cannot step into manhood until he first comes to himself (Luke 15:17). Commentators on this Bible passage note that this phrase implies a deranged or crazy person coming into his right mind. Separated or at a distance from God, a man cannot rightly know his true image, self, or manhood.

The truth is that until we understand who we are, *imago dei*, or in "the image of God," we live insane, crazed lives with reference to our true identity or potential. Only when we dare to face God can we see we are made in God's image and discover the men the Almighty created us to be.

A PERSONAL DISCOVERY
OF MATURING INTO MANHOOD

I must warn you: A face-to-face encounter with God can leave you feeling disappointed with yourself. The prodigal son came to realize he had sinned against his father and against God in his rebellion. "I am no longer worthy to be called your son," he confessed to his father when he came face-to-face with him (Luke 15:21). Just like the prodigal, we come to see that much of what the world has accepted about us suddenly shows up as totally unacceptable in God's eyes. We begin to see that some of the things we have been justifying are not pleasing to the Father whom we now want to look on us with favor. First Peter 3:12 (AMP) teaches us that "the eyes of the Lord are upon the righteous (those who are upright and in right standing with God)". We know it benefits us greatly to be pleasing in the Father's sight!

Paul explains the spiritual maturation process in 1 Corinthians 13:11–12 (NLT):

When I was a child, I spoke and thought and reasoned as a child. But when I grew up, I put away childish things. Now we see things

imperfectly as in a cloudy mirror, but then we will see everything
with perfect clarity. All that I know now is partial and incomplete,
but then I will know everything completely, just as God now knows
me completely.

The prodigal son had to "come to his senses" and grow up to
where he could face the truth of what his life had become. He had been
behaving like a child, but it was time for him to mature into manhood.

The Hebrew word for presence is *paniym,* which literally means to
be "before one's face" (i.e., face-to-face). When we say "come face-to-
face with God," we mean developing an intimacy with God, a spiritual
nakedness. When Adam and Eve sinned in the fall (Genesis 3), they
could not stand to be naked—revealed and transparent—in God's
presence.

And they heard the sound of the LORD God walking in the garden
in the cool of the day, and Adam and his wife hid themselves from
the presence [paniym] of the LORD God among the trees of the gar-
den. Then the LORD God called to Adam and said to him, "Where
are you?" So he said, "I heard Your voice in the garden, and I was
afraid because I was naked; and I hid myself."
GENESIS 3:8–10, NKJV

In daring to face God, you come naked into God's presence. You
cannot hide your past. Your every thought and feeling is known to
God. Naked before God, you are stripped of your self and must then
be re-formed and reshaped into the form intended by your Creator.

Coming into the presence of God is like looking into one of the
most intense mirrors that you will ever be called to face. You are
keenly aware that because God made you, you are to be a reflection
of godly character. The interaction you have when coming face-to-face

with the Almighty reveals not only your current inadequacies but also your failings of the past. Daring to look into the face of God means you must take a serious look at your history.

Consider the courage, albeit tainted with desperation, it took for the prodigal son to turn around, look his father in the face, and confess all that he had done. He probably expected to see disappointment, maybe even condemnation, in the eyes of his father. Yet he knew in his heart he had to come face-to-face with his past in order to move into his future.

You may be tempted to concentrate only on your own current image reflected in the mirror. You begin to see the signs of physical maturity reflected there and think you are moving into manhood. But if you will look to the side, there you will see that everything that's behind you also is reflected in that image. Moving into manhood and reflecting the image of God in your life means confronting your past and dealing with it. Only after you have been willing to look deeper and repent (change, turn away from, and leave the past) can God begin to reveal the man you were designed to be.

Like the father of the prodigal son, your Abba Father still looks on you with love, no matter how far you venture away from God. He has been waiting for you to come to the realization that the path you have been traveling is not the right one. Once you look back and admit your failings, God can begin to build and shape the man you were meant to be.

MOUND OF ACCUMULATED RUINS

The building of a man is similar to the building of a city like Tel Aviv. Any city in Israel with the word *Tel* in its name indicates it was built on the ruins of another city. The archaeological meaning of *tel* is a "mound of accumulated ruins." What God does when building a man who dares to face Him is to reveal the ruins of his life. Once those ruins are exposed, He uses them for the only thing that they are good for, the foundation of a new life.

Why do you need to dig up and look at those ruins? God wants you to mature and grow on a sure foundation. You have become very attached to some of those things buried in those ruins. Left unexamined, they could cause impurities in your new foundation. There may be parts of your character or personality that need adjusting—perhaps some old habits that you're still holding but that need to be eliminated before the next level of your maturity can be built.

A word of caution as you dig through the old ruins of your past: You can find yourself in love with an era of your life, saying, "Those were the good old days." Listen to yourself as you talk with others in the same age bracket. When you sit around and reminisce, do you celebrate the past? Even though it was not a very good life, you look back fondly at that era, and the hard times seem erased from memory. You compare those times with today and think things were so much better then.

Why spin the past? Because it's easier to remember the good times. Like most people, you may have distanced yourself from the problems of the past in order to minimize the emotional impact of trying times. You can hide from the persona created during that period, while attempting to distance yourself from the people involved in that part of your life.

All of us have thought about or even tried to establish a new history we hope those who love us will help us affirm. That leads me to a truth that has served me well for many years: You cannot unscramble scrambled eggs; all you can do is start fresh. We desire to undo the past when we have an encounter with God, forgetting that the Almighty knows our past even better than we do. A face-to-face meeting with God is about the future rather than the past.

God says, *"It's time for a reality check."*

When you look in the face of God, you suddenly see yourself and your past plainly and are called to deal with it truthfully, perhaps for the very first time. Come to the place where you can say to your Father, "I have sinned against heaven and against You. I tried to do it my way and I was wrong." At some point in our lives we come full circle. The Bible gives us more wisdom concerning this problem.

The prodigal son's choices led him to live in the worst conditions he had ever known. But the worse the situation got, the more his perception of home, his situation, and his identity changed. When he was at his lowest, he came to himself. The young man became reflective, repentant, and appreciative of the provision, protection, predictability, and security of his father's house.

He saw his past in a new way. He began to cherish the things he once rejected. He assumed total responsibility for his present situation. He positioned himself for restoration by deciding to humble himself, return to his father, and apologize. The decision to go back home was his first step beyond the shame of his failures.

In order to reach the other side of shame, you may have to retrace the steps of your life. That means taking a walk down the dark pathway of deeds you would rather not admit to and a look at past decisions that you have hidden under the blanket of unaccountability.

JUST THE WAY YOU ARE

Many times we men will use an excuse to distance ourselves from the responsibility of our past decisions. A look into God's face demands accountability. I have heard people attempt to excuse their faults by saying God loves them the way they are—implying that anyone who doesn't is being judgmental and unreasonable. Let's have a look at this negative self-perpetuation.

It's true; God does love you the way you are. You can rest in that assurance. But God is never satisfied to leave you in the condition you are in. Understand that people who say they love you but are willing to watch you wallow in negativity, inferiority, the pain of the past, wacky thinking, or self-pity do not love you the way God does.

If God simply loved you the way you are, there would not be a need for any action that transforms human life. There would be no need for salvation, forgiveness, deliverance, or grace. God would simply leave you alone. But God's love includes your deliverance. His love requires change and growth. His love is transformative, effective, and strategic. He has a "you" in mind that the Creator of the universe knows you can become. God is never content to leave you alone, and never tires of inspiring you or giving you the strength to change. God *loves* you the way you are but will not *leave* you the way you are.

Facing God necessitates self-examination—an open-minded look at the past and the present produced by that past. Then a different kind of future is possible. God will give you a new sense of who you were created to be and what you are able to accomplish. The you that has been hidden from everyone is clearly revealed in the presence of God. An intense reflection occurs and you either run and hide or change. God loves you enough to challenge you to change.

A different future is only possible if you are willing to change. That change will open new horizons in all of your relationships. A face-to-face meeting with God demands transformation. The encounter reveals the old negatives. Facing God leaves you completely open, but it can also leave you with a lot of questions. How do we deal with the shame that you feel once you are fully exposed before God? What should you do with your past once it is examined and revealed?

When you dare to face God you will discover that He doesn't reject you for what you have done. You'll realize God knows absolutely everything about you, yet still includes you in the all-inclusive invitation for a personal relationship with the Almighty.

TEARING DOWN WALLS OF DEFENSE

We are very quick to notice the faults of others but are sometimes hesitant to address the things we see. I recently had a conversation with a colleague who had a rather strange idea about relocation but had not considered the personal costs. He obviously had given no thought to the change he needed to make within himself and whether the move would produce a different set of outcomes than had occurred where he currently lived. He had not been nearly as successful in his life as his potential suggested. This man had great ideas but little action-producing results. I asked him if I could have an adult conversation with him.

Many times a man like this has built a wall of defenses—protecting what I call a false ego, built to hide feelings of personal failure. While this phenomenon is found in women also, the man trying to hide a lack of accomplishment is generally trying to project confidence by being aggressive or overly assertive. He tends to major in minor things—not speaking to people, demanding courtesy from those he interacts with, and being highly insulted when he doesn't receive it. He is usually in a job he feels is inferior and expects those who are more qualified to look down on him. He anticipates that others will perceive him negatively.

Have you ever known someone who did not want to go to an event but was insulted nevertheless because you did not invite him? I have found that many people in my profession—preachers—have low self-esteem. They use the trappings of success, title, and position to mask their very real insecurities. Many times, men (and women) in leadership are defined by their roles rather than having a well-developed sense of who they really are. Men tend to hide behind machismo, a very ineffective cover.

Our church hosts an annual Power of God Convocation, which pastors from all over the world attend. Held in June, the event includes world-class preaching and teaching, instruction, creative fine arts, music, and support for all phases of ministry. It's also a time for unprecedented networking. Each night of the event, I invite all the pastors in attendance to my office area for a time of fellowship. It's like an old-fashioned house party, with people elbow to elbow holding plates of good food, a lot of laughing, and a great opportunity to meet and connect with people. It is a rare opportunity in our circles. Even though I extend an invitation to all the pastors, I still have to patrol the hallways immediately after each night's event to make sure they respond to the invitation.

I often see pastors going out the exit doors. When I ask them why aren't they joining us, they usually respond, "I didn't think I was invited because I have a small church."

Then I ask, "Did my invitation at any time include the size of the church or did I say all?"

"I just didn't think 'all' included me."

My response, edited for this writing, "Will you just go back!" It's amazing to me that they exclude themselves from an invitation based on past rejections in that kind of setting, along with an inner voice that supports a negative self-image. Their sensitivity to being offended was so acute that they found a way to reject themselves.

So what do you do if you love someone like this? You have to love them enough to challenge them to change and have the kinds of conversations with them that may be uncomfortable but necessary for their change. You have to care enough not to leave them trapped in a self-defeating mind-set that can make them difficult to maintain a relationship with. This is what God does—He loves us enough to not leave us unchanged.

You may know someone who is an offense waiting to occur. You can do little to help a person who believes the world should adjust to his or her distorted point of view. Remember that your desire to help will only be received by one who is not in denial concerning his or her self-perception. This type of self-perception finds its validation in petty things like being easily offended if someone waiting a counter does not gush courtesy all over them. The irony is that this same person is usually picky about bestowing courtesy on others.

A man who is easily offended usually tries to hide behind a bravado that has no real accomplishment. He is offended within himself and looks for others to offend him, too. He gets insulted by trivia that would not bother a more accomplished man who is secure in his identity. Everything seems to challenge his fragile identity.

This man looks for confirmation or rejection in something as simple as another person's glance. You probably have heard someone say, "He looked at me like I was dirt." My response usually is, "How do you look at dirt?" or "How long have you been under the impression that people are paying that much attention to you?" When a man has this narrow perception of himself and life, he tends to respond as if he is the center of most people's attention. This is actually his inner desire and is often a sign of a man deeply wounded by rejection.

His rejection mechanism is rooted in a very strong emotion, making it extremely difficult to persuade him with the facts of a situation. This type of man has a difficult time accepting and changing because the facts of the present do not support the emotions attached to past hurts.

UNCOVERED IN HIS PRESENCE

God will not force you to uncover yourself to Him. The act of confession really is a great illustration of this dynamic. God wants you to come to Him no matter what the issue is. He is faithful, or consistent, in His desire to forgive you. When you uncover yourself, it means you tell him everything. One of the things I love about Him is He knows how to keep a secret.

It could be in traditional prayer or simply a conversation with Him while you are washing the car, but tell Him, talk to Him. You should have no problem talking to Him, because you talk to yourself more than you would like to admit. If you present a problem to Him and you no longer want it, He will take it from you. The Bible says throw all your stuff to Him. He cares for you. God will not force you to uncover yourself, but He wants you to and extends an open invitation to do so. He wants to lift the burden of your low self-image from your shoulders. He wants to take away the heaviness of your painful past.

In Matthew 11:28–30 (NIV), Jesus calls for the weary to bring their troubles to Him:

> *"Come to me, all you who are weary and burdened, and I will give you rest. Take my yoke upon you and learn from me, for I am gentle and humble in heart, and you will find rest for your souls. For my yoke is easy and my burden is light."*

When you look at your tattered past, you may try to approach God wearing the same mask of pretension you've used with others. You think you can "run game" on God, because it has worked on your peers and loved ones. You can't. You only "run game" on yourself when you try to do this. God knows your faults. God simply wants to hear you confess them to Him, as your Abba Father, so that you establish the right relationship, so that you begin to know yourself and forgive yourself.

God loves you so much that He gives you time to uncover yourself in His presence. It happens two primary ways. The more you love Him and the more you learn about Him, the more you understand who He has created you to be—something I call corrective knowledge. God shows you who He is (His honesty, integrity, consistency, His sacrificial love) and invites you to imitate Him.

Emulating the character of God challenges your present methods of interaction and provides you with new ones. Because it is a process, He gives you time and ability by helping you with His Spirit. The Bible says God gives us all things freely to help us (1 Timothy 6:17). The problem with change for a man is hardly ever strength. The problem is often knowledge of God and wisdom concerning what and how to change. Thankfully, God is patient with our progress.

Once you realize the great love God has for you, you will begin to feel safe with your Abba Father and you will begin to remove your masks. With self-exposure comes an ever-increasing revelation of who you are and who you are not. It reminds me of the story in Genesis 27, when Isaac's son Jacob comes seeking his father's blessing by trying to cover up who he really is.

Isaac was the son of Abraham, the famous Biblical patriarch. Isaac had twin sons, Jacob and Esau (Genesis 25). Esau grew up to be a skilled hunter, while Jacob, the more cunning of the two, was an indoor sort of guy. As the firstborn, Esau was first in line for his father's inheritance—what the Bible calls a birthright. The birthright automatically gave two-thirds of the estate to the oldest child.

Jacob persuaded Esau, hungry after a day of hunting in the field, to trade his birthright for a pot of soup. Esau did not understand the full value of his birthright, but Jacob certainly did. Esau swore an oath and agreed to the trade, giving Jacob the birthright.

Some years later, when their father had grown old and weak, he called for his son Esau, to give him the blessing of his birthright. Before Isaac would give the blessing, he wanted Esau to prepare a special meal for him. Esau obeyed his father and went off hunting.

Rebecca, their mother, overheard the conversation between Isaac and Esau. She called Jacob to tell him what she had heard and plotted with Jacob against Isaac and Esau. She wanted Jacob, her favorite, to get the blessing. They forgot the words spoken at the twins' birth, "The elder shall serve the younger."

The two planned a scheme for Jacob to go before his father pretending to be Esau—but to pull it off they needed to do some costuming. Taking advantage of Isaac's advancing age and blindness, Jacob covered himself with lamb's fur to imitate his hairy older brother. He killed two young sheep to replace the venison Isaac had requested from Esau.

Jacob donned his brother's robe and took the cooked meat to his father. Even in his old age, Isaac had a moment of clarity. He discerned the voice as Jacob's voice but the back of his hands and his neck felt like Esau. "The voice is the voice of Jacob," Isaac said, "but the hands are the hands of Esau" (Genesis 27:22, NIV). Jacob was accepted into the presence of his father because he was wearing his older brother's coat. Jacob was accepted because he had disguised himself as Esau.

There is a spiritual reality I must address at this point—the reality of Christ as a covering is being illustrated in this story. The Bible teaches we are in Christ. It is a garment illustration used in the Bible to explain a spiritual truth. We are more like Jacob than we are like Esau. Jacob came to Isaac as a son, but in disguise. We come to God as sons and daughters, but we arrive less than honest. The fortunate thing for all of us is, unlike Isaac, God does not age and His vision is crystal clear. He sees precisely how we are, but He chooses to see us through Christ and His love. So once we are in a relationship with God, he receives us with all our faults because we are dressed in the garment of our older brother (Christ). God gives us His righteousness so He can have a relationship with us.

When you come to God trying to impress Him with your righteousness, He sees you as if you are standing naked before Him. When you come to Him, having a relationship with Him through Jesus Christ, you are covered in Christ's coat of righteousness. This coat is not a disguise that fools God into thinking you are someone other than who you really are—far from it. God chooses to see us this way and made the provision for us to be seen in this way through the death and resurrection of His Son. Christ covers you and shields you, much as an older brother protects his younger, weaker siblings.

FOR WOMEN

THE NEED FOR A DIFFERENCE

Your man becomes transparent when he feels secure and intimate in his relationship with you. A man receives little affirmation or confirmation that he should develop traits like transparency and humility, but a man must be transformed by God's image in order to develop true humility.

When he is uncovered by God's presence, he begins to worship with greater intensity. This uncovering is a crucial step in his ability to become more transparent and open with you and your ability to relate to him.

He begins to see things differently. Don't take away his ability to see things differently, and differently from the way you, as a woman, see them. If you have successfully henpecked the man in your life, you have successfully taken away his ability to see things differently.

It is the difference that initially attracted you to that man. It was his masculinity, not femininity, that turned your head. He was distinctly different.

That distinction is what attracted you to him or what will make you love him more as he comes face-to-face with God, unless you came from a mama-dominated household. If you came from such a household, something strange happens. You will watch your mother dominate your father and say, I never want a man like that. But then when you choose one, you choose one you can dominate. You look for someone to think like you and be like you, which means you don't get a real man.

If "no" is not half of his vocabulary, you don't have a real man, because he is only telling you half of the time what he is really thinking. We men don't agree with a whole lot of what you women say. We go along with a lot. The reason most men agree with what they don't agree with is for peace. But that kind of peace costs you what you need. If a man is close to you, he needs to be able to tell you when you're not making sense. Not because he wants to argue with you, but because he is being real, he is being transparent.

A man who is becoming intimate with God is going to be more confident and vocal. He will tell you when you're not making sense, because he doesn't want you to go out and say that same crazy thing to somebody else. If you embarrass yourself, you embarrass him. If he corrects your diction and your grammar, it's not that he is offending you, it's just that he doesn't want you saying that to other people. If he tries to correct your emotionalism, you've got a real man on your hands. If he attacks what's wrong, you've got a real man on your hands.

A man who is face-to-face with God is not concerned about peace. A man who is face-to-face with God doesn't care if you get mad. A man who is face-to-face with God will tell you you're old enough not to mix up your wants and your desires. A man who is face-to-face with God will sometimes hurt your feelings. You think he's picking you apart, but he's trying to make sure you're representing God—and him—well. He doesn't want anybody looking at you like they're looking at hoochies. He sees you as a reflection of himself, and that is Biblical. The Bible says that the woman is the glory of the man. (When he starts giving you suggestions—for example, "You know, I love you, baby, and just because they sell that dress in your size doesn't mean you've got to buy it. I think you look better in . . ."—you need to listen. When a man wants to dress you, it's because he cares about you. See what happens when you heed what he says about stuff that doesn't matter much, like a dress or something, because he's really sizing you up for some diamonds. But if you reject what he says about something small, he knows you won't listen to him on the major things. This is how a man's mind works, especially once he develops a strong relationship with God.)

When a man who is face-to-face with God comes into your life, he's usually popular. People like him. He's the life of the party. People respect him and everybody knows him. He talks to everybody. He doesn't even have to know anybody, but when he comes into a room full of strangers, he just says hi to everyone. When you first meet him, you like that. Because you're with him when you walk in the room—you're not a stranger—everyone is speaking to you and being nice to you because of him.

A man who is face-to-face with God takes you places you wouldn't go on your own. He talks to you about how you should see things. Don't think he's trying to control you—he's just trying to expand your horizons.

A look into the face of God also removes the excuses a man makes for himself. It also removes any excuse you may have for any victimization you feel you have experienced from him. He's accountable to God. You must hold him accountable for his actions toward you. Generally, a man will use an excuse to distance himself from the responsibility of a decision he has made, while a woman may blame her actions on another person. This is a Biblical reality revealed by Adam and Eve.

Looking into God's face demands accountability from the man in your life and positions you to be free from excusing your behavior by blaming your incorrect decisions on someone else. This uncovering is a crucial step in his ability to become more transparent and open with you and your ability to relate to him.

A man who hungers for God begins to develop a heart for Him and for you.

BE READY TO FACE HIM AND FIND BALANCE

Even with all your issues, whatever they may be, you are allowed in the presence of the Father because, if you believe in Christ, you are wearing the covering of your older brother Jesus. If you are pretending with God, the problem may be that you are not living in this truth. Instead, you come to God wearing masks and trying to hide your weaknesses, hoping to expose only what you consider to be your strengths. Understanding that God will never be impressed by your strength is a revelation of God's mercy and how much more work you need to do.

In life we naturally present the best to the people we meet, but God wants you to bring to Him your weakest, so He can make you strong. This truth is revealed in a story of a man whose right hand was withered. In the story, Jesus was visiting a place of worship and encountered a man with a disfigured hand. He told the man to come forward and stretch out his hand. The man did the opposite of what most people would do. He extended the problem hand when most people would try to hide the problem. His honesty was rewarded. Jesus performed a miracle and healed the hand, bringing it to wholeness, like the other hand. Jesus gave him the ability to live a balanced life.

When you face God, hiding nothing, He is able to bestow balance in your life. Balance in life is usually understood as giving the major components in your life the same attention at the same time—God, spouse, family, work, parents, and so on. This traditional definition of balance, however, is a formula for failure. True balance is not a straight line.

Achieving successful balance in life is more like juggling several balls in the air. All of the balls are in the air, all at varying heights, but in control. Life is just like that when successful balance is exercised. Priorities shift, causing one component to receive more attention than another for a moment, but the priority for the moment will eventually normalize. That normalization brings the priority back into balance with the other important interests of life.

At times, life seems to pile up on you and you can feel overwhelmed. In very stressful times, you may feel tempted to chuck your whole life when the items on your plate are piling up and running off the sides. Or the items on your plate have reached their shelf life and you need to take them off. Like cans of food, some things were not meant to stay with you forever and you have to let go of them.

Some things in your life are constant; those usually are not the items causing the stress. It's usually the extra stuff like a demanding project at work or the season of your child's chosen extracurricular activity or a stressful time in the life of someone you care about that demands your involvement.

The stress can feel so overwhelming you feel as though your entire life has gone crazy. In reality, it may be only one or two issues causing the overload. Some people consider major changes in lifestyle or vocation when the things causing the stress have a natural shelf life and will migrate off the shelf by themselves. For example, you may feel stressed fighting rush hour traffic to pick up your daughter from day care by 5:30 so you won't get fined. But your child will not always be in day care. The temptation is to throw out the entire plate when the project at work has a completion date, but the overtime demand at work will conclude in a month, or soccer season will end. The wisdom of God is a great help at these times.

My own life is very full and demanding. Some components are constant; others are what I call projects. I am often asked how I handle the demands of so many major responsibilities. I apply the plate principle along with the submission principle. Instead of rebelling against the weight of my responsibilities, I submit to it. Every time I accept the weight of the season in my life, I find I have the strength to handle the tasks. Submission to the weight of a task reveals my ability to handle that task. When I don't feel up to it, I rely on the strength of God. I tell God about it and ask Him for strength. By telling God, I am honestly confessing my weakness in search of His never-ending power.

God is looking for you to willingly expose your weaknesses to Him. Be ready, once you dare to face God, to reveal all your inadequacies and then be willing to allow Him to begin a radical transformation of all the things you believe represent who you are. As you truly examine your past, you will see an image you have manufactured for yourself and others to believe.

God desires you to be shaped in His image, not that of the world or your own imaginings. He already knows everything about you, so exposing yourself isn't really about revealing your weaknesses. It's about trusting Him enough to stand before God naked and vulnerable and surrender yourself to Him, giving Him all that you are, and allowing God to do with you as He pleases.

TRANSPARENCY BETWEEN FRIENDS—YOU AND JESUS

This Biblical story in 1 Samuel 18 serves as an example of the type of relationship we should have with the Lord. It especially illustrates the beginning of the relationship between Christ and any man. It is a relationship that joins you and Christ firmly together in a brotherly love for each other, similar to that of a man's love for a woman. To demonstrate the type of relationship the Lord desires with us, the Bible reveals the relationship Jonathan desired with David and took steps to initiate such. He began to take off the things that represented who he was and give them to David. Christ gave up His heavenly role and His life on earth for you. God requires that we take off the trappings we think represent our manhood and our identity and give them all to Christ.

Notice what Jonathan was willing to do as his soul bonded with David's in 1 Samuel 18. Jonathan became extraordinarily transparent in his friend's presence. Saul, Jonathan's father, was the king. David, then a shepherd boy, demonstrated his love, loyalty, and devotion for Saul. When David met Saul's son, Jonathan, the two became immediate friends. They were as close as any two brothers could be. The Bible says they were "knit" in their souls, even though at the time Jonathan was a prince and David was a lowly shepherd. The two exchanged pledges of friendship for the future, but something else occurred. Jonathan took off his robe, his bow, and his sword, items that represented his title, his strength, and even his masculinity, and gave them to David (read 1 Samuel 18:1–4).

Jonathan was sending a message: "I am giving you my identity. I trust you with who I am. David, I see in you all that I want to be, all that I admire, and the only way I know how to get it is to trade my identity for yours." Jonathan surrendered his total self to David.

One of our biggest issues as men is the surrender of our perceived authority. Jonathan recognized something in David he felt it was appropriate to submit to. It is an example of a man submitting himself to Jesus; it is not, as some have interpreted it, God illustrating a homosexual relationship. The underlying principle you can adopt is this: There will always have to be an act of submission and therefore a feeling of vulnerability in every relationship.

It happens in your work, sports, clubs, church, or other endeavors; you will never experience promotion or maturity without a period of vulnerability. It is quite natural when you leave something familiar to get involved in something new. A man must learn how to manage these emotions so he will not reject new dimensions of opportunities, relationships, and maturity. I say dimensions instead of levels because levels are usually comparisons with other people.

When you first come into the presence of God, it is like seeing through a cloudy glass—your own image is not clear to you. But the longer you stay face-to-face with God, the clearer your reflection becomes. Ultimately, the Bible says, we all are going to be just like Him, because we will also come to see Him as He is (1 John 3:2). Meanwhile, we go through a process of handing Jesus what we have labeled as our masculinity and our machismo. We turn over our defense mechanism and our mantle, or the image that we have for ourselves, to Jesus and then something totally opposite of what the world expects happens to us—we begin the discovery of true manhood.

In the world, if I hand you everything that represents who I am, I lose something. But in Christ, the more of my life I lay down, the more of my life I gain. It is similar to what occurs when a piece of sand gets stuck in the shell of an oyster. The sand becomes an irritant, but the oyster covers the irritant with something precious. An oil is released from the oyster that begins to transform that irritant into something very valuable.

Your sin, like the grain of sand, is attached to Jesus. Jesus, in His death at Calvary, transformed your sin into a relationship between you and God.

When a man gets face-to-face with God, he makes a decision: "I see clearly that everything I've attempted to build in my own image and in my own mind is inadequate. I am now ready to trade all that I have and all that represents who I am, and put those things in the hands of Jesus. I am willing to trust Him with everything that I am." Only then can he truly understand the transforming power of God. This man understands that no matter where he has come from, no matter what his background, he can be called *a man after God's own heart.*

TAKE ON THE MIND OF CHRIST

That radical transformation is available to you once you commit yourself to the Lord. The real man in you can only be discovered through a relationship with God. The transformation is possible only if you are willing to trade in the non-productive characteristics of your life. Trust is the key that unlocks the transfer. Like Jonathan did before David, turn the identifying aspects of your life over to God. Let His way become your way—your mind, your emotions, and your will.

The Bible says to let the mind of Christ become your mind (Philippians 2:5). Become willing to exchange your mind for His mind. This means trading in your selfishness for consideration; it means allowing this new mind-set to remake your personality. When you trade in your identity, you are committing to emulate the character of Jesus, rather than the macho man you may have established as your image. You become committed to trusting God for wisdom, endurance, strength, commitment, and all the other character traits that reflect the image of God. You turn over the management contract of your life to the Lord.

Give the Lord your agenda-driven personality by taking on a servant's posture. This means becoming more concerned about others and how to serve them.

When Jesus is the brother-friend, the Lord, of your life, you will have a new sense of accountability. A new standard for your decisions and lifestyle happens, impacting not only the decisions you make but the process of making them. The ultimate concern is doing what pleases God. After the mind comes the will.

When you trade the inconsistency of your emotions for the consistent, steady heart a man must possess, you become the standard of emotional consistency in the lives of those connected to you. When you have adopted the self-control of Jesus, you become a symbol of strength in your community. Once you are in control of your mind and emotions, the application of your will ultimately changes your decisions and involvements. Your conscience leads you to right decisions. Your will no longer leads you into error, because you have exchanged your will for His will.

While Jesus was in the Garden of Gethsemane, He asked God if there was any away He could avoid the cross of Calvary. God did not answer because He had not changed His mind. Jesus, understanding His Father, replied, "Not as I will, but as You *will*" (Matthew 26:36–39, NKJV). Jesus traded His desire for the will of His Father. Once you turn your will over to the Lord, your decisions, direction, and destiny are transformed. You become aware of the will of God as a guide and reference for all your decisions. You open the door to have what I call a "Gethsemane experience."

When you decide to imitate the mind of Christ, you gain control over emotions previously seen as a challenge and direct your will toward reflecting the image of God. Your life begins to change for the better. You start the journey to becoming a man after God's own heart.

BECOMING A MAN AFTER GOD'S OWN HEART

King David was deemed by God to be a man after His heart. This is often confusing to people who know David's life story. From outward appearances, David seemed one of the least likely men in the Bible to become a success. His father and brothers rejected him as not having the potential for being a king. He was probably illegitimate. David had the dirty job of the youngest boy of the family—tending the sheep. Nevertheless he rose from shepherd boy to king. Despite his meteoric rise to power, he messed up—big-time! He was far from perfect: he ate the sacred food reserved only for the priests, he took another's man wife and then had the man killed, he failed to discipline his children. Political intrigue, murder, and infidelity were a part of his administration, yet he is called a man after God's own heart. How could that be? Why did God give David the distinction of always loving him and giving him this special place in the heart of the Almighty?

It's very simple. Instead of running away from God when he made a mistake, David got face-to-face with God and asked for forgiveness. This made him the distinct man that he was, in Israel's history, in Biblical history, and especially to God. His story illustrates a man who understands his God and the nature of their relationship. David proved to be the type of man God is looking for.

Contrast King David to his predecessor, King Saul (read 1 Samuel 13:13–14, NIV). When Saul had used up all of God's patience, He sent the prophet Samuel to confront him about his disobedience to God.

Samuel declared, "You have not kept the command the Lord your God gave you."

A man's background can be overcome by the anointing of God on his life. David revealed his own past in Psalm 51:5 (KJV): "I was shapen in iniquity; and in sin did my mother conceive me." David came to God the way we need to come to God. Despite being steeped in inadequacy and failure, David drew closer to God when most men would have pulled further away. Therefore, God said of David, even after his sin, that he was a man "after my own heart" (Acts 13:22).

David composed this psalm, which reflects his desire to be close to God, even during the lowest times of his life:

> When You said, "Seek My face,"
> My heart said to You, "Your face, LORD, I will seek."
> Do not hide Your face from me;
> Do not turn Your servant away in anger;
> You have been my help;
> Do not leave me nor forsake me,
> O God of my salvation.
>
> PSALM 27:8–9, NKJV

As you dare to meet God face-to-face and expose every area of weakness in your life, your Abba Father will begin to build on even the ruins of your life and move you into maturity. Once that building has begun, you can expect your life to be blessed by God. That blessing isn't your own doing, but rather a work of grace.

■

I dare you to be transparent before God.

- Understand that facing God is non-negotiable if you will reach your potential.

- Come before God in humility; He does not need to be impressed.
- Be uncovered by His presence.
- Give God the things you think identify you as a man.
- Become transparent. Trust God not to reject you after you tell Him what He already knows. Transparency leads to true intimacy.
- Be a man after God's own heart. No matter what, don't run from Him; run toward Him.

13

DARE TO ACCEPT CONSEQUENCES

Denial is the defense of failures.

G OD FORGAVE DAVID. He did not take away the consequences of his actions, however. David retained his kingdom, but drama was a constant problem. He valued his relationship with God and kept the lines of communication open by confession to God. He understood that if we confess our sin, God is faithful to forgive our sin and cleanse us from our unrighteousness (1 John 1:9).

When you appreciate the significance of seeking God's face, you understand that the Almighty is a loving Father. Though God may chastise us, God's mercy always precedes His judgment. Knowing this should eliminate any fears of rejection that have clouded your thoughts. Yes, you will still have to deal with the consequences of your poor choices, but no matter what you do, you are never rejected by your Father in Heaven.

This concept of God is challenging for most people. The best way to understand God's mind is by looking at the ministry of Jesus. The Savior did not descend from heaven and come to earth looking for perfection. If he was only looking for perfect people, he would have never had a disciple. Jesus proclaimed He did not come for well people, but the sick (Matthew 9:12; Mark 2:17; Luke 5:31). Your imperfection, not your strength, is what draws the Lord to you.

There may be some things in your life you find no pride in and will always be ashamed of. That feeling is appropriate for a man who has taken responsibility for his actions. No man is perfect—and most of us are repeat offenders, often deluding ourselves into believing that the context changes the nature of our mistakes.

If you are a man like David and have made many mistakes—imprisoned for crimes committed, caused great pain in the lives of those you said you loved, or lived a life of self-indulgence, caring about little else but the present—God is waiting to accept you. Your sin will not cause God to turn away as you seek His face.

People make mistakes. Recognize that incorrect behavior is not always a mistake. We call them mistakes in retrospect, but at the time our behavior was very intentional and had little to do with how we were perceived or people's disapproval. Only after we mature can we see the long-range effects of our action.

Many times a man will feel entrenched in a habit or behavior—alcohol, drugs, sexual promiscuity, violence, criminal behavior—or a weakness in character that produces consistent unproductive behavior. Perhaps you were mercenary in your career pursuit—dishonest, falsely loyal, agenda-driven or a user in relationships, with a success-at-any-cost attitude. Perhaps the cost of your corporate success meant hardship in another person's life and family—a fellow employee lost his job because of your take-no-prisoners attitude. Maybe a business competitor lost an opportunity because of your all's-fair-in-love-and-war approach to business. It seemed okay at the time, but now it's clear you were wrong in your thinking, implementation, and rationalization of the negative outcomes you perpetuated.

Imagine your life is a house. Don't just invite the Lord into the rooms you have straightened up. He needs to have access to the entire house—especially the rooms that are a mess. That's what he wants you to give Him. Don't present the Lord with your strengths, give him the stuff that's messed up. He has the power to make your crooked things straight. His love, acceptance, and forgiveness can change the things that have been wrong for a long time. God has a miracle of transformation for every man. God wants to make a new man out of you!

God does not take away the consequences of our actions, and if you must face harsh or hurtful consequences, remember consequences are actually beneficial. They are designed to teach you not to repeat the same mistakes again. Remember, consequences, negative or positive, are always educational. Many times we are kind of slow to learn. One important way to learn not to repeat a mistake is to understand the benefit of a negative consequence.

If you work and get paid a week's wages, that is a positive consequence. The paycheck encourages you. The lesson learned is to repeat the same behavior if the same result is desired. It is the same principle with a twist when it comes to negative consequences. If you, as a man, do something that produces a negative result, like not going to work and not getting a check, it should teach you to go to work if you want to get paid. So you learn not to repeat the behavior if you like money. But the consequences are not just a loss of pay, but a loss of perception as a reliable individual. Then, when terminated, and you need a reference from the previous employer, you can't get one, so it's difficult for you to get another job.

The domino effect begins and you experience difficulty in meeting other obligations. You may want to blame this outcome on a variety of factors, but the bottom line is that you did not go to work.

That bottom line—the end result—must always be your consideration when evaluating your actions and outcome. You have to face the consequences of your actions to become the ultimately successful man you can become. When analyzing your actions and the consequences, never ever leave out your part of the success or disaster in your mind. Go to school on your success as well as your failures.

GODLY MANHOOD REQUIRES A CREATIVE MIRACLE

If you will dare to allow yourself to be transparent and vulnerable in the face of God, not only will you experience love from the Father, it also allows Him to complete His creative work in you. There is a Biblical illustration that shows the creative work the Lord will do if a man allows himself to be vulnerable before Him. Of the known miracles of Jesus, He encountered one man who was congenitally blind (John 9:1–12).

Jesus spat on the ground and made a mud paste and put it on the man's eye sockets. A passage in Genesis 2 describes how God created man after the mist had fallen and watered the ground. Understanding this creative process brings clarity to why Jesus used mud. He needed to create something that had been missing in the man from birth. Since the blind man's creation was incomplete, Jesus went back to the Genesis creation, wet the ground with His own saliva, and placed the mud on the man's eye sockets. Jesus sent the man to the Pool of Siloam, the pool of deliverance and miracles, and instructed him to wash away the extra mud, revealing God's creative miracle, a pair of eyes.

Jesus did more than heal the man's blindness. He created something that was missing in the man's life. God will do the same for you if you will dare to expose your inadequacies and weaknesses before Him. Whatever it is that has been missing in your life, once you become transparent in the face of God, Jesus then is able to complete your creation and send you out whole.

It is common for a man to adopt an attitude of doubt concerning personal change. You may have started to believe what others have said about you, but more important, you may have accepted those negative statements as valid and true. Truthfully, it is possible that you have given those who love you all the ammunition they need to make their unflattering assessments. They may be correct in their opinion because of the things you have done, giving reasonable people no alternative but to draw disparaging conclusions about you.

Perhaps you've given your word as a man and broken it so many times that no one believes you now. If this is the case, your loved ones are justified in their negative opinions of your lack of concern for others. You may have acted inappropriately, yet want the respect of a man who lives a life of integrity. Perhaps you did wrong and were publicly exposed, and there is no denying it. No matter what you have done, you are not beyond the help of God. Your life can be repaired.

One of the greatest moments in my life was the day I stopped making excuses for myself. Once I realized my explanation did not change the outcome, I began to be a lot more reliable as a man. Not showing up but expecting people to act as though you did because of your explanation will never, ever change the outcome.

I remember taking care of my brother one day while my mom was away working. I was given a set of instructions to follow and implement that day. My brother had not gotten the memo that he was supposed to follow my instructions. He usually didn't. He insisted on playing in the front yard and the rules were to stay on the porch. I had grown tired of going to get him and decided to let him do what he wanted to do. I would just tell Mom when she got home. He kept running into the yard and throwing himself into the grass. I did not see the shard of glass. He dove in and cut his hand. It was my job to watch and correct him. I did not do it. He got cut and I caught it when Mom got home. My excuse was he would not listen. Mom was not buying it at all.

I had not fulfilled my assignment. My reasons did not change the outcome and I had to face the consequences. It taught me a lesson. In a world of expectation, excuses will never alter the effects of the consequences. If you shoot me by accident, apologize all day, and promise never to do it again, I will probably forgive you but I am still shot.

Our church is full of men from diverse backgrounds, with all manners of criminal pasts—and I do mean all. Drug addiction, murder, and federal, state, and local infractions are representative of the crimes committed by men who made a lifestyle of irresponsibility and unaccountability. Yet today, these men are radically transformed into productive, committed, serious men who are billboards for transformed manhood.

God wants to create the real man in you—a man of responsibility, integrity, consistency, reliability, and productivity. This life is available to you if you will make yourself available to God. In looking again at Jesus' miracle performed on the man with the withered hand (Matthew 12:13), we see another example of God's creative miracles. By showing Jesus his deformed hand, the man was acknowledging his deficiency and his desire to be made whole.

Think about it for a moment. The man also had to possess a measure of faith in order to dare to stretch out his withered hand to Jesus—revealing all his imperfections—and giving Him room to perform a creative miracle. He had to believe that Jesus was a healer who had the power to take what was useless and make it useful. Therefore, a man of faith who is not afraid to get in God's face will receive a creative miracle, no matter what is lacking in his life.

Once his hand was restored, it brought balance into that man's life. Imagine how difficult it must have been for him, especially in those days, trying to accomplish even the simplest tasks with only one functioning hand. Everything that man tried to do would have been out of balance. God will bring balance back to your lives, bring you to wholeness, and give you the ability to get back to His purposes if you are willing to stretch out your imperfections to Him.

I dare you to give God all the unbalanced, weakened, and withered parts of your manhood and watch Him restore the balance in your life.

- Believe God for a creative miracle in becoming a new man in Christ.
- Show God the bad hand, the weak side of your life.
- Give God a chance and He will provide the balance.

14

Dare to Worship Vulnerably, Without Doubt

Relationship requires discovery.
There is no discovery without an element
of doubt and vulnerability. When trust
develops, there is vulnerability but
there should be very little doubt.

I N PREVIOUS CHAPTERS, I shared how cultivating a heart of praise and worship was a challenging growth process for the men in our church. It challenged me as well. Worship takes you further in the display of emotion and intimacy. You, like most men, may be challenged in publicly displaying intimate emotions toward your spouse or a family member, let alone toward God. Publicly exposing the intimacy of your spiritual relationship will deepen you as a worshipper. In worship, you become highly vulnerable and exposed to others.

Worship exposes your heart. Your inner man becomes a public picture for other people, not just God, to observe. Daring to worship out of a deep, private, personal, and intimate relationship with God becomes one of the greatest "dares" of your relational life. Worship marks the beginning and the continuation of a relationship-building process with God. Your relationship with your Abba Father impacts all your other relationships.

Every significant relationship requires real vulnerability. For years, I had very few real relationships with men. This was probably because of the failed relationship I had with my father, even though my grandfather was an extremely strong symbol of manhood to me.

As I entered professional relationships with other businessmen, I found myself being extremely cautious. Because my father was such a promise breaker, I tended to expect to be let down by men. This was not very logical but it was emotionally real. I inadvertently began to look for relationships that had no period of vulnerability. Impossible!

So when I began to have a relationship with God, I realized one of my biggest drawbacks was my emotions. There is no relationship as significant as the one I have with God, and looking back I see that there is none that required a higher degree of vulnerability. The learning curve with God is extreme. Worship requires relationship. What fills the gap with God and with people?

Faith! It is faith that fills the gap where vulnerability needs to dwell until your knowledge of the focus of your attention increases enough for you to be vulnerable. The vulnerability needed in every relationship can only be compensated for with faith. Once faith is born in you, you will worship with vulnerability and not doubt.

BE VULNERABLE WHEN YOU WORSHIP

One of the greatest battles any man faces is allowing himself to become vulnerable. To willingly become susceptible to another requires a high level of trust in the relationship. Therefore, for you to build a lasting and fruitful relationship requires both time and effort. The more you know about someone, the more you feel you can trust that person. The more you can trust, the more vulnerable you allow yourself to be with the person. How often have you heard or given the advice, "Take it slow, take your time, and get to know someone before you trust your life or your future to them"?

Worship is the beginning and the continuation of a relationship-building process with God. It is prudent to ask yourself some questions:

- How do I get to know an invisible God?
- How do I form a relationship with the Creator of the Universe?
- How do I connect with a God who seems elusive and untouchable?
- How do I build the level of trust needed to overcome my feelings of insecurity?
- Who can teach me how to accomplish this with both men and women who seem to be dealing with similar issues of vulnerability?

Herein lies the root fear of every man's pursuit of understanding and articulating true worship.

OVERCOMING THE FEAR OF REJECTION

As men, we tend to approach a relationship with God in the same way we would with another person. We start out trying to impress Him with our strength, our maturity, and our ability instead of seeking to really *know* Him. We come to God hoping that those things we have accomplished that have amazed other people will also impress Him. Deeper into the relationship, though, we find God is more interested in our *inabilities* than He is in our so-called *achievements*.

Uncovering your inabilities before a righteous God will produce acute feelings of vulnerability and insecurity that are deeply rooted in the fear of rejection. This fear of rejection is one of the primary reasons we men work so hard to hide our inabilities, our insufficiencies, and our infirmities from the world, even from those closest to us. It is an absolute truth that most men have become masters at wearing masks and hiding their true identities. Many times those closest to us feel they know us, but deep inside there is a part of us we are afraid to reveal. We fear that should this weakness or characteristic be unearthed, it will sharply contradict the perception we have created of ourselves for most of our lives. Therefore, the thought of coming into the presence of an all-knowing God, allowing the mask to come off and your inabilities to be exposed, can present a real dilemma.

Overcoming these fears means daring to admit to God and yourself that you are dealing with the fear of rejection. You must dare to stand before Almighty God clothed only in your vulnerability and insecurity and refuse to allow the fear of rejection to come between you and Him.

TRUE WORSHIP RISKS VULNERABILITY

The interchange between God and Moses at the burning bush in Exodus 3 clearly illustrates how worship risks vulnerability. The first thing God said to Moses is, "Take your sandals off your feet, for the place where you stand is holy ground" (Exodus 3:5, NKJV). Moses' shoes represented all his issues and insecurities plus all his reasons for fearing rejection:

- the home he was released from prematurely
- the river where he was cast that placed him in the hands of his enemies
- the palace where he was raised and where his identity was exposed

- his eviction from a place of relative comfort
- his season of confusion in the wilderness
- and even his being accepted by strangers in a foreign land

As Moses stood before God and heard his assignment, all of his insecurities and issues with rejection surfaced through his questions. "Who am I?" Moses asked. "What shall I say? Who shall I say sent me? Who shall believe me?" In the presence of God, he saw only his physical inabilities and his perceived failures. He already had been rejected by the very people God now wanted him to help. What an insecure place to be! Moses reacted as most of us would in such a situation.

As a mere mortal, how do you dare to do something you don't know how to do and don't feel adequate to accomplish? What is your first step? How do you deal with issues of rejection, persecution, and low self-esteem that have been cultivated over a major portion of your life? When you study the way God answered Moses and how He dealt with all those insecurities, you learn the depth of God's desire to help you overcome them and move you into your proper position and authority. Through this story, you learn that you can trust the love of your Heavenly Father to not send you in alone or leave you unprepared for the assignment at hand. You also learn the very real need to depend on God for direction and guidance every step along your journey.

REVEALING YOURSELF BEFORE GOD

When you begin a relationship with God, it is natural to want to conceal your inadequacies, but you know deep within that God knows everything about you: all your fears and pain, successes and failures, thoughts and feelings—everything!

The confidence-building truth Moses' interaction with God reveals is that despite what God knows about you, He welcomes you into His presence. The insecurity and unworthiness that you feel is simply spiritual confirmation that you are in the presence of a holy God. A holy God inspires in us feelings of both insecurity and intrigue. God's holiness draws us to Him. What's fascinating and intriguing to us is that as Abba Father, our "Daddy" can love us in spite of ourselves.

When Jesus addresses God as "Abba," He demonstrates an intimacy in our worship devoid of outward ritual or form. God invites us first to relationship before our behavior, intimacy, and outward expression change and develop toward Him. To speak of God as "Daddy" is never an affront to his Holiness; it is only an offense to the religiously self-righteous.

If you truly desire to make yourself vulnerable and enter into true worship, you cannot do so without understanding that God is already aware of your insufficiency and insecurity. When you are weak, it is at that juncture that God stands up and is shown strong (see 2 Corinthians 12:10). God wants to have a Father-son relationship that acknowledges your need for His guidance and direction as well as one that openly articulates your thanksgiving and praise for what He is doing in your life. In John 4:24, Jesus expands this by explaining that we are to worship the Father *in spirit and in truth*.

LOVE: PATIENT WISDOM

You cannot talk about relationship-building without discussing the interesting and complicated concept of love. Love is both exhilarating and frightening at the same time. Love is exhilarating because it gives you a sense of purpose and security. But it can be frightening, because your happiness is connected to the behavior and commitment of another person. Any time you profess to love someone, you position yourself under that person's direct influence. Love's vulnerability opens you up to the risk of hurt and gives another the authority to chastise you and even grants them the power to impact your hopes and dreams.

In every relationship in a man's life, there is a season of vulnerability and insecurity while both parties begin to learn about each other. As you strive to shore up your position in each other's life, you both may go through periods of jealousy and even experience unsettling feelings of inadequacy. This sense of insecurity and vulnerability your man feels in earthly relationships can transfer into his relationship with God.

Does your request that your man go to church with you trigger an automatic argument? Recognize that there are many reasons why he may be slow to commit to regular opportunities to worship God. It's not just to aggravate you! You can support your man's moving to become a man who worships. Understand that men naturally tend to resist situations that produce vulnerability, like worship. His resistance to vulnerability is rooted in his lack of experience with intimacy. Encourage his steps toward intimacy with God, understanding that your man must love God passionately before he can love you sincerely.

As he takes steps toward consistent worship, allow him room to worship God in the way that fits him. Men tend to worship relationally and reject the superficiality and meaningless ritual that so often accompany religious services. Be patient and flexible. Your man shouldn't go to a worship service just to get you off his back. Most important is that his worship is pleasing to God. It will be an encouragement to you.

TWO FRONTIERS OF WORSHIP—
SPIRIT/TRUTH AND
BELIEVING WITHOUT SEEING

In John 4:21–24, Jesus teaches that the Father is looking for those who will worship Him in spirit and in truth. It is the Spirit of God that allows us to enter into a relationship with God, which then produces true worship of God. "The Spirit itself beareth witness with our spirit, that we are the children of God" (Romans 8:16, KJV). All true worship is a result of an ever-increasing relationship with God. Daring to boldly go to the throne of grace in a time of need (see Hebrews 4:16) requires that you first overcome your insecurities.

God desires that you—and every other man—realize He is seeking those who dare to be true worshippers. Men who dare to worship are those who understand who they are and willingly acknowledge who God is. In the Abba Father equation, God says He will cover our infirmities, support us, restore us, resurrect us, and begin to transform us into the men that He has created us to be.

One of Jesus' twelve disciples, Thomas, had walked alongside Jesus but was marked by doubt and believed only what he could see with his own eyes and touch with his hands. After the resurrection, he fell at the feet of Jesus and worshipped him, saying, "My Lord and my God!" Jesus accepted Thomas' worship. He didn't chastise him for doubting; in fact He blessed him. And added, "Blessed are those who believe without seeing me" (see John 20:24–29, NLT). There is an even greater blessing in store for those who will believe before they see a physical manifestation. A multiplied blessing is available to those who dare to be vulnerable enough to worship God in spirit and in truth.

Many men live with a self-sufficient, wanting-to-be-in-control attitude that says, "I need to see it to believe it." You can bring this same attitude into the presence of God, all the while doubting the integrity of the self-reliant person that you've worked so hard to create. Jesus knows all about you, understands your doubts, and still accepts you, as He did Thomas. It is at this intersection that you can have a revelation of true worship. It's when you see the nail-scarred hands of Jesus and realize God loved you long before you ever knew He was your Father. Like Thomas, we can do no more than fall at His feet and declare, "My Lord and my God!"

Many men have difficulty allowing themselves to enter a place of vulnerability in worship and intimacy with a father because of their childhood experiences. If your childhood haunts and hinders you, make an intentional decision to move from doubting to trusting your heavenly Father and knowing that He loves you with a depth that is beyond your full comprehension. Stretch yourself beyond your human experience into a spiritual realm that involves risky faith.

■

I dare you to worship out of deep and passionate love for your Abba Father, coming to God with a love that is all-consuming—your heart, mind, soul, and strength.

- Risk vulnerability.
- Embrace intimacy with Abba Father.

- Abandon doubting God while risking trust through a leap of faith.
- Love God passionately—with all your mind, heart, soul, and strength.
- Worship relationally in spirit and truth, not ritualistically or religiously.

15

DARE TO RECEIVE
A BLESSING

*God blessed them and said to them,
"Be fruitful and increase in number;
fill the earth and subdue it."*

—GENESIS 1:28, NIV

A MAN'S DISCOVERY of his uniqueness empowers him to achieve success by the total utilization of his ability. Once you discover your uniqueness, you will understand that God has empowered you in your own special area of ability. God has designed an environment for you that will attract the blessings and the resources appropriate to your talent. Within you lies a distinctiveness and uniqueness that equips you to access the blessing in your particular marketplace, family, polity, and community. The Biblical principle is this: God gives you all you need to receive the blessing.

Will you receive it?

ACCESSING THE BLESSINGS
DESPITE COMMON BLOCKS

Jesus taught that "it is your Father's good pleasure to give you the king-dom" (Luke 12:32, NKJV). Ed Cole, noted Christian author on men's issues, succinctly commented, "God's good pleasure is to give us His Kingdom. The issue is not to convince God to give the Kingdom to us, but to where we can receive it."

God equips a man to be blessed and places him in an environment to receive that blessing. Whether the man chooses to be blessed or not is up to him. He has to *dare to receive the blessing*. The problem for most of us with accessing the blessing is the process we must "go through" to release it. We resist going through the processes of growth that God has for us, like trusting, learning, being equipped, and changing.

Faith takes you through God's process for receiving blessing. The Bible teaches that the only way to receive your blessing is through faith (Galatians 3:13–14). That which God has prepared for you to use can only be released according to what you believe. Generally speaking, the blessing you desire appears to be outside the realm of your capability, something you cannot do on your own. Generally, you do not register as blessings the achievements that you can easily bring to fruition. What you perceive as blessing are the things God has to release or personally reveal to you that are above and beyond your capability. But, that desire for blessing has to start as a promise you heard you were entitled to receive. "So then faith [*trust, believing*] comes by hearing, and hearing by the word of God" (Romans 10:17, NKJV—emphasis added).

Once you *hear* (i.e., learn, discover, and understand) God's prom-ise to you, a desire begins to grow inside of you. When you reach the point where you believe blessing is available to you, the faith you will need to access it begins to be cultivated from within.

When you develop a hunger for your blessing, you then begin to hope for something you cannot yet see. The process progresses like this:

- **Hear!** You hear or read God's Word to learn more about His promises.
- **Learn!** The more you learn about His promises the more you begin to believe.
- **Declare!** As your faith grows you declare the promise to be a possibility in your life, which releases more blessings to manifest in your life.

When you understand this process and make the choice to trust God and His Word, you are choosing to be blessed. Abraham was such a man. He dared to receive a blessing.

Hear!

Abraham was a picture of faith. Abraham's beginnings were remarkably commonplace among men of his time. His choices, not his origin, set him apart from mediocrity. Birthed a pagan and living in a non-religious environment, he heard a divine word and chose to learn and declare. When God personally spoke to Abram, he was then seventy-five years old and living in a place called Haran. God's instructions to Abram were "Leave your country, your people and your father's household and go to the land I will show you" (Genesis 12:1, NIV). The command came first and then the promise of the blessing followed. "I will make you into a great nation and I will *bless* you; I will make your name great, and you will be a *blessing.* I will *bless* those who *bless* you, and whoever curses you I will curse; and all peoples on earth will be *blessed* through you" (Genesis 12:2–3, NIV— emphasis added).

DARE TO RECEIVE A BLESSING 177

Seemingly out of the blue, God incredulously promised to give unbelieving Abram a wealth of blessings. He promised to establish a great nation from this childless, seventy-five-year-old man and his wife, who was well past her childbearing years. What is almost as astounding is the fact that Abram did as the Lord had instructed. The Bible says that Abram left his homeland and started his journey based on this monologue, this unilateral promise from God. Packing up his wife, Sarai, his nephew, Lot, and all their possessions, Abram set out for Canaan.

Abraham is called the "Father of Faith" because of his trusting obedience to God's instructions. His life paints a "picture of faith" with brushstrokes applied with obedience and risk. His wife and companion, Sarai, in this context, represents grace. Grace gets in a relationship with whom the Father assigns. Grace is silent and follows even when she does not agree with where faith is going or what faith is doing. Grace is often given away by faith but never complains. God always returns Grace to faith even though faith has not merited her favor.

Fear and integrity impact faith as polarities. Abram walked into a tight situation and found his faith wavering. The Egyptian pharaoh desired Sarai—a picture of grace. Grace is always attractive to people. Rarely do they understand that while Grace is free, she is made available at great cost to the Giver. Abram imagines that the Egyptian king will take his life; fear sets in and His integrity is challenged. He tells Sarai—who was quite beautiful even for her age—to pretend she was his sister rather than his wife.

In essence, Abram says to Grace, "Tell them you are something other than Grace," because Grace is attractive, even to the unsaved. Grace does what faith instructs her to do and she is taken away. But God turns the kingdom upside down to get grace back in partnership with faith.

Abram is the picture of a man of faith who finds his character challenged in the midst of two types of situations—fear and famine. When Abram got into a tight spot, fear set in and he forgot the promises of God. Suddenly, Abram gave Sarai away. (He takes a chance on losing Grace, but Grace simply waits for God to send her back to the man of faith.) The man of faith gets reacquainted with Grace, and they set out on their journey again. Affliction reveals not only the positive aspects of our character but also the negative.

Abram (whose name by this time had been changed to Abraham) has to go through a similar test with another king named Abimelech, and for a second time he let fear challenge His faith in God (read Genesis 20). Afraid of what might happen to him if it was discovered that Sarah (her name had been changed also) was his wife, he again pretended that she was his sister. Fear is perhaps the greatest enemy of faith. He didn't consider the fact that his life was not in any real danger, because the promise of God had not yet been fulfilled in him.

After the second test, Abraham finally understood that God's promise covered three people—him, his wife, and their promised son Isaac, the person through whom his God-ordained destiny was to be accomplished.

Abraham, father of the Hebrew nation, discovered that God was ultimately concerned with the plans and future He had for Abraham and his descendants. An eternal God had little concern for how much time it would take for Abraham to achieve success through faith. God had made provision for Abraham's character development so it would be completed by the time he received God's promises for land and legacy.

Learn!

Circumstances and situations are designed to reveal your character to you, not to God. The key is to react correctly to that revelation and allow God to transform you so you don't sabotage your own destiny. God will reveal who you are so that you can see yourself as God and others see you. In knowing yourself, you can no longer deny or ignore your character flaws. In our weaknesses, God reveals His strength and power to transform us and ensure His purpose in and through us. God promised, "My grace is sufficient for you, for My strength is made perfect in weakness" (2 Corinthians 12:9, NKJV).

When you dare to face your weaknesses, you discover that God will not reject you, but rather will use that confrontation to cause you to grow and mature. Over and over, God used situations and circumstances to mirror Abraham's character flaws, not for the purpose of condemnation but for transformation.

Moving beyond the familiar is also illustrated in Abraham's story. Abraham had two other challenges he had to face early in life, challenges common to many men. First was pagan authority over his life. Abram brought his pagan father with him as he left his homeland and journeyed toward his promise. This meant he still had pagan authority over his life. Pagan authority works in your mind to mute God's voice of truth and hinder your growth and maturity.

Parents are to be honored and respected for what God has done through them. At the very least, they have birthed us, and we can honor them for that. If they transgress God's laws, however, they pass on their sins, curses, and unbelief to future generations. We who are in Christ do not have to receive that legacy, however. In Christ's cross, every curse is broken and its pagan authority is replaced by a spiritual authority that guides us in all truth.

The second challenge was troublesome relatives in his life. Abram had not separated himself relationally from them. His nephew, Lot, would introduce a number of tribulations into Abraham's life. Lot's poor decisions created crises in his own life, which in turn had a negative ripple effect in Abraham's life.

At times, a man of faith allows his compassion to overrule his common sense, and he takes along people who will delay his destiny and interrupt his progress. Such relatives need your prayers and wise, godly counsel, but they don't need your advice or rescue. You cannot fix them or their problems. Only God can change others; you can't. You cannot take responsibility for their wrong decisions. You cannot cover or excuse their mistakes. What you can do is speak the truth in love while staying fixed on the plans and purposes God has for you. Abraham eventually had to separate from Lot in order to fulfill God's purposes for his own life.

Abraham represents the challenges of having to move out of familiar dimensions and away from negative relationships. It is human nature to cherish the familiar and love the very people who are most troublesome to you. God does not necessarily require that you abandon those relationships, but rather that you move away from the power of their influence in your decision making. When you are willing to do that, you begin to walk in blessing.

FOR WOMEN

CHANGE OFTEN DEMANDS CHANGE

Your man can only dare to be blessed by learning to trust God for what he wants and needs to accomplish in his life. As he learns to trust God, he will learn to trust you and help your relationship grow into one that is pleasing to God. He also becomes a man who is more worthy of your trust. He grows to trust God and His promises out of his own relationship with God; he cannot do it through you. In trusting God, he learns patience for God's ways and God's timing.

Cultivate your own level of patience, knowing that he needs a partner like you to wait with him. Your man is unique and cannot be motivated by your comparing him with what other men are doing.

As he learns to wait in faith, his character is revealed and strengthened through trying circumstances. His faithful waiting teaches him to speak good news to you rather than bad news, because he knows God is in control.

Ultimately, in order for him to exercise godly authority with you in co-regency, he must come out from under pagan authority. That means separating from troublesome relatives and friends—both his and yours.

Declare!

The learning part of the process has just been described. Declaration involves speaking what God has promised and proclaiming His truth instead of constantly bemoaning your circumstances. His promise is always good news. If you aren't careful, you can major in bad news, talking much more about what's difficult instead of what's promised. Stop complaining about God's process in your life! Start declaring what He has promised instead of what you think or feel. The truth is, your opinion simply doesn't matter. The only opinion that counts is God's.

Many men fall away before receiving the blessing because they don't understand God's timing and the process required to actually possess it. Receiving a blessing requires desire, patience, process, and possession. Declaration begins the possession. We cannot possess what we don't believe, speak, and then act upon. The process is necessary; without it, we cannot find lasting success and significance in God's timing.

Relationships can be a distraction along the way, but so can impatience. Once you have seen the promise, developed the faith needed to receive the blessings, and dealt with relationships that could impede your progress, your human nature steps up and demands, "I want it now!"

THE TIMING OF GOD

You may not always understand the correlation between your circumstances and the timing of God. Time, unfolding as history, is the stage on which God acts and accomplishes His purposes. God's purposes and plans run parallel with human circumstances like a set of railroad tracks. In the natural, if you look at a rail line into the distance, it appears as though those tracks converge down the line. The point at which earthly time and circumstance converge is a *kairos* moment of revelation for man. *Kairos* is a Greek word for a specific time or season. At a *kairos* moment, time and eternity intersect according to God's design and will. You cannot birth or contrive a *kairos* moment. That is God's doing without regard to human impatience or manipulation.

At times you grow impatient with waiting for God's timing and circumstance to come together. The challenges you face while waiting for that *kairos* moment are the multitude of choices that emerge along the journey. Most men will agree that whenever there is a godly choice or "God idea," there are always "good idea" alternatives to consider as well. Good ideas are for the moment, but "God ideas" are for eternity. (Evangelist Tim Storey, in *Good Idea or God Idea?*, introduced the concept of a God idea versus a good idea. Storey asserts that good ideas keep us busy but rarely move us forward. Good ideas make a dent in things but fail to make an impact. Good ideas may make a man appear successful but cannot take him from success to significance.)

Conversely, a God idea embodies wisdom, knowledge, and understanding. A God idea takes the long look, seeing how the thing will end up years later. A God idea focuses on pleasing God instead of pleasing man.

Good ideas randomly bombard you, distracting you from discerning the very God idea that can move you from confusion into clarity. A God idea actually shocks your erratic life-beats into a steady, consistent rhythm, moving you from dysfunction into progress. God ideas flood into time at *kairos* moments to transform chaos into order.

Several things can affect your decision-making process along this railway path toward your *kairos* moments. As you attempt to make the righteous choice, you may allow the impatience that rumbles in the volcanic people around you to influence your decision-making process. There was no overt indication of impatience on Abraham's part, but Sarah became impatient with the time it was taking to see God's promise for an offspring to be fulfilled. Sarah had a good idea: conceive a son with her maid, Hagar.

So Abraham had a son through Hagar. He discovered in the natural that he still had the natural ability to receive the blessing. The problem with his son, Ishmael, was that he was produced through human effort—a good idea but not a God idea. Patience is essential to receiving a divine promise. Isaac, the true and promised heir, was the long-awaited, only-begotten son of Abraham and Sarah.

The couple had to go through the process of God's planning, purpose, and timing before they could be renamed Abraham and Sarah, reflecting the needed change in their character. Through the Hagar episode, Abraham developed in character and became the stronger leader he needed to be to possess the promise.

WAIT WITHIN OUR WAITING

The most difficult attitude to embrace is the willingness to wait. "They that wait upon the Lord shall renew their strength," God declares in Isaiah 40:31 (KJV). You must wait through your feelings, beliefs, experiences, relationships, and circumstances to receive God's idea for your next step. The right choice is found within His timing, not your desire to "get on with it."

Even the great apostle Paul dealt with the issue of choices: "For I have the desire to do what is good, but I cannot carry it out. For what I do is not the good I want to do; no, the evil I do not want to do—this I keep on doing.... So I find this law at work: When I want to do good, evil is right there with me" (Romans 7:18b–19, 21, NIV).

Choices are a natural part of life. You may think it easier to pluck unripe fruit off the tree than to wait to see what God's ultimate, ripened fruit is for your life. It's always easier to choose the instant, good-looking choice and call it a miracle instead of waiting for God's miracle-birthing process—which often takes time, trials, obedience, steadfastness, and painful growth.

Seeing God's purpose manifested requires patient, obedient faith. When you dare to be blessed, you have to dare to "wait within your waiting." This is not just waiting with impatience, but waiting with the confidence that He is able to accomplish what He has promised. "And I am certain that God, who began the good work within you, will continue his work until it is finally finished on the day when Christ Jesus returns" (Philippians 1:6, NLT).

When God's promise is revealed, you must go through His process to possess that promise—you cannot take shortcuts. The man who dares to be blessed must believe that God will preserve him through His process—hear, learn, and declare.

DO YOU WANT TO MAKE A DIFFERENCE?

The time from when I accepted God's call to ministry until I took possession of it took all of ten years. When I compared myself with my peers—who were being called, licensed, and ordained within six months—I began to ask the Lord why. He answered me with a question, "Do you want to make a difference?"

At about the third year of my journey, I became frustrated with waiting and wanted to quit. God wouldn't let me. Around the seventh year, I became quietly frustrated again and decided I would like to go back to secular work. God let me know that I couldn't do that either. It was three more years before God called me to pastor the church I presently lead in New Jersey.

Looking back, I realized that had I launched out on my own when I thought I was ready, I would have missed the lessons I needed to learn between the third and the seventh year. I would have circumvented the specialized training I need to handle what's happening in our church right now. If I had quit between the seventh and the tenth year, I would have bypassed the equipping I lacked for the work God has now placed in my hands. I have come to understand that through God's process, not only did I develop patience, I also acquired the expertise to utilize my unique God-given abilities.

As I looked back on that time of process, God revealed a very profound principle to me: The height of a building is directly related to the depth and the width of the foundation. I realized that the reason God made me wait so long for ordination was that He was widening and deepening my foundation to build the ministry He was going to place under my stewardship.

God first builds the man, then He builds the ministry, the vocation, and the profession. Like Abraham, I can look back and see that everything I went though was essential to inheriting my blessing and to maintaining it as well. If I had not had certain challenges—the

186 DARE TO BE A MAN

famines, the afflictions, the setbacks, and the disappointments along the way—I would not have developed the character needed to preserve the blessing.

I have also come to understand a final dynamic in daring to be blessed: possession and security are the most difficult parts of this process. The Bible says that we will have blessing *without* sorrow, but the Word also warns we will have blessing *with* persecution. If I had not learned how to endure the persecution that is automatically a part of being blessed, it would have produced sorrow in me. I might have gotten to the place of promise and been totally dissatisfied instead of being able to inherit and possess the full blessing.

God wants to show you in a very profound way that, throughout the journey, He is equipping you. Once you understand that the wilderness is actually a refining school, then you can face the process with a lot more integrity. Once you recognize the need to walk through the *entire process* of God, you will be more patient and learn how to do what the psalmist says, *wait within your waiting.*

> *I wait for the Lord, my soul waits,*
> *And in His word I do hope.*
> *My soul waits for the Lord*
> *more than those who watch for the morning—*
> *Yes, more than those who watch for the morning.*
> PSALM 130:5–6, NKJV

When you have certain assurance that God has given you a plan and recognize that you have been created to do a certain thing within His Kingdom, then you also must realize that the waiting times, with all your trials and wilderness experiences, are vital parts of your process. A man who cannot wait, and who will not endure through each progressive step, will never get the chance to participate in the ultimate will of God for his life.

Your waiting and developing time is necessary to bring you to a place where you can understand who the Father says you are and what you are capable of accomplishing.

I dare you to receive your blessing, and walk in the destiny and anointing of your position.

- Discover that your uniqueness empowers you to achieve success by maximizing your abilities.
- Know that faith will take you through God's process to receive His blessing.
- Listen to God's promises for you.
- Learn about God's timing and plans for you.
- Declare the good news of His promises.
- Discover that circumstances and situations are designed to reveal your character to you.
- Come out from under pagan authority over your life.
- Separate from troublesome relatives and friends.
- Be willing to wait within your waiting.

16

Dare to Wear Your Coat of Destiny

Think, speak, and walk in the
direction of your goals.

I HAVE MANY ROLES, but I am clear that those roles are not my
identity. I am a businessman, banker, pastor, husband, father,
bishop, son, and church leader—but they are not who I am. My
identity and destiny are not determined by my skills, associations, or
memberships. My credentials and résumé do not validate or establish
my past accomplishments or future dreams.

Nonetheless, I meet people daily who ask me what I do instead of
wanting to know who I am. If I responded, "I am a man," they might
respond incredulously, "Of course you are. I can see that." But the
fact that I look and dress like a male doesn't mean I have a secure or
appropriate understanding of myself as a man created in God's

image and destined to be a new creation in Christ. Only when I shed the coats of my past and dare to wear my coat of destiny do I really start becoming the man God knows me to be.

God's destiny clothes you with uniqueness and worth, potential and prestige. The coat of destiny—or cloak, as it is referred to in the Bible (2 Kings 2, NIV)—has to do with the identity and anointing God has placed over you. Elijah's mantle represented his calling, anointing, and prophetic office.

The difficulty you face as you begin to realize the uniqueness of what God has placed within you is that, like most men, you probably grew up hanging out with a crowd of peers who dressed, talked, and acted alike. If you never outgrew that need to belong in order to achieve your identity, you may still be operating from that peer-group mind-set. You will introduce yourself based on the clique, social club, or business organization you belong to. Your identity at this level is established through your group memberships or based on the work you do. You believe your associations validate your existence as well as your status in society.

MAN AS A NEW CREATION

The apostle Paul writes, "Therefore if any man be in Christ, he is a new creature: old things are passed away; behold, all things are become new" (2 Corinthians 5:17, KJV). The Greek word for new, *kainos*, literally means "previously unknown." In other words, when God gives you a new identity in Christ, you are unique, one of a kind, and radically new.

When you dare to become a man of God, a radical transformation begins that may require a degree of separation from those with whom you previously derived acceptance and validation. You begin to take on a new identity, and to abandon the old identity, which may have been one of the most insecure places in your life. You may have invested years cultivating an image you believe has made you acceptable in certain cultural contexts. You may have sewn a coat for yourself that has come to represent everything you aspire to achieve.

Suddenly, having dared to face God, you are required to take off that old garment of identity and put on your new coat of destiny. You feel disoriented and out of place. Change is always uncomfortable, but without transformation there can be no growth.

If you look back honestly, you will realize there were times when an internal voice tried to tell you there was something different about you. But your need to belong was so intense that you attempted to quiet or distort the voice. You may have tried to make your uniqueness fit within the acceptable mode of behavior determined by your circle of friends. You even may have believed your social organization was the vessel that was going to carry you into your destiny. But these feelings were circumvented when what you were created to be began to generate an irresistible force within, encouraging you to let go of the old and drawing you in to test the waters of new beginnings.

As you emerged into adulthood, the more you began to discover your unique abilities, the more you saw yourself walking along a different pathway of life. As this new path unfolded before you, and you began to walk toward your destiny, subtle divisions and slight detachments began to occur in peer relationships that lacked transcendent accountability. You slowly began to realize the need to move from being "one of the boys" into the maturity of manhood.

PUTTING ON A NEW IDENTITY

What happens when you discover who God says you are and realize you don't know how to transition from being one of the boys to becoming your own man? It is quite an upsetting day when you realize the people you thought were comrades for life may no longer be viable voices of influence. At this point, you begin to see that some of those who've participated in all the major events of your life thus far may not be the friends you are going to take into your future. You begin to realize these relationships may not be God-ordained to help you fulfill your destiny.

Part of the problem with being a man is the inordinate number of years you spend molding and fixing yourself into a shape that you think is acceptable to other men (who also are unsure of who they will one day become). We men tend to depend on peers, stuff, success, wealth, status, or popularity to get to where others think we need to be. But you eventually come to realize just how much you depend on your group to determine what you can and cannot do. God wants you to break away from your dependence on human beings and come to rely on Him for your true identity.

Jesus calls us to throw off our old cloak, jump up, and move on like the blind beggar who sat by the Jericho roadside did when he met Christ in a *kainos* moment. Blind Bartimaeus and other beggars came every day to seek aid from those who traveled a major roadway (Mark 10:46–52). This group of beggars found comfort and even acceptance in one another's company. One day, Bartimaeus learned Jesus was among a crowd of passersby. He called out to Jesus. Despite the crowd's rebuke, he continued his impolite shouts in a desperate attempt to gain Jesus' attention. We are not told how many other beggars sat with him, but it was only Bartimaeus who threw off his coat, jumped to his feet, and ran to Jesus.

There is great significance in the order of events here. Bartimaeus called to Jesus, who stopped and called for this blind beggar to be brought to Him. Before Bartimaeus even approached Jesus to ask for his healing, he threw off his cloak and jumped to his feet (Mark 10:46–52). The cloak he was wearing is called the *himation*, which represented everything that he was, including his position as a beggar. Everyone understood what wearing that cloak meant.

When Bartimaeus threw off his coat, he threw off his beggar's identity and aggressively separated himself from those associated with that image. They all had resigned themselves to living as powerless beggars, sitting by the roadside without a real or productive identity. But Bartimaeus dared to be different. Something inside of him convinced him that he no longer needed that cloak. He dared to run to Jesus to receive his true coat of destiny. Jesus told Bartimaeus, "Go, your *faith* has healed you" [emphasis added]. Immediately, the former beggar received his sight and followed Jesus along the road (Mark 10:52, NIV). His life was changed for the better. He willingly threw off his old coat and stepped forward to accept his true coat of destiny.

All of this happens when you discover your true mantle, your own coat, which symbolizes reaching your true manhood. You learn that you cannot allow another to tell you who you are or what you are destined to be.

SAUL AND DAVID–BOTH CALLED TO ROYALTY; ONLY ONE BECAME A TRUE KING

Young David is another example of one who refused to allow another to limit his ability to step into his destiny. When David declared he would fight the giant Goliath, King Saul attempted to put his own tunic and his royal coat of armor on David. But even as a young man,

David had sense enough to know he could not defeat the giant wearing Saul's coat (1 Samuel 17:1–40). Though Saul ruled a great nation, David knew wearing another man's identity could not affirm his own empowerment, his anointing, or his destiny.

David could, however, draw some things from Saul as he prepared to do battle with Goliath: (1) Saul could fight; (2) Saul was a king; (3) Saul was a leader of his nation.

But David could not accomplish what God had called David to do using Saul's identity. He could not adopt Saul's envious nature, his insanity, or his inconsistent faith. He could not face a giant in adopting Saul's unconcern for the emotional and mental state of his children or the cowardice he had publicly expressed in the face of this challenge.

God called for David to be ready to step in as the next king-in-training. David had to face Goliath in his own garment, wearing his own coat of destiny. He defeated the giant without the help of Saul or his armor (1 Samuel 17:38–50). David was secure in who he was, knowing what he was called to accomplish on that day. His sense of duty arose out of his God-given destiny, not his allegiance to a man. He did not need another man's identity in order to move into his destiny.

THE COAT REPRESENTS THE PROMISE

Do you remember the story of Joseph's beautiful coat in Genesis 37? It represents the promise of the fulfillment of a vision. If we compare his story to that of Jesus, we see that Joseph's brothers actually represent the Pharisees and the Sadducees at Calvary. They stripped the coat from Joseph, just as Jesus was stripped prior to His crucifixion. When Joseph's brothers decided their dreaming brother had to go, they stripped off the symbol of Joseph's dream and his father's favor. Joseph's coat was a Technicolor, cinematic, futuristic, destiny-oriented coat. Great insight emerges from the soundtrack of *Joseph and the Amazing Technicolor Dreamcoat*, because the lyrics reveal that what kept Joseph going, despite all the adversities in his life, was the fact that he had a vision and a revelation of the significance of his coat of destiny. That vision and revelation reassured him over and over that the Lord was with him. When you know who you are and hold on to that knowledge, circumstances will not alter your self-perception. You will be able to traverse the difficulties of life and hold on to your true identity. At each juncture, Joseph was able to say, "This doesn't look like the life that God has shown me."

While he was in the pit he remembered, "This is not the promise." Even as Potiphar's wife tried to seduce him and he was unjustly incarcerated, he held on to the truth: "This bears no resemblance to the vision God has given me."

When you understand that your coat of identity produces a vision of who God has created you to be, then circumstance and time will produce patience rather than discouragement. Living in recognition of what God has created you to be keeps you consistently headed toward the place of your destiny. You can move from the pigsty to the mansion when you realize who your Father has created you to be and begin to walk in that identity.

FOR WOMEN

HIS OWN COAT

Your man has to wear his own coat, one that has been designed for him by God. He cannot wear a coat you have designed for him. You cannot clothe him with your faith. He cannot fit into your father's coat, your pastor's coat, or the coat of any other male role model you may want to project onto him.

Realize that along his spiritual journey, he can still seek the promise of his coat of destiny even if his is stripped from him. If his dreams seem to have been taken from him, he needs you to support and believe in him even more as he looks to God and believes in Him for his destiny.

If your man needs to return to the Father's arms, your encouragement is everything! Your criticism only serves to discourage him from pursuing his faith journey. He can put on Christ only for himself. He can't do it—and won't do it—just because you want him to.

REESTABLISHED IDENTITY

While Joseph embraced his identity, the prodigal son rejected the man he was called to be. Unlike Joseph, he chose to leave the environment that his father had created for him and deliberately set out on his own path. Despite all his self-inflicted agony, the wayward son remained confident in his identity as his father's son, a distinction he'd tried to run from.

The Biblical story also implies that the prodigal's father never stopped looking for his son to return. Even though the young man landed himself in a pigpen—an even greater shame because he was Jewish—far from the place he was called to be, the image of the father confirmed that he was a still a son and still had a destiny.

On his return home, his father saw him before he had even reached the family compound. The father repositioned him back as a member of his household by putting shoes on his feet and a ring on his finger, and a coat on his back (Luke 15:11–31).

That's what God wants to do for every man who is willing to come back to His waiting arms. It doesn't matter if you have foolishly squandered all your inheritance. God wants to reestablish your identity, your authority, and your position.

In addition, the Father has a fatted calf that He has been preparing for each son's return. This represents the love of God always anticipating and eager to celebrate the return of a son to his true identity.

God wants you to have your rightful identity in Him. This is such an amazing kingdom principle, such a place of hope for every man. It doesn't matter whether you've lost your way or your identity. You can return to the Father and He will reestablish your inner image. But only God can grant this coat of destiny to you.

This parable gives infinite hope, because there is no indication of the duration of time between the son's departure and his return. It could have been a few years or a very long period of time. Whether a man comes back to get his coat after a year or five years or fifty years, the time passed is irrelevant to God. The coat is still there waiting. The Father always has the coat, the mantle, ready.

PUT ON CHRIST

In the story discussed earlier about Isaac's twin sons (Genesis 27), you will recall, Jacob deceived his father into giving him the blessing of the firstborn son by pretending to be his older brother and wearing his coat. In the sight of God, once Christ is in your life, He willingly exchanges garments with you, allowing you to receive your inheritance through a legitimate relationship with Him.

Throughout Paul's literary imagery describing our relationship with Jesus, he says to *put on the Lord Jesus Christ* (Romans 13:12–14, NKJV). It is like taking off an old garment and putting on a new coat. You are to not just cover up the old man; you are to remove that old identity and put on the new man, complete with a new identity.

The coat of destiny can also be understood as a mantle, which has to do with identity, position, and anointing. When the prophet Elijah's mantle fell, it represented the transfer of the office of prophet as well as the passing of the anointing from one man to another (2 Kings 2:13–18, NIV). So the cloak, or the coat, represents not only the identity but also the capability and the authority in God. Elisha had dared to put on the mantle—which had once belonged to his mentor, Elijah—his coat of destiny, in order to access all that God had destined for him. So did Joseph. So did David. So did the prodigal son. And so can you.

I dare you to don the coat of destiny that your Heavenly Father has designed for you, and step into the fullness of your position and authority as a son of God.

- Seek God's destiny, which clothes you with uniqueness and worth, potential and prestige.
- Separate from the boys, who are content to live in ignorance of their divine destiny.
- Refuse to wear another man's coat of destiny.
- Remember the promise of the coat, even when others strip it from you.
- Return to the Father's arms, as He wants to reestablish your identity, authority, and position.
- Put on Christ.

DARE TO RELATE
GOD'S WAY

~~~

Relationships reveal!

Y EARS AGO, business was conducted with a handshake and a
verbal agreement. A man's word was his bond, and parties
didn't feel the need to put everything in writing with signa-
tures, witnesses, and notaries. Today business is conducted differently. In the field of banking, for example, there are a multitude of
contracts for loans, mortgages, installment agreements, investments,
and the like. Banks make contractual agreements with customers,
clients, employees, and investors. In today's world, an enforceable
and accountable fiduciary relationship is defined by contract.

This legalistic mind-set has permeated our other relationships—
prenuptial contracts, separation, divorce, and parental rights contracts.

Parents can adopt children through legal contracts and children can divorce parents through contracts. Churches contract with ministers for professional pastoral services. Parents contract for child-care services. Sadly, most of us even view marriage as a contract that can be terminated or broken when either party is unhappy or dissatisfied.

God's way of defining relationships is different from man's way. God speaks of relationship by using the word "covenant." A covenant in the Old Testament (in Hebrew, *berit*) represents a pact, alliance, or *relationship* that is built on certain Biblical qualities and lasting value (e.g., communication, agreement, trust, loyalty, friendship, acceptance, affirmation). A primary attribute of covenant relationships that distinguishes them from contractual agreements is *love*. Banking and business contracts have no provisions for love, but every God-formed relationship is defined by love. He is love and all He does and commands reflects love—unconditional acceptance. God expects us to love one another in this same way, with equal intensity and devotion (read 1 John 4:7–11).

DARING TO LOVE UNCONDITIONALLY

Daring to relate God's way means treating people the way God wants us to. Jesus explained it for us by saying we are to love others as we love ourselves (Matthew 22:39). The principle we need to grab hold of here is that the depth of a man's character and all that he really is can be seen in the significant relationships in his life. A man will have several significant relationships throughout his lifetime, many overlapping in the same time frame. He is a son and a brother. He is a husband and a father. He is an employee and an employer. He is a disciple and he makes disciples.

If you want to determine whether a man is responsible, account-able, and consistent, or if you want to know whether he exhibits the love of God in his life, just observe his primary relationships. Especially look into the relationship he has with the important woman in his life. It has been wisely noted that you can determine how a man is doing by observing the countenance of his wife.

FOR WOMEN

THE WAY WE TALK

Men and women have different styles of communication. Style speaks of the way we mix verbal and nonverbal language when we communicate. In male-female relationships, women have to pay more attention to learn men's communication style, and men have to pay more attention to understanding the needs of a female in communication.

As a woman, you are likely to use more words to communicate one point, while a man may use a multitude of nonverbal signals and only a few words to communicate. Strive to understand his style and seek to move toward him in both style and understanding. When these two things happen, your communication gap will steadily shrink.

Be patient and affirming as he tries to learn your style of communication and what your nonverbal cues mean. Your man cannot read your mind. He doesn't intuitively know what you want. Strive to communicate your needs and desires to him in a way that he can hear and understand. Recognize his unique verbal and nonverbal communication.

Developing strong communication in a relationship requires

work and patience. Work with him, not against him, in developing an effective process of communication that will help you both build a stronger relationship.

The example you set as a man will be imitated by those with whom you have a significant relationship. The way you interact as a husband with your wife models the standard for the kind of relationship your children will expect to have with their spouses. The father/son relationship you grew up with determines how you approach parenting as a father. The way you have honored your parents is the way your children will honor you. The unselfish or selfish way you relate to your siblings will be copied by your children with their brothers and sisters. The apostle Paul dared to make this statement to those around him, "And you should imitate me, just as I imitate Christ" (1 Corinthians 11:1, NLT). As a man, would you dare make such a statement to your family, friends, or colleagues in the workplace?

GOD'S PLUMB LINE

Our Heavenly Father sets the standard for every relationship we enter. The measuring stick of God's loving nature keeps our relationships in alignment, both with Him and with each other. There are ways you can measure how well you are doing in holding true to God's standard. First is comparing your ways with His through consistent study of His Word.

Jesus taught His disciples that the key to relating God's way is *love.* "So now I am giving you a new commandment: Love each other. Just as I have loved you, you should love each other" (John 13:34, NLT). He described how others would know that we are His disciples using this same standard of measure. "Your love for one another will prove to the world that you are my disciples" (John 13:35, NLT).

Love, from God's perspective, manifests at a higher standard. We can say we love hamburgers, and then we use the same word for describing our relationship with our children. The world teaches us to love stuff and use people. God's way is to love people and use stuff. "This is my commandment: Love each other in the same way I have loved you. There is no greater love than to lay down one's life for one's friends" (John 15:12–13, NLT).

God set the standard high when He gave the ultimate gift of love, His Son. "God so loved the world, that he gave his only begotten Son" (John 3:16, KJV). There are times we may wonder how God could love *everyone,* but His Word is very clear on that point. Paul reiterated the importance of understanding God's definition of love in 1 Corinthians 13:4–8 (NLT):

> *Love is patient and kind. Love is not jealous or boastful or proud or rude. It does not demand its own way. It is not irritable, and it keeps no record of being wronged. It does not rejoice about injustice but rejoices whenever the truth wins out. Love never gives up, never loses faith, is always hopeful, and endures through every circumstance. . . . Love will last forever!*

Love is more concerned with the well-being of another than with self. Love desires God's best for others. This is definitely not the standard the world has set, even for our most intimate relationships.

Imagine a relationship where you truly regard the other as superior (read Philippians 2:3). Most human beings seem unable to handle such an assignment. Only through the work of the Holy Spirit in you, constantly refining your character and maturing you in the fruit of the Spirit, can such an attitude of humility be produced within you (read Philippians 2:4–5).

The apostle Peter gives us practical advice on how to handle the significant relationships in our lives. He concludes that we cannot even pray effectively if we do not learn to relate God's way within our earthly relationships (read 1 Peter 3:7–8).

LOVE COMMUNICATES

How can we expect to communicate effectively with God if we cannot communicate in love with those closest to us here on earth? God is love. To expect to have an intimate relationship with God, then, we too must love, and show it in our speech.

There is a difference between talking and communicating. Many people consider talking as communication. Talking may not resolve a concern that arises between parties; however, communication is geared toward resolution. Talking does not necessarily reveal a person's thought process, but true understanding and conflict resolution can be achieved only when we take the time to reveal the process of our thoughts.

Have you ever been in a relationship with a person who talks in fragments, as though everything is a secret? You ask question after question, because you are receiving one-word answers that offer no detail. In that kind of relationship, you are not being treated like a person who is part of a loving, covenant connection. Responses like "Just trust me" or "That's none of your business" breed distance rather than closeness in communication. It is impossible to feel secure in this type of relationship. Security is cultivated in a relationship when communication produces familiarity with your thought processes. Love that informs cultivates a safe place in the heart.

When you feel informed, you are inspired in your relationship.

Creativity, sensitivity, and a considerate atmosphere are built. When a person is not communicative, however, those in relationship with him or her alter their perception of the person's moods, anxieties, struggles, and challenges. Those around him or her become less and less concerned, which is actually the last thing the noncommunicative individual wants. In general, this type of person desires a level of communication he or she is not willing to give. By the time a non-communicator decides to talk, significant others have given up hope of ever having true, meaningful interactions. Loved ones then learn not to care deeply.

COMMUNICATE TO RELATE

Effective, resolving communication is one of the keys to providing a safe place to dwell called love. In reading the story of Adam and Eve in Genesis chapters 1, 2, and 3, we gain insight into God's way of relating to His people. He gives an example for us to follow in developing earthly relationships. God begins by asking questions. He then listens to the answers, analyzes the situation, and responds to the situation. God's relating process is to then question, listen, analyze, and respond. Many times we sabotage our relationships by not following this simple formula of communication. We tend to react to the situation rather than responding to the real problem.

A man I knew, Jay, was upset, disappointed, and angry when he discovered his teenaged daughter was pregnant. He held such high hopes for her. While Jay and the girl's mother had never married, he wanted more for his only daughter. Almost since the day she was born, he had been making provisions to send her to college. He felt that the pregnancy would dash all her hopes and dreams—his, too. Jay was reacting to the situation, but the real problem was his daughter's unresolved issues related to the fact that her parents were never married and she was raised by a single mother. He needed to communicate with his daughter in order to help her and himself.

The way we learn how to relate God's way to others is by uncovering the secrets of effective communication. Communication requires the following C's:

- **Clarity:** Use clear, simple, and direct communication. Keep your sentences brief and to-the-point. Don't try to confuse or complicate the discussion with blame, manipulation, intimidation, or domination.
- **Consistency:** Keep on point and don't change the subject or the direction. Say what you mean, not what you think the other person wants to hear.
- **Clean:** Don't throw mud at the other person. Refuse to condemn, profane, or defile the other person with your words. Decide to speak life to them. Remember, "Death and life are in the power of the tongue, and those who love it will eat its fruit" (Proverbs 18:21, NKJV).
- **Caring:** Effective communication is caring and kind. Love must permeate every word and action as you communicate.
- **Confronting:** Failure to confront problems and concerns sends a message that dysfunctional behavior and poor communication are okay. Speak the truth in love directly, avoiding denial or hope that the problem will go away.

The way to communicate more productively with one another is not through trial and error, not through hurting and learning, but through a strategic questioning process following God's guidelines. His way of communication is through interaction. Our desire must be to come to know what the other person is really saying. For instance, in every communication process, there ought to be three questions:

1. **"What are you really saying to me?"** Clarify and paraphrase what is being said. Repeat what you heard and have your friend, colleague, spouse, or family member confirm that you have heard correctly. Don't be so intent on hearing your own thoughts and formulating what you are about to say that you miss what the other person is saying to you. Be quick to listen, slow to speak, and slow to anger, according to James 1:19. Hold in abeyance your emotional reactions and words. Communicate with the intent to understand and *then* be understood.

2. **"Am I understanding you correctly?"** Understanding goes beyond simply hearing the words spoken and knowing what they mean. Understanding implies that you also discern the nonverbal communication signals sent out by the other person. Pay attention to nonverbals—facial expression, tone of voice, silence, appearance, eye contact, body language, gestures, and behavioral signals. All of these contribute to your ability to really hear and understand what the other person is communicating. In turn, be careful with your own communication, both verbal and nonverbal, so that what you communicate doesn't obstruct or distort the other's ability to convey thoughts and emotions.

3. **"What do you want from me?"** As is true for most people, much of your communication arises out of your needs rather than a desire to meet the needs of others. It's positively disarming in communication to respond without being defensive. This question is another way of asking, "How may I serve you?" Scripture commands, "Submit to one another out of reverence for Christ" (Ephesians 5:21, NIV). Instead of trying to guess what another person wants or needs, ask him or her directly. Often spouses or friends play guessing games. Don't assume that because you have been in relationship

with a person for a significant period of time that you can know what another person is feeling or wanting without asking or being told. That's simply not true. Even lifelong friends have to communicate what they want. You are not a mind reader!

A good rule of communication to remember is what I call the 500/300/150 rule. Most people involved in a conversation think at least 500 words a minute. In a normal conversation we speak at about 300 words a minute. When you are upset, speaking drops to about 150 words. So in a normal situation at least 200 words a minute never reach your conversation.

In a fifteen-minute conversation that's 7,500 words thinking, 4,500 words speaking. In a crisis, 2,250 words may reach your mouth. During an argument, most of what we think never makes it out of our thoughts.

So in a crisis, we become less effective communicators than we tend to be under normal conditions. No wonder men and women have trouble communicating with each other.

Using this process, you learn how to discern the true meaning of a person's conversation, and the other person learns how to speak more accurately. By clearly asking what you can do for the other person, you let it be known that you are listening and truly interested in what is being communicated.

Effective communication requires consistent, concentrated effort from both parties. Listen to the words, understand what the other person is saying, and remember what has been spoken.

I dare you to become a great communicator and a man of your word, for whom contracts and agreements are testimonies to your integrity, not instruments to make you keep your word.

- Love and accept others unconditionally.
- Use God's standard of covenant for relating instead of relying on contract relationships.
- Work at communicating effectively by listening and seeking to understand others.
- Use the three-question process to communicate.
- Understand that others may not know what your nonverbal communication means.

18

DARE TO
BE FATHERED

The novice doesn't hunt. He takes a walk.
The quickest route to experience is instruction.
Someone must show you where
to wait, watch, walk, and hunt. Trial and
error takes too long and is often painful.

EVERY SON NEEDS a father. The lessons are submission and faith for the son and reliability for the father. Having been failed by my natural father, I had a natural reluctance to be fathered again, but I knew I needed one. After the passing of my second dad, my granddad, I was afraid to trust again.

I was ordained, made official in my vocation, around 1990. I had a need for a father but often made assumptions concerning the capability of several senior men in my life. To be fathered, you have to find a man who possesses the character traits and or experience you need for the future. Fathers should have a capacity for sharing and sacrifice without feeling as though you are an imposition. They are great listeners, problem solvers, mentors, and teachers.

I met J. B. Dicks as an ordination student. He was my teacher. I spent many weeks with him learning all the necessary material for my ordination test. He was knowledgeable, kind, wise, hilarious, a little salty at times, and, in my eyes, a great man. I submitted to his teaching, and as the weeks passed, my respect and admiration for him grew. He became my teacher, friend, and later on my defender and war counselor. But most of all, he became the father I had been looking for.

Instead of letting my past disappointment sabotage the potential for a new relationship, I took my time, not testing to see if he would fail but exercising patience until the relationship developed and my fear of rejection and disappointment was alleviated. J. B. Dicks was equipped to be a father. I dared to be fathered.

Reverend Dicks died several years ago. There is a void but not like the one he had to fill. He helped me through some of the toughest times in my life. His legacy to me is wisdom, a calm demeanor, and a balanced approach to life and work. I miss him and our weekly visits.

My dad was not equipped for the responsibilities of fatherhood; he simply didn't have the tools. At some point, however, I realized I needed to learn how to forgive him for not being equal to my expectation of his job description. When I received this revelation, forgiveness was so simple that it was amazing to me. I realized that long before my father ever procreated, he was a man with strengths and weaknesses.

Putting away childish and unrealistic expectations of natural fathers is part of becoming a man. In order to recognize the person my father really was, I had to change my perception of him and realize he was an inadequate parent figure falling far short of fatherhood. My expectations of him changed as I reconfigured my image of him, and I saw he was just a person who happened to be my father. The one thing that became really clear was that my father, although he had not been equal to the task of fatherhood, had always been consistent. He had never, ever deceived us. He never tried to perpetrate a fraud of who he was. He had been this person for our entire lives.

I realized that as long as I kept him in the dad category, I would have a childlike expectation of who and what this individual was supposed to be. Paul wrote, "When I was a child, I talked like a child, I thought like a child, I reasoned like a child. When I became a man, I put childish ways behind me" (1 Corinthians 13:11, NIV). I had to put away my childish hopes and dreams of a natural father and adopt realistic expectations about who my Father really is.

The only way for me to remove childlike expectations was to have an adult-adult relationship with my father, rather than trying to force a child-adult relationship that had never existed. The expectations I had for him had not come from an adult-adult dynamic. They had come from a child-adult dynamic. The child in me had been longing for a child-adult relationship with a person who had consistently proven that he was not equipped for the task, nor did he want to be.

I had a choice at this point: either try to make him into what I perceived a father should be or adjust my perspective. I chose to adjust my perspective, since he had proven for nearly sixty years that he wasn't going to change. Like many other children, I had the misconception that parents are supposed to be perfect. I didn't expect a dad to make mistakes or have bad days. I expected my father to forgive me for every mistake I made but I did not extend the same forgiveness to him. When I moved from the parent-child dynamic to an adult-adult relationship, I was suddenly able to forgive and forget my list of expectations. We were able to establish a functional relationship.

CHOOSING NOT TO BLAME

Establishing a functional relationship with my father also meant choosing not to blame my father for my own inadequacies. I had to search within myself for what I lacked, for whatever reason, and receive a personal revelation of what I needed to do to become a godly father. I learned to turn what appeared to be a negative in my life into something God could use for good.

For example, my father was an alcoholic, so I learned early in life that if I wanted to be successful I couldn't drink. My dad used drugs, so I knew drug abuse could not be part of my life. My father was physically abusive toward my mother. I realized that a godly marriage could not tolerate spousal abuse. Rather than emulate my father's negative characteristics, I decided everything my father did that was negative would be my springboard to doing better. I purposed to learn from his negative experiences what not to do in my own life.

My next step in this process was to find a Biblical role model for a father, so I went to God's Word. God says He will be a father to the fatherless (Psalm 68:5). When we go to God to give us what is lacking in our lives, we allow Him to be the father who was absent or inadequate. Daring to be in the Father's likeness also means daring to be a weight bearer, shouldering the responsibilities He has placed in our lives, which I'll discuss at length in the next chapter.

A TRUE IMAGE OF FATHERHOOD

When we are born we have physical resemblance to those who birthed us, signified in the Greek word *teknon,* which literally means "offspring." It refers to a child who is birthed in the physical image of a parent. As we grow and mature we enter another level of sonship, called *huios,* meaning "son," which is bestowed on the son by the Father. Most men struggle to mature from the state of *teknon,* created in the likeness and image of a natural father, to *huios,* a son who reflects the image and likeness of the Father. A son of God is a new creation—a transformation, not a reformation, has taken place. The old man isn't reshaped. A new creation is birthed by God's Spirit.

When God the Father births a child by His Spirit, something radical and transformational happens. A relationship becomes integral to the whole process. That relationship includes the heart, anointing, and character of the Father, so that we relate spirit to Spirit, heart to heart, person to person, not simply in roles but in intimacy. Any man can be part of birthing an offspring, but only a father can impart his character, image, and anointing to a child through relationship.

The whole premise of *huios*—having the father's character, image, and anointing—actually begins in the book of Genesis with Adam's two sons, Cain and Abel. Even though he is the oldest son, Cain does not have his father's heart. Abel, the younger, is like the Son (Jesus) who made the perfect sacrifice, who laid down his life. We can also look at the sonship of Solomon, who became king after receiving his father's anointing, even though he was born outside the traditional circles of royalty. Sometimes the one who has been in closest proximity to the father may not have his father's anointing, because he does not have his father's heart. Another may come from the outside who possesses the father's heart and thereby receive his anointing.

This has happened to many would-be pastors. A minister may have served in a church for years, assuming himself to be the "heir apparent" to senior leadership once the aging pastor retires or passes on. Be he does not receive the pastor's anointing because he does not possess the pastor's heart. A minister from outside the fold may receive the anointing because he has the heart of the one who leads.

Look at the prodigal son's older brother, who stayed home with his father while the younger went away to squander his inheritance (Luke 15). One would assume that the older son had the father's heart and anointing. But as the story unfolds, we discover he had no compassion. The younger son exhibited his father's heart, though he traveled far away from home before discovering his true identity.

Understanding true sonship is critical, because it is revealed by the degree of fellowship we have with the Father. In Romans, it says that "those who are led by the Spirit of God are sons of God" (8:14, NIV). The Father offers "sonship" to his offspring, all those created in His image, to have a relationship with Him through Christ (John 1:10–13).

The more consistently you follow the leading of His Spirit, the stronger your relationship with Him. The strength of your bond with the Father and the development of your obedience to Him has several benefits. One of the greatest is that once you learn how to be an obedient son and mature from *teknon* to *huios* with the Father, you also learn how to be a godly father to your own children.

FOLLOW ME AS I FOLLOW CHRIST

Jesus speaks very clearly about how a man's life is transformed. "Follow Me, and I will make you become fishers of men" (Mark 1:17, NKJV). This transformation only occurs as a man answers the call to become a disciple of Christ. Living in close proximity to Jesus, a man will develop the characteristics of godly fatherhood. Fathers, therefore, are trained by example and experience.

Paul set an example as he "fathered" Timothy (read 1 Timothy 1:2). Paul took Timothy on his second missionary journey and involved him in his work. "But you know that Timothy has proved himself, because as a son with his father he has served with me in the work of the gospel" (Philippians 2:22, NIV). Paul then sent this "son" to Ephesus as a teacher and leader of that church. Paul continued to give Timothy help and encouragement so that this son would grow into a powerful man of God (read 2 Timothy 3:10).

In setting a fatherly example for Timothy, Paul instructed him to be an example for others and to "set an example for the believers in speech, in life, in love, in faith and in purity" (1 Timothy 4:12, NIV). Paul boldly challenged Timothy and all who desired to live the godly life,

"Follow my example, as I follow the example of Christ" (1 Corinthians 11:1, NIV). "Join with others in following my example, brothers, and take note of those who live according to the pattern we gave you" (Philippians 3:17, NIV).

THE IMPACT OF THE FATHER

One of the misconceptions in the world today is that fatherhood is simply being able to sire another individual. The ability to procreate does not prove fatherhood. Fathers have to be like shepherds. They have to guide, feed, protect, and train up a child in the way he should go (Proverbs 22:6). A father has the ability to impact the development of his children through his voice, through his presence, and through his example. He is vital to their development.

The problem today with most men, and women, is that they did not have a good father example to follow after. As Sam Keen explains in *Fire in the Belly,* "By the time they reach adolescence, 60 percent of the children born since 1987 will not be in the physical or emotional proximity of, or be financially supported by, their natural father."

The question then becomes, how does a man overcome the lack of exposure to a godly example? The teachings of Christ set the foundation, but we need human examples to exemplify the teaching that prepares us to move into fatherhood ourselves. The problem we face is how we choose a man to become our example, a mentor who will ultimately speak godly purpose into our lives.

There are mentors for both good and evil. Before you are saved, your mentor can be ungodly—an unrighteous person you attach to because he is the model of success within your circle of interaction. Perhaps there was a businessman or politician who appeared to be a worthy example who in truth had an unscrupulous or dishonest lifestyle. The difference between righteous and unrighteous mentors/fathers is that a righteous father does not want to impart his weaknesses to you. An unrighteous father/mentor makes it his business to impart his ungodly ways into your life. His pride leads him to want to reproduce his own unrighteousness in another.

A father has to be in control of his emotions so that when the problem and crisis times come, he sets a godly standard while he has his children's attention. The example a man sets during a crisis will impact his offspring for years, even generations, to come. The way a father navigates crises teaches his son how to handle troubling situations in his own life.

FOR WOMEN

ONE OF HIS STRUGGLES

A man who is raised without a mature father will lack an image or likeness needed for fatherhood. You may have struggled with this in your relationship with your own father, as well as in your relationship to the father of your children. Understand that the man who raised you only could be a father to you if he has been fathered in the Father's likeness. That is true for any man.

A man can only be expected to imitate the behavior of the man who mentored him—whether that influence was positive or negative. A man who lacked mentoring will probably treat you more like a mother or an object than a woman loved and fathered by God. Though he will resist, don't buy into relating to him as if you are his mother or just an object!

A man who has not been fathered in the Father's likeness has to go through trials to develop into full manhood. That is true for your own father, your husband, your child's father, your significant other,

and your son. If you rescue a man from the things that build godly
manhood, he will never develop to the level of maturity he needs to
assume the role that God designed for him.

PUT OFF CHILDISH THINGS— FROM OFFSPRING TO SON

When you desire to grow and put away childish things, a father or
mentor can help you mature from the *teknon* to the *huios* stage of life.
When I was a child, I talked like a child; I thought like a child, I was
a *teknon*. To become a *huios* I had to put aside childish ways and
move into manhood. God calls every man to mature into full sonship
(*huios*).

Christian recording artist Jason Upton has written a poignant
song, "Father of the Fatherless," that calls on God's promise to be a
Father for the fatherless. In the song, he questions how many sons have
cried for their fathers and how many fathers have cried like a son.

God, the ultimate example of fatherhood, understands that fathers are not born, they are developed. In order to mature from *teknon*
("offspring") to *huios* ("son"), a man has to put aside certain childish
characteristics, immature agendas, distorted mind-sets, worldly perceptions, and selfish reactions. There is a maturation process that teaches
a son how to serve and overcome the selfishness that characterizes the
self-centered, childish stage of growth.

Any man who tries to become a father before he has become a full
son is headed down a rocky and unstable path. God's process to sonship teaches maturity through reorganizing and reassessing priorities. When a son follows and emulates a godly father, essential fatherly
characteristics transmit to the son, enabling him to mature and be-

come a father himself. It is similar to Enoch (Genesis 5:22), who the Bible says walked with God, and who in the process evolved from youth to sonship to manhood.

The way to truly walk with God is to realize that He can see farther than you can and to acknowledge that He is leading you through life with your best interest at heart. God allows the trials and tests that will best shape your development as you travel the path of maturity. Along the journey, God may block you from things that are prematurely timed for you. In other instances, He allows situations and circumstances to develop you and give you the strength to make mature judgments. Each test or trial you complete helps you to put away more of the things that denote childhood and grows you into manhood.

MEN MATURE THROUGH TRIALS

Paul clearly describes the flow of the maturation through trials process:

> *Therefore, since we have been made right in God's sight by faith, we have peace with God because of what Jesus Christ our Lord has done for us. . . . We can rejoice, too, when we run into problems and trials, for we know that they help us develop endurance. And endurance develops strength of character, and character strengthens our confident hope of salvation . . .*
>
> ROMANS 5:1-4, NLT

A man who has matured into fatherhood knows how to walk with, coach, and mentor a child, and guide him or her through problems and trials. He will not abandon his child either emotionally or physically.

A man who hasn't learned from a father and treats his progeny like offspring rather than his own children will not know how to model, train, teach, and instruct them, hindering their ability to move from immaturity to maturity. A fatherless child tends to resist or complain about trials instead of learning from them. Fatherless children usually want instant solutions and fail to develop endurance, perseverance, and patience. Their expectations are unrealistic and they become easily discouraged and disappointed.

But fathered children know the relational love of a strong man. They feel supported and grounded. Sons and daughters in true relationships with fathers develop strong and enduring character traits—love, joy, peace, patience, kindness, goodness, faithfulness, gentleness, and self-control (read Galatians 5:22–23).

Maturing from the status of offspring to sonship is one of the hardest processes a man has to walk through, because elements of both boyhood and manhood are always present. For instance, when you are in your early pubescent years, there is often conflict within, because childishness is a more dominant influence than the fleeting moments of maturity you experience. As you navigate this time of oscillating childish and adult feelings and actions, you may find yourself behaving childishly but demanding adult respect.

As you mature, you find through trial and error, or godly example, that childhood habits, mind-sets, and perceptions simply aren't productive. Often it is through life's minefield of mistakes and failures that a boy learns how to become a man. How long this process takes depends on your willingness to learn from your mistakes and glean from those who have walked this path before you and are willing to walk beside you—such men are true fathers.

A wise son does not have to walk onto a busy highway and get hit by a truck to know that the highway is dangerous. Immaturity says, "Let me experience it for myself." Maturity and wisdom will reason, "This person already has the tire tracks on his back. I don't need to go through that experience. I just need him to tell me about it so I can avoid it."

This presents a dilemma to us as men, because we are not usually open to the advice of another. This is especially true while we are still in those conflicted years, where we are too childish to be a man and just barely man enough not to be a child. Our identity at this stage of development is often mixed and confused.

Here is where a wise man attaches himself to a mentor or seeks the advice of a father—his biological parent or a father figure. The loving father has been down this road and has reached his destination. If a father is not present in your life, ask God to give you a fathering mentor who can speak life and wisdom into your journey. Once that mentor becomes a dominant voice in your life, the process of putting away childish things becomes easier. Remember, a mentor will stretch you to your limits. A man who wants to be mentored is automatically signing up for correction and stretching.

IT'S ALL ABOUT EXPECTATIONS

Over the years, I have observed some amazing sonship characteristics in young men who did not have a father to be a model to them. When a man has a child and seeks to father as God ordains, he begins to develop godly characteristics that he was unable to acquire growing up because of the lack of a father influence in his own life. As he matures in God, what he lacked begins to build in him and he no longer has that deficit in his character.

Jake learned what it meant to grow in sonship and the ability to be a godly father. An early life of criminal activity—as a gangbanger and a drug dealer and an addict—came to a screeching halt when he faced a possible seven-year prison sentence. But God was merciful to Jake even before he knew God as his Abba Father. Sentenced to probation and community service, Jake entered a Christian drug rehabilitation facility and eventually gave his life to Christ.

In his first year as a believer, Jake teetered between the old man of sin and the new man in Christ. He journeyed down a sometimes rocky path, but he kept going. Then his girlfriend announced she was pregnant. He kept going with the help of a Christian counselor.

As Jake grew in his faith, he and his girlfriend started having problems and ended their relationship. Months later, he got a phone call from her. She didn't feel she could raise the child. She asked Jake if he wanted to raise the child. Her question caused him to do a lot of soul-searching. Now a college student, he had no idea how to care for a baby as a single father. He prayed, "God, if I can't be the father my baby needs, please send someone who can."

While Jake looked at his newborn son at the hospital, God answered his prayer in a most unusual way: "If you want a godly man in your son's life to teach him about the Lord, you are going to have to be that man."

By the grace of God, Jake has persevered, with the help of a strong support system of church and family. "I am able to love my wonderful son and care for him the way he deserves to be loved and cared for—in a way that I never was, when I was growing up."

Jake reflects, "I was a criminal, a drug dealer, and an addict, nothing more than a walking menace to society. Today, I'm trying to be the best father I can be and give my son the father I never had. Only God has the power to change someone like me from what I was to who I have grown to be."

Even though God gave me a role model in my grandfather, until I became a pastor I still felt a void in my life in the area of fathering. I missed what I felt should have been that dynamic of fathering that I had been denied. What I lacked as a son, learning to be a father from a father, I now experience as a spiritual father over other men and women. It's a spiritual dynamic that only God could have accomplished. What I was unable to experience in my natural growth was supernaturally supplied as I sought to serve my Heavenly Father and fulfill His call on my life.

Even as God has worked in me, growing me and grooming me, I still have to deal with overcoming the disappointment I experienced, feeling I had been denied a father-son relationship as a young man. What I discovered was that the role of parent seems to carry with it a preconceived list of lofty expectations. The titles "father" and "mother" appear to have a host of historic expectations, which are harbored either consciously or unconsciously. Therefore, we expect that list of expectations to be satisfied when we are interacting with our own parents. Disappointment arises when a parent is not equal to the title and the job description that we have attached to it.

SETTING ASIDE EXPECTATIONS OF PERFECTION

Setting aside expectations of perfection may be more subtle than you think. Expecting perfection doesn't just mean expecting that a person will do everything right; it's expecting that a person will be more whole, mature, and wise than you are. Just because a man is older, educated, skilled, or more experienced doesn't mean that he is in a position to father you. Growing in sonship means setting aside fantasies about infallible parents—including such factors as age, experience, or education in making a man a man.

Flawless expectations of a father figure can burn an imprint of perfection in your head. You are left in constant search of the perfect father image, meanwhile ignoring imperfect but genuine and loving role models. When you attempt to compare your ideal with the real people to whom you relate, you generally find them falling short of your expectations. The people who raised you as parents were not necessarily equipped to meet those high expectations, often having experienced the same deficiencies in their growth and development years.

My experience has taught me that seeking fathers other than the Father is a stretching and demanding search.

TEN THOUSAND INSTRUCTORS, NOT MANY FATHERS

As I began to pastor, God instructed me in the area of spiritual fathering—for the sake of those I was to oversee and to move me into a higher level of maturity as His son. In pastoring, I discovered there was a misguided expectation that has evolved within the church: a pastor is expected to father all those he leads to Christ and make up for the deficiencies they experienced in their parent-child relationships. Most pastors, however, are instructors. Paul says, "For though you might have ten thousand instructors in Christ, yet you do not have many fathers" (1 Corinthians 4:15, NKJV). Yet some, like Paul, are called to be spiritual fathers. We haven't given natural birth to them and may not even have been around when they were spiritually born, but God puts them into our sphere of influence to father them.

When a man dares to take on the mantle of spiritual fatherhood, it demands impartation, consistency, discipline, and grace. Fatherhood requires obedient and faithful sacrifice to the Father. A spiritual father has to have enough of himself to share. He has to have the capacity and desire to serve in a way that's sacrificial and not feel as though he wants something in return. An instructor will have a difficult time sharing strength without expecting compensation. Conversely, a spiritual father's compensation is the success of those he has fathered.

THE HEART OF THE FATHER

A father has to be many things. At times, he is friend, counselor, adviser, partner—but he is *never not* a father. Once a man understands that he has been created to be a father, he has to look at the prototype God the Father. Until you understand the spiritual condition of fatherhood and the qualities of God that make Him an effective father, you may misunderstand God's method of fathering.

God has said, "I will never leave you nor forsake you" (Joshua 1:5, NIV). He has also promised that he will be a mother and a father to you (see Psalm 27:10). During those crisis times, if you don't realize that the presence of God is always with you, you will compare God with your earthly dad, who might have failed in his role as father.

The biggest issue most men deal with regarding fatherhood is sacrificial serving. It is impossible to be an effective father without accepting the need for sacrifice and service. A father who has mastered sacrificial service places himself closer to the heart of God, because sacrifice is at the heart of our Heavenly Father. Strength to be a father is intensified through the act of fathering—not in the contemplation of it but in practical action.

As a father engages in sacrificial serving, he draws closer to the heart of God and realizes he is not losing anything in the process. Instead, he is imparting generational strength, knowledge, and maturity to those for whom he is responsible. When looking at fatherhood, we must bring to the definition some of the Hebrew names by which God the Father is known: *Jehovah-Jireh* (which means "the Lord will see and provide") or *Jehovah Shammah* ("the God who is present").

DEALING WITH FATHERING MYTHS

Along with the unrealistic list of expectations many of us have for fatherhood come many myths and misguided beliefs. One myth is that effective fatherhood is confined to marital circumstances. If this were true, then a widower would have a problem being a father and any man who experienced divorce would have to abdicate his role as father. In truth, a man still has both the role and the responsibility of a father, whether or not he is in a marital relationship.

There is another misconception: All men and all women are created to be parents. This is simply untrue. Society shows us, in both Christian and non-Christian homes, that the capacity to procreate is not an automatic qualification for the role of mother or father.

Timing is an essential element in the fatherhood equation. A man has to mature both spiritually and naturally before he is ready to be a father. It takes time for a man to work through his selfish side. He also has to deal with the fact that his life literally is not his own once he takes on the responsibility of a father.

In *The Father Connection,* author Josh McDowell suggests that the Biblical qualities imparted by the Father for effective fatherhood include unconditional love and acceptance, purity, truth, trustworthiness, comfort and support, refuge, friendship, discipline, forgiveness and respect. While there are certainly other qualities that could be added, McDowell's list gives us insight into the maturity needed by a father figure—a mentor, coach, spiritual father, or natural father—who desires to become closer to the likeness of the Father.

If you are struggling with fatherhood, that discomfort generally comes from not having a clear understanding of your own image, your own capability with God in Christ. You have not yet become comfortable with the life of sacrifice that fatherhood requires.

Fathering is about the ability to impart strength to another human being and positively affect his or her development. A father carries responsibility; he is a weight bearer, something we will discuss in the next chapter.

I dare you to seek the Father's image within your own character, to grow and mature in the qualities that He has as described in

Galatians—love, joy, peace, patience, kindness, goodness, faithfulness, gentleness, and self-control.

- Move from childish to mature ways.
- Release unrealistic expectations of your biological father.
- Form a personal, intimate relationship with the Father.
- Understand the process of maturing from trials to character.
- Become a "son" mentored by a father in whom dwells the Father's likeness.
- Live out the character qualities of the Father.

DARE TO BE
A WEIGHT BEARER

*You will become all you are destined
to be if you bear the weight of your
responsibility; facing your responsibility
after an apparent failure is essential
to progress and success.*

THE THINGS WE TEND to avoid as men are usually the things that would benefit us the most. In retrospect, I can see the benefit of the weight of responsibility. Men were created to develop under the weight of responsibility. But it is easier at times to avoid responsibility than to accept it. The society we live in seems to applaud avoiding all you can, not taking on more responsibility than you must.

During the past eighteen years of my ministry, I have been chided for working too much. I work a lot of hours each week. I very readily accepted the responsibility of my work, and I've gone from doing just about every leadership job myself to having a wonderful staff. I did not avoid the weight of the responsibility, and it has paid off. I was advised by many not to do it that way, but the weight and the stress has built my stamina.

I understand an assignment is designed to reveal to you capability you were unaware of. A man will never discover his full potential until he dares to shoulder increased accountability.

Jesus sent His twelve disciples into the marketplace with a list of specific ministry instructions and a word of caution, that "anyone who does not take up his cross and follow me is not worthy of me" (Matthew 10:38, NIV).

Jesus was explaining the concept of weight bearing to His early followers. This same principle is true for men today. If we are not willing to deny ourselves and shoulder the responsibilities God has placed on our shoulders, we will not be successful in fulfilling our purpose here on earth. Jesus willingly shouldered His cross. Had he rebelled against the weight of His responsibility, He would never have fulfilled God's will for His life. Jesus' prayer, "Thy will, not mine, be done," pointed him to the cross—to bear the weight of the sins of the world.

After Peter's declaration that Jesus was the Messiah promised by God, they were again warned, "If anyone would come after me, he must deny himself and take up his cross and follow me" (Matthew 16:24, NIV).

Too often men shy away from responsibility, some feeling as though these responsibilities diminish their identity. But Jesus disproves this mind-set. Jesus' purpose is seen fully in the cross. Jesus is recognized for His unselfish choice to shoulder the responsibility for the sin of humanity, carry His cross to Calvary, and submit to His full assignment, which meant death upon that cross. Jesus taught that he who lost his life would gain it (Luke 9:24).

Losing his self-centeredness doesn't diminish a man's identity or life. The truth is this: Losing his selfishness makes room for that man's true responsibility and identity in life! When we shoulder the cross, the challenges we then face help us discover our identity. When you accept the responsibilities of manhood that have been put on your shoulders, you do not lose yourself. Truthfully, there's a dimension of your identity that you cannot reach until you accept responsibility for the *weight* that has been assigned to you. When you accept that *weight*, you discover God has already given you the capability to carry the responsibility. Accepting your assignment shows you things about yourself that otherwise could not have been discovered. In the process, you also learn that God never gives you an assignment without first giving you the ability to shoulder it. At times when the weight may cause you to stumble—as Christ stumbled while carrying his cross to Calvary—you will always stagger in the direction of your destiny.

THE PURPOSE OF WEIGHT

The weight you are called to shoulder as a man is not designed to pull you back or press you down, but instead to push you forward and raise you up. It is absolutely essential, if you are to be the man God has called you to be, that you submit to the weight that has been assigned to you. Out of this weight bearing, your true identity is revealed. You will become known as much for the weight that you have carried as the weight will become known for you. Jesus is known as much for the cross He carried as the cross is known for Him.

Society, on the other hand, seems to suggest that man should avoid taking on responsibility. This has created a serious gap in the development process God has designed for building a man's character. Society focuses on delegating responsibility and relationships, blaming and avoiding life's sticky problems and confrontational issues. But escape mechanisms do not build a man.

Many times parents who have led rough lives try their best not to unduly stress their sons, not realizing that men are created to be developed through accountability and responsibility. The longer a young man is delayed from accepting responsibility, the more his growth toward maturity is impeded. It is virtually impossible for a son to develop into a man without being given ever-increasing responsibility—progressively heavier weight to bear. His real manhood and true identity will not be revealed until he is put in situations where he is ultimately accountable and responsible for himself and others.

One of the great dynamics in this process is that God continually places us in environments larger than we have previously experienced in order to expand our responsibilities and develop our character.

It begins when an infant is born into a family unit. As a child grows from infancy, he is required to expand his vision beyond his own selfish needs and grow in productivity to the familial unit. An infant is solely concerned with having his needs met. As he grows to be a toddler, he can learn to pick up his toys and put them away when he is done playing. This teaches him that his toys are his responsibility and should be kept out of the way of others when not in use. This maturing reveals certain characteristics exposed through interaction with other members of the family.

The next phase of the human growth experience occurs when a mother sends her child off to school, placing the child in a context that is much larger than his little family unit. In this expanded environment, the child learns some significant aspects concerning his strengths and weaknesses. He begins to understand the consequences of certain behavioral patterns.

At each level of his educational experience, he gains understanding, and more of who God designed him to be is revealed to him. When he moves from elementary school to high school he enters an even larger organization, where another level of maturity is revealed that never would have developed had he stayed in an isolated environment with only his parents. In high school, with the support of parents, teachers, and other caring adults, he learns to handle peer pressure and ever-increasing areas of responsibility, such as time management—to balance studying and extracurricular activities, dating, or even a job.

Moving from high school to college expands his world to an even larger field of discovery. Having left the security of home and school, he is required to become more responsible for his own time and begins to seek direction concerning the overall plan for his life. Decisions made during this phase of growth begin to shape the future he ultimately walks into. As he moves from an educational into a business environment, he discovers certain skills that would not have surfaced had he remained in college, high school, elementary school, or at home.

God intentionally places us in increasingly more challenging environments in order to reveal to us what He has already imparted to us. If we have not developed an increasing sense of responsibility throughout this process, we may find ourselves stuck with an image defined by the world rather than establishing our true identity as God has defined it. God's process is designed to prepare us for increasing levels of weight bearing.

EVER-INCREASING WEIGHT BEARING

Society seems to strongly encourage men to concentrate on doing one thing at a time. The world has boxed us in, telling us we can excel at only one task within a given time frame. When we are studying the created image that God has given us, however, this mind-set is in error. Man has been created to be multitask-oriented in a major way. The assignment God spoke to man from the very beginning was to "be *fruitful* and *increase* in number, *fill* the earth and *subdue* it. Rule over the fish of the sea and the birds of the air and over every living creature that moves on the ground" (Genesis 1:28, NIV—emphasis added). There does not appear to be an addendum attached to God's command that stipulates doing only one of these tasks, completing it, and then moving on to the next. Believing that a man is capable of handling only one area at a time actually stifles our development instead of encouraging expansion and exploration into wider dimensions of possibility.

We were designed for more responsibility, not less. If a man, who has been designed by God to be a weight bearer, is not allowed to be responsible for his area of dominion, something will crack inside of him. When we don't fulfill that purpose, there is a breakdown, a loss of identity. There is even the possibility that our true identity will never be discovered. We were made to be strengthened and developed by taking on more and more responsibility for our personal area of dominion.

When you discover this truth, your assignment takes on a different dynamic and you aspire to move into true manhood by accepting more and more responsibility in your life. Rather than avoiding responsibility, which hinders your promotion into manhood, you begin to willingly shoulder each new responsibility, moving you closer and closer to reaching the dimension of true manhood.

To truly become a man, don't look for ways to decrease your levels of responsibility; seek to shoulder more. That doesn't mean taking on responsibilities that will prove counterproductive to you and others or will hinder the growth of another person—that's enabling. Look for and seek through prayerful discernment the responsibilities that God has designed for you to handle, rather than those someone else simply wants to throw on your back.

True manhood and the capacity for becoming the man you were designed to be is discovered through God giving you greater and greater challenges to face and overcome. Attempting to avoid responsibility will never allow you to fully develop into the man God has created you to be. Only the man who willingly shoulders responsibility continues to develop day by day, week by week, month by month, and year by year. Responsibility is not something to be avoided; it is to be welcomed if you will become all that God has called you to be.

As you accept the challenge to dare to be a man, one of the ways that you can become a godly weight bearer is to face the challenges before you head on. Confronting responsibility is your call, not avoiding or delaying it. As you assume more and more responsibility and accept personal accountability for the decisions you make, you will see yourself becoming fruitful in all that you do.

At each intersection there is a choice to be made. You can accept the challenge and establish your authority or you can rebel against it and remain a victim of the circumstances around you.

REBEL OR ACCEPT?

A man who rebels against the weight of his work never will establish his identity in that work. He will spend more time trying not to be identified with that area of responsibility than he will trying to discover his full capability. His growth will be stifled and his life will become more and more frustrating and unfulfilling. In order to be fruitful at his work, a man has to submit to the weight of the work to which he has been called, accept the responsibility God has given him, and trust that God has already prepared and equipped him to fulfill that assignment.

I've been asked many times how I am able to handle work that is so demanding and requires such a high level of responsibility. My answer is that I decided fifteen years ago not to rebel against the assignment. I chose instead to willingly submit to the weight of the assignment, and at each juncture of my life I discovered that God had already given me the ability to carry it to completion. This church's ministry is known as much for me as I am known for the ministry. This can only happen when the pastor submits to his given assignment and accepts his responsibility.

Submitting to your assignment lifts you to the place of your God-ordained destiny and purpose. If Jesus had not submitted to the weight of the cross, He would never have been nailed to it and would never have been lifted up to become the Christ. The whole spiritual dynamic of a weight bearer is that the submission to the assignment God has given you will ultimately propel you to fulfill your purpose in life.

Most men, quite inadvertently, identify themselves by what they do. For example, when asked who he is, a man will reply that he's a truck driver or a teacher or a lawyer or a doctor. In a man's world, in a man's mind, his work is not what he does; it is who he is. The zeal or drive to stay up all night completing a job assignment comes from a mind-set that in completing this assignment, he is developing his identity.

Rather than a job, a man's character defines who a man is. But responsibility, or weight bearing, is integral to a man's identity. Character comprises the core values and beliefs dictating a man's feelings, thoughts, and behaviors. But weight bearing actually puts into practice who a man is through what he does. Scripture says it this way, that "faith without works is dead" (James 2:26, NKJV). The inner capacity to become a weight bearer, to accept the responsibility that the call places upon a man, produces identity and fulfills purpose in his life.

FOR WOMEN

IDENTITY CRISIS

A man's whole perception of the weight of his vocation is different from that of a woman. To the woman, her job is what she does, not who she is. That is why a man has a consistent inner drive for what he does that a woman cannot understand. She will say things like "You are going to kill yourself working like that."

A man's likely response is "No, I'm not killing myself by working hard, because this is not what I do, this is who I am."

Your man has God-given and God-ordained responsibilities that may be opposite from your expectations for him. He needs your support and assistance in determining what things are temporary and what's permanent in his responsibilities.

Pray with him and for him, that he can discern God's will and know that God has already equipped him to do all that He has ordained.

Most men in pastoral ministry will sacrifice everything for their call, while a woman may not. Not many men will give up their call because their woman does not want to be involved in that ministry. Many relationships have dissolved because the woman did not want to be a part of her man's ministry. Conflict can occur with the woman in his life if the weight bearer/warrior character does not understand the concept of balance. A man who is performing his God-given responsibilities is likely to be involved in many things. Stop complaining to him that he is multitasking or working too hard. Your man has to work with you in setting boundaries and limits as he balances all his responsibilities within and beyond the relationship. Find ways to make the time you do have to spend together special and enjoyable.

UNDERSTANDING BALANCE

When does the weight-bearing warrior aspect of a man's character become a conflict with his role as father, husband, friend, or loved one? The conflict generally arises out of a distorted concept of what balance is supposed to look like. Attempting to keep everything evenly balanced along a straight line brings tension rather than order into the lives of everyone concerned. Real life means juggling many balls, keeping them all in motion, but never feeling the need to keep them all at the same height at the same time. How does a man determine whether he has the correct mind-set concerning balance in his life?

Consider how you would respond to each of the following scenarios:

- If one of the children in the family gets sick, does it throw the whole house out of balance until that child gets well?
- If a big project comes up at work and the man of the house has to pull a double shift, does the home tip out of balance for the next two or three weeks?
- How long does it take for balance to be restored once the project ends?
- What causes our pursuit of purpose to be injurious to us and those around us?

If family life is easily disrupted by one or more changes in your normal daily routine, then you have a precarious form of balance in place.

God, however, is the God of order, so the problem is not that man is called to be a weight-bearing warrior but that we have the wrong perception of balance. We have to train our household in the art of juggling the varieties of responsibilities and activities associated with the family unit. God has placed within the man the ability to establish order in his environment.

Therefore, during soccer season, when the kids are required to be at each and every practice and game for a period of about fourteen weeks, the household does not have to fall into stress. If we are living in the straight-line version of balance, there will be tension in the household for at least fourteen weeks, because we are trying to do something that is unrealistic. Balance is the ability to shift priorities when we need to and to bring things back to an even keel when the need for the shift is over. So instead of stressing out the entire family during the fourteen weeks of soccer season, we adjust our priorities to accommodate the temporary requirements of certain members of the family for this particular time frame. Everyone is aware of these shifts in priorities and responsibilities, and therefore the household still functions smoothly in spite of the change in the normal routine.

When the plate piles up with activities, most people get frustrated and are tempted to just toss the whole plate out and start all over. What we need to do is to evaluate each item on that plate and determine the length of time each activity will actually be on the plate. As stated previously, but it's worth repeating here, there are some things that have their own shelf life. There are things that will terminate on their own. Soccer season has a designated time frame and special projects at work will have a deadline for completion. So when we start to get overwhelmed by the number of activities on the plate, we check to see what is permanent versus what is long-term, what has its own shelf life and what is temporary. Once we do, we will get a different perspective of what the overall picture really looks like. Some of these activities will migrate off your plate within a very short period of time. Thinking that the adjustments needed for this season are always going to be there brings stress. Adjust as needed and readjust when something ends its designated time, and balance will become a way of life.

Men either don't understand how to build a comfort zone with the people in their sphere of weight bearing, or they don't take the time to learn to build it. As the head of the household, you need to establish this mind-set of balance within your family unit, and then your weight bearing will not be an area of conflict with your wife or children. It is your job to establish the boundaries and limits to what is allowed on the activities plate for your family. As you assume this responsibility, your life will move into mature manhood and you will begin fulfilling the assignment God has given you to be fruitful, increase in number, fill the earth, and subdue it.

I dare you to be a weight bearer, a man of responsibility.

- Take up the cross and follow Jesus.
- Lose your self-centeredness and begin to serve God and others.
- Accept various and multiple responsibilities at work, in your family, and in spiritual and societal leadership.
- Become fruitful, multiply, subdue, and take dominion of your sphere of influence.
- Evaluate and prioritize your multitude of responsibilities.

20

DARE TO EXERCISE
YOUR SOVEREIGNTY

*True authority and power are never
dissuaded by a negative situation.*

A S A PASTOR, a man seeking to reflect the image of God, and a weight bearer, I believe that every person born again through this ministry becomes my responsibility. As pastor, when God assigns "sheep" to me, those sheep do not come with a guarantee of stellar behavior, so it is also my charge to function as a true shepherd when my sheep are in trouble. When they are not in a crisis and are doing well, I preside over them.

The heart of a true shepherd is revealed when one of his sheep is in peril. A person knows whether or not he or she has a true spiritual father when that person is lost, stuck in a dark crevice. The unspoken question is "Is my shepherd coming to get me? Is he sending someone to look for me?"

When I went in to retrieve my sheep who had resumed her career as a stripper (see Chapter 5), I had taken her return to her former life as a personal affront against one of my own. I saw it as a plot orchestrated by Satan to impugn the work of God in my life and in hers. I believe God has assigned people to my care as members of our fellowship and given me responsibility and authority to impact every facet of their lives. As I interpret the scriptures, the pastor's role as shepherd involves more than just feeding the flock. It also involves providing, protecting, preserving, and sometimes doctoring those sheep.

When the enemy attempts to draw one of our people away from the flock, away from the direct influence of the shepherd, I know I have to go out and look for that person to bring him or her back. Since God has assigned these people to me, I am responsible to help them stay on track to accomplish God's purpose for their lives. That assignment has caused me to go after and retrieve many sheep that have been tempted to wander off.

Even as I strive to protect my sheep, I have struggled with certain aspects of that responsibility. At times I have struggled with when to rescue and whether the person needing assistance actually wants me to step in. One of the hardest things to do is to help someone only to have that person reject that help by going back to the situation.

The problem you may face, as I have, is reluctance to be a weight bearer to others who may need but not want your assistance. The bottom line is you must try, within reason, for your own conscience's sake.

In order to do this with some success and as little personal hurt as possible, you have to have an adult conversation with the person you desire to help. That dialogue will equip you to figure out whether the person has a seasonal problem or has adopted the problem as a lifestyle. You have to ask them the hard questions and listen for the truth. You then have to lay down the rules for your assistance.

I have a relative who is a career criminal. He called one night from jail, wanting bail. I paid the bail and had to take care of him for the period of his probation. After gaining an understanding as to why he, with the brains and ability he possessed, was acting like a criminal, I told him it was the last time I would help him in this way. We agreed on the house rules and responsibilities, but he soon took my kindness for weakness. When he got into trouble again, my response was a resounding "What did I tell you the last time?" He eventually got out of prison and went back to the same lifestyle. My decision, though heartbreaking for me, was the right one. He was determined to have it his way, so I let him.

On the other hand, I have had the same conversation with others who have gone on to do well. Since you cannot know until you try, you must try for your own state of mind.

You have a God-given responsibility to exercise your sovereignty. It is the expression of the consistent, committed, obedient, and loving leadership every man has been created to exhibit. You exhibit this in some form in some arena of your life, whether it is at home, work, or church, in the community, or recreational. And you have done so with some measure of success. It's time for you to use those same success characteristics in the significant relationships in your life.

The role of a man has many faces. You must be a leader, father, son, brother, friend, husband/lover, employee, employer/adviser, sometimes parent to your parents—a picture of consistency and strength. A man daring to reflect the image of God can effectively take back what the enemy has stolen, reversing the curse many men feel overshadows their very existence.

I believe that part of a man's mission in God is to make up for the shortage of fathers in the community. It is not an uncommon practice for me to show up at a school to check in on children who have no father figure in the household. These children need to know that God loves them enough to send a shepherd to encourage and support them.

As the head of our household, my mother did it well, but she was not a man. Nevertheless, I did not adopt that as an excuse for failure, brooding into dysfunctionality. As discussed previously, my father's failings did not become a part of my personality and negatively affect my ability to approach life. While I do have to resist certain genetic tendencies, I always look to take on the good part of who he was.

Environment and genetics work together. You will find yourself with tendencies passed down by relatives whom you love but do not want to emulate. Awareness of this reality helps you have a conversation with yourself to correct yourself before the thought develops into action.

Think of the times you considered engaging in behavior you disapproved of for others but justified for yourself. When this happens, it is time to ask yourself, "Am I pleasing God or myself?" You can probably list times you did not operate in the sovereignty God has given you over your own life. We all have. The sovereignty God has given you is for you to operate according to His will. Sovereignty gives you a tool for self-control, consistency, responsibility, and accountability. It allows you to be a weight bearer.

Always use the tools God gives you as a man, first to give leadership to yourself, then to others. In doing so you will have greater success when others tempt you in ways you know are not pleasing to God. We all struggle with this, especially when the heart is involved.

MANAGING MISTAKES

Have you petitioned God to send you a man who will treat you the way that you want to be treated? Understand that the man you love, or the kind of man you want to love, must be in obedience to God before he can relate to you in a godly way—the way that you deserve. But there are some things you can do to help him on that journey.

Encourage the men who are important to you as they travel the sometimes rocky road to surrender themselves to pleasing God. Understand that means you will take second place—sometimes in tangible ways.

The significant man in your life needs your forgiveness as well as your correction, and support when he is right so that he can dare to be the man God has called him to be. Help him and support him as he takes the steps that cause him to grow in love and grace. A man needs to know when you think he has done something well.

A woman must be able to come to her man and admit his decision was the correct one, the obedient one, and honor him because he dared to obey God. When she does, the man must have the grace to forgive her, accept her apology. A woman and a man must understand their relationship is a safe place to make a mistake.

If you are prayerfully seeking a man to have a special place in your life, look for God to send you a man who has a proven history of accountability, responsibility, and commitment.

Some years ago, I had a building maintenance business. A few of my relatives worked for me. One of them would not come to work regularly and did a poor job when he was there. Around holiday time, when the family came together, I was faced with a very sensitive problem: Terminate the relative and give the job to someone who would appreciate employment or hold on to a non-productive employee because of blood ties.

My perception of the business was that it was a gift from God. I operated it with integrity and serviced each contract as a blessing from God. My relative's actions were beginning to draw criticism from the client, however. My dilemma was this: Terminate the relative at holiday time or let him continue to work to please my extended family. The spiritual problem arose when I asked myself if I was being a good steward of the business by having an unproductive employee.

I knew what needed to be done, but I didn't like my choices. I could please God and draw the obvious displeasure of my relatives at the holiday dinner table or let the him stay in position through the holidays. I asked myself a life-changing question: If I lost the contract, could he replace the income? Did this person care that he posed a threat to my welfare? Would God be pleased with me for taking a risk for someone who was not concerned with my welfare or the blessing God had given me to be a blessing to him? The answer to all my questions was a resounding No! So I fired him. I chose to please God in a business situation.

The family dinner was another matter, however. I had to defend my decision from a spiritual-stewardship point of view. Several of the female members of the family were extremely upset with my action and timing. I was told what I should have done and why I needed to carry him. A few of them, including the terminated relative, had very little to say to me for quite a while. Even after I explained the business framework and all the implications, my actions still were not completely understood.

Months later, I began to receive apologies from some of them, including my own mother. Mom had never left my side on the issue, but she initially felt I should have carried him. After observing the relative's lifestyle and behavior, however, she realized my decision was correct. I had acted to protect my business and my employees, and had honored the opportunity God had given me. But the decision was still a hard one. Taking action that pleases God may be misunderstood by others initially, but the wisdom of the decision will triumph.

You must be prepared to be misunderstood as a weight bearer when you obey God and act in your sphere of sovereignty. It is not always clear to others why you are not bending to popular opinion. At times, standing in the will of God gets lonely, but He never fails to validate your obedience.

By looking at the example of Jesus, you can see that God often places you in an apparently isolated place when you are obedient to His Word. Your decisions often make you appear vulnerable and seem to validate the doubts of observers. It is for such seasons that you must build a habit of committed obedience, responsibility, and accountability, so that when others doubt, you will not be deterred from your faithfulness to God.

In every relationship there will be times when the more appealing solution to a problem may be something that would not please God. During those times you, as a weight bearer, may have to take an unpopular stand. A man who dares to obey God will have these experiences from time to time. You must be prepared to forgive those who did not understand the decision at the time but saw the wisdom in retrospect. Be prepared to extend forgiveness when your actions are misunderstood. Surrender yourself to God so that you can have sovereignty in your sphere of influence and develop a personal history of accountability, responsibility, and commitment. Through surrender, you can exhibit His love and grace to those around you.

I dare you to exercise your sovereignty as you obey God.

- Realize that consistent obedience matures and disciplines you.
- Discover that God alone knows what's best for you.
- Take initiative and control instead of passively reacting to life.
- Forgive others as God has forgiven you.
- Take up and exercise the authority and sovereignty God has given you.
- Let God empower you to relate to the woman in your life in a godly way.

21

DARE TO ACT FROM PURE MOTIVES

Self-inventory will usually identify the cause and the motive for an emotion.

MAN WAS NOT CREATED to be controlled by his environment; he was created to exercise authority over it. Man was not created to be ruled by his situations or his circumstances; he was created to have dominion, sovereignty, over them. Authority is the ability to influence the outcome of any situation or circumstance. Dominion means having the authority, power, capability, knowledge, and wisdom to positively affect the environment.

A carnal man (a man whose sovereignty is self-generated) uses power and authority to dominate, intimidate, and manipulate. He has a self-centered vision and agenda.

So how does a renewed man move from the inappropriate use of his authority to exercising godly dominion over his environment? He submits his vision to God and partners with the Father in pursuing that vision, allowing God to alter, expand, or reduce it as He sees fit. When he truly partners with God, he walks with a righteous Governor who keeps him on track, bringing fruitfulness and blessing to his environment.

AUTHORITY IS GRANTED AND PRESCRIBED BY GOD

A man's dominion and authority are *always* prescribed by God and are to be used within the confines He has set for them. Therefore, a man's vision must be in agreement with his Abba Father's vision. When a man's vision and God's vision are aligned, the fruitfulness of that vision comes forth.

The first hurdle to achieving this crucial alignment is realizing that God really has given you this authority. Most people spend their lives reacting to their circumstances. They are reactive rather than proactive, unaware of the dominion they have been given over their environment. Understanding the divinely mandated empowerment God has given you to govern your circumstances is the next step to effectively and properly exercising that authority.

EXERCISING SUPERNATURAL AUTHORITY

When a man understands that it is the presence of God in him that gives him dominion, he will begin to walk in his supernatural authority. The problem with expressing that level of authority is that a godly man also must accept accountability and responsibility for the outcome.

Suppose I'm in the middle of the desert, completely lost. I find you and ask for directions, but you are afraid to accept responsibility for your answer. So you advise, "Just go in the direction you feel is best for you." Let me tell you, you haven't helped me at all!

God has given men the ability to exercise authority over their environment and to impact people's lives. Many men are leery of possessing that level of responsibility. Once you are willing to accept the responsibility that accompanies supernatural authority, your God-given dominion will be expressed in your circumstances and you will positively affect your environment.

Walk in supernatural authority. It is essential to realize that you have supernatural authority but also that you walk in that authority. To do so, however, requires social interaction with those within your area of influence.

Jesus said we are to be like salt and light (Matthew 5:13–14), having an impact and exercising influence over the environment in which we are placed. Salt and light are interactive with the environment. Salt has the ability to transform, to preserve, and to improve whatever it is applied to. Light has the ability to influence any landscape it falls onto.

So when you understand the principles of authority and dominion, you realize that you can influence and impact your circumstances. If you release them and walk in your God-given authority, you will be able to interact with and cause significant changes in your environment, whether church, home, workplace, or community.

SPIRITUAL AUTHORITY AND DOMINION IN THE FAMILY AND WORKPLACE

A man's authority within his marriage and family is exercised in obedience to God, who has given him dominion as co-regent in his own household. When a man submits his vision to his Heavenly Father, he is giving those following him an authority that is worthy of submitting to. It is a man's submission that releases God's authority in his life.

A carnal man may believe that giving orders and acting macho authenticates his authority. In God's Kingdom, a man's authority is released through his submission to God. Jesus set the example when He told His disciples, "My food is to do the will of Him who sent Me, and to finish His work" (John 4:34, NKJV). Notice Jesus did not say He needed to finish his own work. A man's submission allows God to use him for *God's work* and release divine authority and anointing within him.

As you walk in the authority He has given you, you will discover that the problems of your household are under your realm of authority. Your ability to institute corrective action when needed confirms that you are operating within your domain of authority. Exercise your authority to correct.

Never lose sight of the fact that the ultimate purpose of your authority is to shepherd and mold those under your care to reach their full potential and purpose in God's plan for their lives. When you aspire to have authority in your domain, it will be released automatically as you set an example of submission and obedience to God, demonstrating your desire to see your family achieve their full potential.

Submission to God is also the key to exercising your authority in the workplace. If you are a supervisor, your submission to God will produce what I refer to as "stellar work character." That means you will show up for work on time, do your job to the best of your ability, and treat coworkers with respect. As you do this, you fall into the godly model of superiors and subordinates that Paul explains in Ephesians 6:5–9.

Only after you have submitted to God can you exercise proper authority over the people that have been assigned to your oversight. In the workplace, your submission to God produces the voice of authority in a leader others can follow.

In the Kingdom, God expresses Himself through submitted men, allowing Him to activate fruitfulness, multiplication, restoration, and replenishment in their specific environment. When you dare to exercise dominion and authority, you dare to submit to the King, your Abba Father, in every area of your life.

FOR WOMEN

BALANCE AUTHORITY

Men can only exercise authority as they have seen it done. The man in your life may have a distorted understanding of authority based on what he has seen or how he imagines a man in authority behaves. He can exercise authority with integrity and blessing only as he receives that authority from the Father.

If married, affirm your husband as he exercises authority as a co-regent, not a superior, in marriage, without jealousy, domination, manipulation, and intimidation. If single, look for the signs. Each time he dares to exercise authority and dominion, as designed by God, it is an opportunity for him to grow in godly manhood.

Jealousy and insecurity—whether his or your own—will hinder a man's ability to effectively exercise authority and dominion. He will benefit from your prayerful input and feedback as he exercises authority as God intended. Pray with him and for him as he seeks God's direction.

A Profound Lesson on Authority

Exercising authority and dominion is a man's God-given provision; however, it is one that requires wisdom, insight, forethought, and sensitivity. I learned to consider the long-range effects of my decisions, even when operating within my established area of domain. I had purchased a restaurant franchise knowing I was well equipped with business acumen, but I had never actually worked as a short-order cook. The cooks were trained to do their job, but I attended one of their training modules in order to get a broader understanding of the business.

It was not until I was operating the grill alone, however—with twelve orders sitting in front of me, each with twelve or thirteen different items on the order—that I realized the full impact some of my authoritative decisions could have. I began to appreciate what a simple command from a manager or simple question from a waiter might actually involve and what type of stress it produced. After that experience, I began to exercise my authority with more sensitivity, understanding what it would take to implement each command that I gave.

Giving a command simply for the sake of exercising your authority is immature and counterproductive. Exercising godly authority and dominion is exemplified through careful consideration of the time parameters, the capability of the individual, and the practicality of your request. When you and those over whom you have authority understand this principle, God can work through you to achieve fruitfulness and prosperity in your environment.

Understand Authority and Anticipate the Outcome

A high-ranking officer in the Roman army came to Jesus, asking that an ailing servant be healed. The centurion's understanding of military authority helped him to understand Jesus' spiritual authority and dominion. He knew that Jesus could simply speak the command and the servant's sickness would have to flee in obedience. Jesus was amazed that a Roman soldier understood his spiritual authority while the chosen people of God had never exhibited such faith (read Matthew 8:5–10, 13). When you truly comprehend this vital principle, your faith will join with the power of God's authority and command victory over any circumstance you face.

God gave me a great visual of this principle while I was working with a talented musical prodigy. I had obtained sheet music of some interesting classical music. I showed it to her and asked if she had ever played it. She told me she had always wanted to play this particular piece. As I watched her prepare to take on something she had never done before, I learned an important lesson on anticipating a desired outcome. She asked me to turn the pages for her so she could move through the piece without breaking her concentration. I watched in utter amazement as she played the music on page one while she was obviously looking ahead at page two. When she was playing the middle of page two, she told me to turn to page three. As she completed the complicated arrangement, I asked her how she did it. The only explanation she could offer was that she was fully aware and fully comprehended the assignment in front of her. She was able to anticipate the outcome of what she had set out to accomplish.

After my musically gifted friend showed me the principle, I fully understood what it took to do what she did. To properly exercise godly authority, learn to anticipate the outcome before issuing the command. If I ask a question, it is to confirm what I already know, not to inform my ignorance.

EVERY LEADERSHIP SITUATION IS AN OPPORTUNITY TO HELP ANOTHER GROW

I also have discovered that every leadership assignment is actually an opportunity to invest strength and life into another or to equip that person to better handle future situations. The ultimate outcome of every leadership decision should be to help another to grow. Authority in leadership must be exercised with grace, benevolence, and a mind to teach, instruct, and develop another.

The world expects a leader to say, "Do what I say and don't ask questions." That is not leadership; that is domination and it is definitely not exercising godly authority. The leadership of a godly man includes grace, judgment, and personal interaction. This is the salt-and-light type of interaction Jesus taught in his Sermon on the Mount (Matthew 5:13–16). Godly leadership includes ongoing interaction to determine the status of the project and an explanation of what is expected. A man begins to exercise dominion over his environment when everyone involved understands the expectations.

I was recently at a huge national convention, with all types of people—actors, politicians, musicians, writers, and just plain working people. A recently divorced lady from Chicago began to ask me questions concerning men. She was still upset about the breakup of her marriage. She asked me why men do the stuff they do.

We began to talk about the motives of people in relationships, why people do what they do. I told her men, like women, are sometimes reluctant to voice their real motives. The average woman will not tell you she is looking for a husband on the first date, when many actually are. The average man is not going to reveal he is initially attracted to a woman physically, rather than to her personality. It is not incorrect to conceal these thoughts. Hiding these thoughts is considered the right thing to do. Men simply conceal different thoughts from women. But the thoughts are not the problem. Motive is the problem.

When the thought is concealed because it is not pure, as a man, you must analyze your motives. When your motives are pure it gives integrity to your actions. Purity of motive gives you the ability to relax as relationships develop. When your motives are pure, as a man you will resist being unduly influenced by a society that feels covering the real motivation is preferred over revealing motive from the beginning.

As I talked to the lady from Chicago, she began to ask me questions about myself, the ministry, my media involvement, and my status. She would ask a question, I would answer her; she would then voice her skepticism as it related to my answers. This happened for about fifteen minutes of conversation. I realized she thought I was trying to impress her.

Then a photographer who was familiar with my work came into our area and began to talk to me about my involvement in the convention. She listened as the photographer and I talked. Then the lady from Chicago introduced herself, now realizing my motives were completely honest. Perhaps I broke the stereotype of men that had been set by her husband. My motives during the conversation were pure. I sensed she was extremely vulnerable. So I protected her by refusing to be molded into her very narrow view of men and resisted being shaped by her perceived possibilities of the moment. I began to address the misconceptions she had based on her experience by exercising the authority a man was created to express.

■

I dare you to exercise dominion and authority from pure godly motives.

- Set aside all jealousy, domination, manipulation, and intimidation.
- Exercise authority over your environment.
- Seek God's direction for exercising your authority.
- Receive authority from your relationship with the Father.
- Anticipate the outcome before you act or speak in authority.
- Grow from each time you dare to exercise authority and dominion.

22

DARE TO
PROSPER

*The key to wealth and success in all
things is wisdom. Wealth and poverty,
sufficiency and insufficiency are usually
the result of someone's choices.*

I REMEMBER THE DAY I decided that failure was no longer an option. I was living in the Fairground Projects in Chester, Pennsylvania. We had very little money and only the bare essentials. My dad was not sending money. Mom was doing it with guts, determination, and faith. My brother and I needed clothing and there was nothing to buy it with. I promised myself that day I would not live life as an unsuccessful man. I made up my mind to work hard, get an education, and use all the negatives my father represented as a springboard to greater things.

You can learn a positive lesson from just about any situation, but God added to my life the balance and the divine favor I needed as a man, to overcome my disadvantageous beginnings. I began to operate the faith-works equation necessary to achieve the goals I set for myself.

As I think back and reflect on my own personal victories in daring to be a man, I realize they were all rooted in:

- hearing revelation
- reacting in faith
- responding by action

When these things are done, success is guaranteed. Before I was saved, I enjoyed a measure of success as a banker. One of the early lessons God taught me was that the thing you are doing when God anoints you for your purpose is the thing you are to continue to do. He showed me how King David was called away from being a shepherd boy. God anointed him for his purpose and sent him right back to tending his father's sheep. What David learned as a shepherd equipped him to become the king of Israel.

So when God called me to ministry, I continued in the vocation where I was demonstrating ability and success—banking. This is an important point in the equation of success for a man of God and cannot be overlooked. So many times I have heard men come from a mountaintop spiritual experience, having heard God's call, and say, "I've been called to the ministry. I'm going to quit my job, leave my responsibility, and go off to school."

I can't emphasize this strongly enough: The call of God *does not* disconnect a man from maintaining his responsibilities. Most people feel a call to the ministry is an escape from secular work. God would not call a man into His service and instruct him to send his family into bankruptcy. When a man is called, he is to continue to do what God has empowered him to do and continue handling his assigned responsibilities. The skill God has been developing within that man will continue to serve him as he gets to the place to where God is leading him.

Any endeavor you choose as an assignment for your life can be considered a call. A call is something you have a passion for and feel you have a talent or gift for, and also something that provides for you. Remember, when you are called to a thing, it will always provide for you.

Before my mountaintop experience with God, I realized I needed to start my own business. One of my bank clients, a high school dropout, had made a million dollars a year for twenty-five years. I began to consult with him about a profitable business in which to invest my time and energy. He had built a very successful janitorial business, so I asked him to show me how he did it. Two years later, I was making a half million dollars and three years later I'd built a million-dollar-a-year business.

It was at the height of my janitorial business that God called me to pastor a church. I was finally making some real money, and suddenly God changed my season. The day He spoke to me about this change, I'd received a call from a university, offering me a huge contract. I broke out in a sweat. I started rationalizing, going down the list, logically weighing the pros and cons of this decision. As I sought to understand God's plan, He told me, "I'll give you three years to get out of all your commitments." I called the university back and told them, "Thank you very much" but I could not accept their offer. As I hung up, I thought I might have made one of the biggest mistakes of my life.

I made a choice to trust in God and His plan for my life. I called two or three of my best employees and asked them if they wanted to start their own business. I explained that I would be done in this business in three years and that I would get them started if they were interested in learning how to take it over. I planned to seed the equipment into their new business and give them two or three contracts right away to get them started. As my other contracts came up, I explained to each company that I was not going to rebid, told them I was going into full-time ministry, and referred them to the other business I was seeding. All my clients thought I was crazy; they had a pretty good idea of the kind of money I had to be bringing in.

I went from making hundreds of thousands dollars a year to about fifty thousand, and that included benefits. Fortunately, I had been a good steward over what He had given me. I obeyed the Father's voice, and as I heeded Him, I began to grow and learn even more about His plan for my life. In just a little while, the church exploded—expansion came each and every month. God began to send all kinds of people into my life and He locked me into an income that was not threatening to my family's economic stability. I began to see how He wanted me to use all my experience, all my gifts, and all my business connections to become an entrepreneur again, but this time with an expanded agenda.

I heard what God said I could do, reacted by faith, and implemented His plan using everything He had set in place to bless me and everyone I was connected with. I began to form those entities and opportunities that were consistent with my talents and gifts as well as my anointing. I could not have done all this if I had not been in the right environment and formed the right relationships using everything God had in place for me. God had moved me into a kingdom business.

Every man is equipped to cultivate the environment where he has been placed and to be blessed by that environment. God has uniquely endowed every man to prosper. But rather than seeking to understand our uniqueness, we tend to compare ourselves with other men to evaluate our personal success rate. The apostle Paul calls this foolishness. "When they measure themselves with themselves and compare themselves with one another, they are without understanding and behave unwisely" (2 Corinthians 10:12, AMP).

Instead, every man is to "carefully scrutinize and examine and test *his own* conduct and *his own* work. He can then have the personal satisfaction and job of doing something commendable [in itself alone] without [resorting to] boastful comparison with his neighbor" (Galatians 6:4, AMP—emphasis added). When a man discovers that God has given each of us the power to create wealth (Deuteronomy 8:18) and placed everything we need within our designated environment, he then understands his created ability to be fruitful and to multiply.

CHOOSE TO PROSPER

God puts a man in a place where he is ordained to prosper, equips him to prosper, and then commands a blessing over his life. God then releases that man to use his gifts and abilities to be fruitful and multiply within that environment. We are to grow and become fruitful where God has planted us.

We are not victims of our environment; poverty and prosperity are really just choices. Proverbs 10:4 (AMP) says, "He becomes poor who works with a slack and idle hand, but the hand of the diligent makes rich." God's Word does not qualify this tenet by saying it is true *unless* the man is born into a poor family or in a bad neighborhood. The man decides for himself whether he will be poor or rich. God's Word lets us know that in His Kingdom, a man has been created with the ability to be blessed, to be fruitful and to multiply within his environment. It is our choice whether we live a life of prosperity or poverty.

A man must discover his uniqueness and attract God's blessing. First he must discover what God has created in him that gives him uniqueness. Then he moves to unveil what God has embedded within him that will attract the blessing to him. Most men are seeking the answer only through secular means. Only God can reveal what each man has been created and equipped to do.

God's Word will connect you with your ability. "The Lord will make you the head and not the tail" (Deuteronomy 28:13, NKJV). Therefore, the first step is to discover what you are gifted to do. The second challenge is not to become bored with it. People have a tendency to become tired of doing something they can do with ease when God has blessed them with that very skill to connect them with success.

BECOMING AN ENTREPRENEUR

Once a man discovers what it is that makes him special, no matter what that skill may be, he must move his mind-set from that of punching a time clock Monday through Friday to that of an entrepreneur. If you are good at cleaning and work as a janitor and God reveals to you that you are able to do this better than anyone else, then you must adjust your thinking to how this uniqueness can become your business. Take that job mentality and cultivate it into a corporate mentality. Shift your perception from working at that job for the rest of your life to understanding that God has given you this ability to make you special and successful. Begin to seek ways to enlarge your territory so you can be blessed and prosper the way God has created you to be.

I knew God had called me to be a pastor, even though I had been a very successful businessman. God had gifted me to multitask on a major scale. I realized I had this gift for a purpose. So I began to pray to find out the kind of ministry that would benefit from a leader with a major multitask orientation, along with experience in business. Well, God did show me. Our church now has a record company, an employment agency, a professional janitorial company, and a security agency as part of our ministries. When I discovered what God had put in me that made me special and connected it to His promise, I was able to attain prosperity and step into the fruitfulness He had prepared for me.

MAKING IT HAPPEN

There are a lot of talented, gifted people in the world. And ironically, some of the world's most gifted people are not necessarily the most successful. Have you ever looked at somebody and said, "Wow, he has so much potential," and then wondered why the person seemed consigned to a life of mediocrity?

It is simply is not enough to be anointed to be successful, just as love alone won't make you successful in a relationship. You must work hard at discovering what's in your anointing that empowers your natural abilities into another dimension; you must discover what makes you special. The road to discovering your uniqueness in God involves five components:

1. receiving the revelation of who God says you are
2. accepting what God says about you
3. readjusting your perception of your life and your circumstances based on what God has said
4. seeking God's vision for your life
5. walking in the direction of the vision, acting and speaking in ways that are consistent with the vision that God has shown you

It is not until these five things are accomplished that you will come close to actualizing the gifts and talents God has given you. Actualization is the bridge where you move from giftedness to fruitfulness—making it happen. When you have gone through the process of discovering your uniqueness, and then associate with people and an environment that support you moving in the direction of your vision, something happens.

"The steps of a good man are ordered by the LORD" (Psalm 37:23, NKJV). The biggest hurdles to crossing this bridge are inactivity and negative self-talk. Don't fall into the trap of looking at the vision God has given you, becoming full of great ideas, but then saying, "It'll never happen to me!" Be careful you don't become a man who remains camped out on the gifted side of the bridge and never crosses over into the fields of fruitfulness.

I have attended numerous pastors' conferences on church growth and have discovered an interesting phenomenon. The problem most pastors are dealing with is not whether our we've got a building that's big enough or an anointing that's powerful enough to handle an increase in our flock. The real issue for most pastors is our inner secret doubt.

Whether you are a pastor, doctor, lawyer, or Indian chief, let me assure you that you will never achieve what you don't have the faith to believe you can accomplish in your own life. Negative self-talk and secret doubt will keep you from crossing over into your Promised Land of fruitfulness.

FOR WOMEN

AFFIRMATION AND AGREEMENT

Whether he talks about it with you or not, every man wants to step into his Promised Land, though he may not be sure of what it is from the outset. Be in prayer with him that he will be open and hear God speaking his purpose into him.

A man who hears revelation from God needs affirmation and support from you. Sometimes God's revelation may be frightening to him, despite his best manly efforts to disguise his feelings of uncertainty or insecurity. Support and encourage him as he moves toward his destiny.

He needs agreement from you when appropriate. Your affirmation and agreement will be well rewarded, as the man who responds in obedience to God will bear fruit that will bless and add to your life as well as his own.

AVOIDING HINDERING, NEGATIVE SELF-TALK

Moses is known and celebrated for leading the nation of Israel out of Egypt and positioning them to enter the Promised Land. But there was a time in Moses' life when he was more like the Father of Negative Self-Talk than a picture of confidence and trust in God. When God called him to accept the challenges of his assignment, Moses had a laundry list of reasons why he was not the right man for the job (Exodus 3:11–4:13).

Negative self-talk is one of the greatest hurdles to productive activity. Inactivity keeps you from moving into your Promised Land. Moses learned that a man may have to dare to be different to step into the full blessings of God. You may have to break with family tradition, cultural tradition, or personal tradition in order to get to where God is trying to take you and to be blessed. The time may come to distance yourself from those who can't see themselves going in the same direction you are and can't see you heading in that direction either.

I discovered another interesting fact about church growth by studying the pastors whose churches were growing. I found that the majority of them were isolated in their cities; they didn't fear solitude.

Their isolation was not an escape or intentional withdrawal; rather, it was the result of emerging from the pack into unique or innovative leadership. My research led me to determine I would rather have the favor of God and fewer friends than a host of friends and failure to acquire all the blessings that the Father had planned for me. If you dare to choose to be in the place of blessing, you may need to separate from a pool of mediocrity that keeps you from crossing the bridge into fruitfulness.

The group gathered at the pool of Bethesda in the Bible represents people who were meandering around a place of mediocrity, discussing their inabilities and finding comfort in their incapacities (John 5:5–9). Jesus called out to a man who had been incapacitated for thirty-eight years. Having been in the company of disabled people for such a long time, the man's first response was negative self-talk. His words speak of the tenor of his environment and aptly describe how his relationships and his negative outlook influenced him.

We have to dare to be different to dare to be blessed. Jesus did not argue with the man, He challenged the invalid to make a choice. Would he dare to receive the blessing of healing and move up into his destiny or would he believe his own negative self-talk and the influence of those around him?

The reassuring thing about God's process is that when you dare to be blessed, dare to be different, and disconnect from those relationships that will hold you back, you will begin to attract like-minded people. People will come into your life who will deposit their blessings and you will, in turn, bless their lives. God will transition you into a whole new set of relationships and send you a fruitful circle of friends who will propel you into a new season of growth in your life.

UNDERSTAND THE SEASONS

A new season introduces a change in our natural environment. When we see this transition, we acknowledge the move from one season to the next.

Spiritually, a new season never evolves through the passage of time, but rather always arrives through revelation. It is a Word from God that introduces the beginning of a new season in the life of one of His children. Accept that your life seasons are connected to revelation rather than chronological time, and learn to wait and listen for a revelation from Him to signal a new season in your life.

You cannot see the seasons of God the way you can recognize the earth's seasons—summer, winter, spring, and fall. Whatever life season you are in, one thing is certain: it is according to your faith. Therefore, your season is not instituted by your circumstances. Each season in your life is the product of a Word from the Father to a child He is in intimate relationship with—a child who dares to believe what He is saying and desires to move across the bridge that will connect him to his fruitfulness.

God's Word will reveal to you, as His child, when a season in your life is about to change. Each season in your life is a distinct work of God designed to equip and strengthen you to move further along your path to destiny. Again, these moves are always orchestrated through your faith and are not determined by your circumstances.

Many people look at their circumstances and allow them to define that season of their life. They begin to believe they will spend the rest of their lives there in that season. Life is actually a succession of seasons. Be particularly aware of this especially when you enter what I call an Ezekiel 28 season of thistles and thorns (read Ezekiel 28:24–26). If you think that is where you are destined to remain, you will become discouraged. The moment you understand that God's reason for a season of thorns and thistles, for example, is to bring you through to a higher level, your hope and expectations change. You move beyond your circumstances into expecting a different season to begin just around the corner.

EXPECTATION AND FAITH

Three things need to occur for a man of God to complete this equation of success: One, you must receive a personal revelation from God. Two, you must react to that revelation in faith by declaring what God has told you even before you see any manifestation in your life. Then three, you must respond by taking action toward achieving your success. Receive + React + Respond = Success.

Faith and expectation are directly connected when a man is working through step two—react. If you are not headed in the direction of expectation, little will be achieved in your life. God's Word, His revelation to you, is designed to birth expectation in you.

If I hear a Word from the Father and it births expectation in me, I have to receive it by faith and then react to it. A problem I have discovered in many men is that after their initial reaction to the revelation, they tend to become docile.

Often, after step two, the reaction, instead of responding we sit back and wait for God to drop manna (blessings) from heaven. One of the key truths we can learn from Israel's journey from slavery to inheriting the Promised Land is that every step they made was part of God's plan to equip them for survival in their new home. Egypt had a purpose; the wilderness experience had a different purpose, but each was a vital step to lead and prepare them for a blessed life in the Promised Land. God requires that we respond through direct involvement in His process. He guides us through that process so that we can achieve success.

Are you ready to move into God's success for you?

I dare you to prosper and be fruitful.

- Hear and receive revelation from God for your fruitfulness.
- Declare what you hear from God.
- Respond to what God has said to you in obedience and begin to bear good fruit in your relationships, your work, and your personal spiritual maturity.

23

DARE TO RISK FRIENDSHIPS

*Relationships influence. Acquaintances
are many while friends are few.
Choose wisely.*

I HAVE VERY FEW REAL FRIENDS. I have learned that friendships are audited during the tough times I face. Friendships can be a very lopsided affair. But they can also be extremely rewarding. I grew up with two other guys I will call Joe and Bob to protect the innocent. We grew up together, fought together, fled together, and faced tragedy together. I thought they would be my close friends for life. As we grew into men, our lives began to take very different paths.

Then I met my lifelong friend, Ron. Ron and I have been friends for almost thirty-nine years. We have seen each other through the greatest days and the worst days of our lives. This type of friendship cannot be built without both of us challenging each other. We have disagreed but never argued. There has not been a moment during these years we have ever had a break in our friendship.

I have had discussions with him that would have broken other friendships. But we continue to challenge our friendship to strengthen it. You must be able to prune each other for the friendship to become more fruitful. Friends who must agree continually in order to get along will never be true friends. Real friends will step into each other's space and comfort zones when necessary. Iron sharpens iron. We celebrate each other's accomplishment and lend a hand in difficulty.

I have been favored with other strong men as friends—like Mark, Al, and a strong group of spiritual sons, many of whom I call friend. But we all risk our friendship with honesty and openness.

True friendship is celebrating each other's success: validating one another's strength. As a man you cannot afford to have friendships that support your weaknesses. You must risk friendship to discover true relationship. Never dumb down, never avoid success, never diminish accomplishments. All of these are designed to test the integrity of your relationships. Your true friends will be revealed.

Walking as a man of God, you may find that once your vision becomes real to you and begins to manifest, there will be unexpected reactions from some closest to you. The problem often arises because valued friends (and family members) may have had a different vision or plan in mind for your friendship, and they are not comfortable with the position they hold in your life now that you are a man of God.

Everyone has a paradigm that he or she finds most comfortable. I discovered this after I'd acquired a VP position in the banking industry. When asked what my job was, I would simply tell people that I worked at a bank. Invariably they would assume that I worked in a position that they were comfortable with, such as a teller or a branch manager. When I would explain that I was a vice president, their entire perception of our relationship changed.

Similarly, along my spiritual journey, people around me had to decide whether they were going with me as I pursued God's vision. If *their* expectation of me was more important than God's, they would not be able to continue having a relationship with me.

THE ORDINARY RISK OF FRIENDSHIP

When a man desires to enter into a relationship with you, it is important that you discover the condition of his heart, particularly his motivations, before you entrust your friendship to him. Success, status, celebrity, and perceived honor are ingredients in a recipe for jealousy, which can create a serious and painful chasm in friendships, even among Christians.

In your relationships with other men, set jealousy aside. Men deal with jealousy completely differently from how women deal with it. If two women are in the same room wearing the same dress, there are a range of emotions that occur, which make no sense to the man. Women compete as if there is only one dress. "You had no right to wear *my* dress."

Men compete for what appears to be a greater piece of the pie. "I don't care about your piece of the pie as long as mine is bigger. I don't care how well you have done as long as my record is just a little better. You can have a great ministry as long as mine is greater." A wise pastor once said, "You can call a man a dog—just don't call him a little dog!"

Men process their jealousy differently, but it is rooted in the same sense of dissatisfaction with self as it is with women. Jealousy is always counterproductive, so beware of this green-eyed monster, whether it erupts in a new or a longstanding friendship.

THE SPIRITUAL RISK OF FRIENDSHIP

The big risk in friendships is whether the relationship will challenge your determination to walk in the will of God. Walking with God automatically audits your relationships. One of the great concerns for a man desiring to walk in God's will is whether he will risk the loss of his closest relationships.

There may be times in your life when you are maturing in God but a valued friend is not. If you find yourself in this situation, it is not necessary to sit down with this friend and say, "I'm maturing in God faster than you are, so it looks as though we are not going to be able to hang out together anymore." As you move forward, becoming what God has called you to be will cause an automatic shift in the relationship.

Moses was called to go up on the mountain and meet with God. When he came down, the people couldn't relate to him the way they did before. As he got closer to God's purpose for his life, changes occurred even in his relationships with his brother and sister. Only Joshua, who had gone up the mountain with him, was able to stand with him. The whole Moses story is a wonderful example of how once the glory of God gets on a man, it mandates a change in his relationships with the people around him. Such changes can even cause offenses to occur between very close friends.

Charles had such an experience. "I've lost friends because of my faith. I was a Christian growing up, but put Christ on the back burner. I had a lot of friends during college, many who were not Christians. But since serving Christ wasn't the most important thing to me then, I didn't think much about it. After college, I began to seek His will for my life. Those same 'friends' who'd accused Christians of being too judgmental began to judge me! It hurt a little at first, but I knew that having my renewed relationship with God was worth losing every so-called friend I had. I have gained so much because of my relationship with God. I have been given a stronger family, better friends, and a peace deep within, because I know I'm moving in the direction where I belong."

The truth is that a person can only be offended when an offense already exists within that individual. The offense actually may be the product of an unrelated, preexisting situation. For example, if a friend takes offense as you progress through God's promotion, it is generally not the result of one isolated event. If there had not already been an issue there, your promotion from God could not have generated negative feelings in your friend.

Here's an example of what I mean: If I am a dishonest person and you accuse me of stealing, I will get offended because you have touched a nerve. I don't want you to expose me. If I've led an honest life, however, and you accuse me of stealing, there is no offense to attach itself to. I'm more likely to laugh in your face and dismiss your accusation without anger or offense.

When your friends are offended by successes in your life, you should question why your progression seems to have caused tension in your friendship. When your promotion is interpreted as an assault on your friendship, it may mean the other person already felt that the relationship was lopsided. It's painful when the people you care for most do not rejoice in your promotion. You don't want to lose friends, especially those who have been in your life for a long time. Seek God's wisdom as to whether the relationship is to continue or if He will replace it with new ones that will move you farther ahead in His plan.

THE TEST OF FRIENDSHIP

The true test of daring to risk friendship comes when friends face betrayal of trust. Jesus gives us the best example of the test of friendship. As a man daring to exercise the authority and dominion given to him by God, Jesus called disciples. He later revealed that His relationship with them was going to the next level (John 15:9–17). His friendship with them did not abandon or overrule His authority and dominion. The fabric of their friendship was interwoven with threads of authority and unconditional love.

The fruit of friendship is ongoing love that accomplishes whatever the Father wills. Now, such a relationship is quite risky. In fact, the more you become open about your feelings and deepest longings, in the way Jesus did with his disciples, the more risks you take in friendship. Alan Loy McGinnis comments in *The Friendship Factor*, "You take risks if you become open about your longings. Once in a while the other person will not respond. But it is sad if you stop expressing them because of occasional disappointment and thereby bed down with disappointment as your constant companion."

The risk of friendship goes beyond simply being hurt—it can become a lasting disappointment. This disenchantment can close the door to openness and intimacy, building walls of unfulfilled expectations between superficial friends. From the cross, Jesus forgave his friends, even though they had betrayed and abandoned him.

At times, men deny their disappointment in friends, trying to disguise their hurt and pain. They withdraw from friendship because disappointment has led them to distrust and become closed and separated from others. A disappointment in friendship may lead a man to withdraw from the offending partner and other friendships as well. He projects disappointment in one broken relationship onto others.

The only healing and proactive approach to friendship must begin with a decision to operate in loving forgiveness, which includes the willingness to confront the disappointments that inevitably will occur. Out of the pain of hurt and the healing of forgiveness, a man's friendships can continue to grow and prosper in the midst of trials and unfulfilled expectations.

DARING TO RISK NEW RELATIONSHIPS

New people who come into your life bring risks as well, and some men are clueless as to how to choose their friendships. Some men are too trusting, and everyone is a friend. Others are so paranoid that no one is allowed to get close enough to become a true friend. When you learn God's parameters and boundaries, it is easier to choose friends wisely.

The book of Proverbs has amazing wisdom for men who dare to risk friendship. It includes wise counsel on virtually every issue of life—borrowing and lending, harsh words, giving advice, true friends versus phony friends, overlooking faults, loyalty, forgiveness, poverty, and wealth (see Proverbs 6:13, 11:9, 12:26, 14:20, 16:28, 17:9, 17:17, 18:19, 18:24, 19:4–7, 20:6, 26:18–19, 27:6, 27:9–10, 17).

FOR WOMEN

SMALL BAGGAGE

Building a mutually enjoyable relationship requires patience and understanding on your part as you and your man become friends. A relationship of true intimacy with a man builds over time and testing.

No matter how impenetrable his façade, he is capable of being vulnerable and therefore hurt. The Bible cautions against being unequally yoked. If the relationship is worth pursuing, however, encourage him as he works through his own baggage of past hurts and distrust. He will risk vulnerability as trust and openness grow between the two of you.

Your relationship with him is best served when you openly discuss, model, and share about friendship with him. Do not allow jealousy to influence his ability to risk vulnerability in your relationship.

Choose friends wisely. God has cautioned against being "unequally yoked." A yoke is a piece of wood that has been hollowed or curved near each end and fitted with bows to place on a work animal's neck and steer him to pull heavy equipment, such as a plow. If two animals shared a yoke that was not designed to fit them both, the results could be disastrously unproductive. A donkey and an ox cannot be joined together under the same yoke, even though both are beasts of burden. By nature, the ox will respond favorably to the weight of his yoke while the donkey will sit down and resist it. Being unequally yoked in a relationship will not help you move forward in God's plan.

Second, two parties in relationship should share a similar perception as to how they are going to plow through to the future. For instance, a man who plans to marry needs to know that the woman can maintain her part of the effort as they both move toward the future. Two people may agree that they are heading in the same direction, but if they are simply two beasts of burden with two different perceptions of how to handle the work, they will continually pull against each other. It is imperative to engage yourself in godly, like-minded, positive, progressive relationships.

As you form new friendships, look for commonality. For instance, a visionary who trusts God for the future may have great difficulty maintaining a relationship with a person who is fearful and clings to what is visible and familiar. One will always be focused on moving ahead, while the other is concerned with holding on to the way things are. Sometimes these personalities can successfully balance each other, but it may be more of a hindrance than a help. Seek relationships based on mutual strengths but also try to determine whether you can each deliver something to the other that you cannot generate within yourselves.

I dare you to risk friendship.

- Risk hurt and be vulnerable.
- Refuse to be jealous.
- Choose your friends wisely.
- Do not partner unequally with someone who doesn't share your kingdom values.
- Learn from past disappointments, but refuse to allow them to become hindrances to future friendships.

24

DARE TO CONQUER YOUR SENSE OF INADEQUACY

*Rewards, success, and victory are for
the disciplined and diligent.*

WHEN GOD CAUSES shifts in a man's life, the first thing that is revealed is his perceived sense of inadequacy. The battle begins, as you ask yourself, "How am I going to do this?" This attack comes out of a self-perception that, left unchecked, will limit your ability to handle what God is about to do in your life.

One of the greatest tests for me was when we moved from our old church building to our new facility. I believed God had directed us to move and that He had given me the gifts and anointing to expand. But, when the reality of what we had done was presented to me, I began to doubt my own ability to handle all that this new phase would require.

At the first Sunday service in the new facility, I looked out over a partially filled house. I remember asking God, "What am I going to do? How could I have even considered that I could handle such an assignment?" I wondered if I had heard God clearly and whether I really had the tools to fight the war I was believing God to empower me to wage. Publicly declaring that this new facility would be filled with the souls of the lost meant I had declared war on the enemy.

God calmly reminded me that He had equipped me with the same weapons He had given me to overcome in the old environment. Further, He assured me He had provided me with some additional weaponry to handle this expanded battle. I realized I simply had to become a more efficient warrior, learn to use these new tools, and become comfortable with confronting whatever came my way.

YOU ARE A WARRIOR

Never forget that God is a warrior and man is created in His image: "The LORD is a warrior; the LORD is his name" (Exodus 15:3, NIV). The Hebrew word referring to a man as a warrior is *gibbor*. It refers to mature men, generally over age thirty (1 Chronicles 23:3). A primary characteristic of a warrior is strength; to be sapped of strength renders a male to be less than a man: "I am as good as dead, like a strong man [*gibbor*] with no strength left" (Psalm 88:4—NLT, bracketed material added). Know that you have been trained and equipped to handle the battle. Your confidence in your commander-in-chief, who is God Almighty, your Abba Father, will make you comfortable with confrontation.

Here are keys to banish feelings of inadequacy:

NO MATTER WHAT YOU MUST FACE, GOD HAS THE ANSWER. But you have to be in control of your emotions. You must be a strategic thinker and not afraid to confront in a righteous, gracious manner. *If we do not confront, we confirm,* thereby allowing the problem to continue. To gain the kind of control over our emotions that we need to wage effective warfare, we must dare to be disciplined.

CONTROL IS NOT REPRESSION. Men often seek to control their emotions through denial or repression. You may often feel that admitting how you feel conveys weakness to those around you. But this is not the case. Confronting yourself with the reality of what's going on inside you requires strength and courage. Authentic friends can help you sort out, understand, pray through, and work through your feelings—casting down negative, defeatist, and destructive feelings rooted in past failures, hurts, and battles you've waged but lost.

DISTINGUISH BETWEEN WAR AND TURF TUSSLES. There will be times in your life when you must face personal challenges and protect the territory God has given to you. If you're like most men, combativeness is something you were encouraged to participate in, starting at a very young age. Most of these early battles have no long-term significance; they are momentary turf battles or the result of slightly injured pride.

Learn to separate minor battles from the war that needs to be waged to protect what is important to your future. Avoid debating or arguing about things that do not impact your transition from boyhood into true manhood.

KNOW ALL YOUR WEAPONS. Judgment becomes a key factor in deciding when to go to war, but not the only weapon God has provided you to do battle. When you consider warfare, you automatically think of physical engagement, but in God's Kingdom battles are fought, and won, through prayer, faith, integrity, and reputation. "The weapons we fight with are not the weapons of the world. On the contrary, they have divine power to demolish strongholds. We demolish arguments and every pretension that sets itself up against the knowledge of God, and we take captive every thought to make it obedient to Christ" (2 Corinthians 10:4–5, NIV).

THE BATTLE WITHIN

The greatest warfare you will wage is the internal battle to become all God has called you to be versus the man that self has worked so hard to create. This battle rages between the new birth and the person you have been.

This conflict has to do with the God-given birthright. The older you are, the more you have assumed the identity created by the world around you. When you are born again, God gives you a whole new identity. As a new creation, you must determine how to overcome your old nature. "Therefore, if anyone is in Christ, he is a new creation; the old has gone, the new has come!" (2 Corinthians 5:17, NIV).

God's Word empowers you to destroy this alter ego and put him under submission—but the old man constantly tries to get the new man to give him back his "birthright." The new man must understand that God the Father has promised that the older shall serve the younger (Genesis 25:23) and that the new man has the authority to supersede that of the old man.

Learn how to pick your fights wisely and wage effective warfare against the real enemy that seeks to maintain your attachment to the old lifestyle. This type of warfare requires an aggressive letting go of the things you used to stand for. Taking off the old man and putting on your new identity in Christ indicates a radically new perception of who you are in the eyes of God.

THE PRIMARY BATTLEFIELD

God uses a spiritual process called "the renewing of the mind" to remove the seeds of old thought patterns and replace them with a new mind-set. The fight of the old mind versus the new mind is spiritual warfare, or an ongoing battle for our personal thoughts. The greatest warfare you face is in your mind, because "as he thinks in his heart, so is he" (Proverbs 23:7, NKJV). As you wage this battle, however, you can do so with confidence, knowing that God in His infinite wisdom has not left you alone or unarmed in the fight. He has given us a Helper (read John 14:26, 16:13).

God has given His Spirit to help you change the way you see yourself and to bring you all truth. The old man in you will attempt to triumph, but Paul reminds us that "the Spirit helps us in our weakness" (Romans 8:26, NIV).

This is not a new battle, nor is it one you should undertake lightly. Pursue a Spirit-led life and refuse to allow the sinful nature of the old man in you to be in control. Paul explains that in this process, you are guaranteed to win this spiritual battle through the help of the Holy Spirit (Galatians 5:16–18, 24–25).

FOR WOMEN

THE WARRIOR SPIRIT

A man is called to be a warrior, not a wimp, so the man who becomes an adversary will fight to win, not simply to engage you. That is why it is important to work in every way to ensure that your man does not become an enemy. He is your ally; treat him as such.

Don't discourage a man's warrior spirit—whether in your man or your son. A man who doesn't have a battle to win or an enemy to subdue will ultimately cease to be a man. Encourage a man's push to break away and be a man—whether it's your man or your son. Don't enable him, discourage him, or baby him. Give him room to grow into a Christian warrior.

Encourage him to channel his warrior energy in ways that are pleasing to God. Above all, affirm his God-given capacity to win the victory!

GRASSHOPPERS AGAINST GIANTS

The new man in you needs constant encouragement and reassurance that God will never give you an assignment that He has not already equipped you to handle, no matter what the circumstances appear to be. Therefore, believe what God says is true, no matter what happens or what people say—friends included.

Before the Israelites moved into the land God had promised to give them, He told Moses to send twelve men out to explore the land where they would be moving. These emissaries brought back evidence that the land was flowing with milk and honey, just as God had promised, and the fruit was so abundant it took two of them to carry a single cluster of grapes (Numbers 13:23–27).

Their Promised Land was all that God had said it would be, but there were major obstacles they would need to overcome. The twelve spies also reported that there were giants living in the land and that the cities were large and well fortified (Numbers 13:28–29). Ten of the spies were discouraged by the presence of the giants and tried to convince their people that battle against them would be impossible to win. But two men were willing to stand up to the challenge for the sake of the prize.

The journey toward taking possession of what God has destined for you will always create a certain degree of conflict—within you and among those with whom you have relationships.

Most people will settle for the status quo to avoid doing battle. Their fear tells them, "You can't," while the voice of God commands, "Yes, you can!" The voice of ignorance always seems louder than the voice of progress and intelligence.

Moses and Aaron listened to the people complaining, grumbling, and afraid to move forward. The majority of the men who had gone into the Promised Land told the people, "We were like grasshoppers in our own sight, and so we were in their sight" (see Numbers 13:33, NKJV).

Joshua and Caleb, on the other hand, understood the promises of God. They told Moses, Aaron, and the rest of the entire Israelite assembly, "Let us go up at once, and possess it; for we are well able to overcome it" (Numbers 13:30, KJV). The two are stellar examples of what Jesus taught about being in spiritual agreement:

> [I]f two of you shall agree on earth as touching any thing that they shall ask, it shall be done for them of my Father which is in heaven. For where two or three are gathered together in my name, there am I in the midst of them.
> MATTHEW 18:19–20, KJV

Any two who come together in spiritual agreement on the outcome and move in alignment with God's plan can achieve the victory, no matter what the circumstances may appear to be. Joshua and Caleb believed Israel was able to conquer the giants awaiting them in the Promised Land.

If there is just one person who will agree with you on the outcome of your situation and you align yourself with God, you can win the battle of self-perception and all things become possible.

I dare you to conquer self-doubt and your sense of inadequacy.

- Become a warrior.
- Break away from a parent's identity and embrace God's identity for you.
- See yourself as a conqueror, not as defeated or crushed.
- Confront your real feelings, do not suppress them.

25

DARE TO
BE DISCIPLINED

*The man who rejects discipline, no matter
how talented or gifted, will soon fail.*

I HAVE A RELATIVE named John who was extraordinarily talented at sports. There was not a field of sports or a game in which he didn't seem to have superior skill. He never had to practice much and was a winner in the school yard and in pickup games. High schools recruited him, then colleges and professional teams were knocking at his door.

The time came for college. The demands of high school were minimal compared with the expectations for a college athlete. In high school, school was not important. His athletic performance got him grades and excuses for absenteeism. College was another story entirely.

He was expected to go to class, take his own tests, and pass them, as well as complete all his assignments. Along with that, he was ex-

287

pected to have a team attitude and team spirit and to cooperate with the coaching staff. He decided his talent should get him a pass on all these requirements.

He would not go to class, did not want to practice, and was generally disrespectful in his lack of cooperation. Oh, by the way, he was attending college on a full scholarship.

He was the best athlete on the team if ability is the measure of ability. He was the worst athlete on the team if you consider all the other requirements. They eventually kicked him off the team and took away his scholarship. He didn't fail because of a lack of ability. He failed because he lacked discipline.

The definition of discipline encompasses a multitude of strong and positive character traits—including submission, consistency, and faithfulness. A man daring to be disciplined is sensitive to the voice of God and submits to him, focused and unwavering in his determination to follow God's plan for his life, and faithful to do what God commands.

Throughout my adult life, as a man both in business and ministry, I have had to be a student. In other words, I am learning for life. I discovered that every problem presents itself as a learning experience, not just an obstacle to be destroyed or overcome. I found this to be true even when the problem wasn't created by me. I had to deal with it and learn. Discipline is more than structure, persistence, and perseverance. It's being teachable.

Proverbial wisdom reveals, "Harsh discipline is for him who forsakes the way, and he who hates correction will die" (Proverbs 15:10, NKJV). The Hebrew word translated here as discipline (*towkechah*) also means to correct, reprove, reason with, and rebuke. Reasoning is a process of examining your beliefs in light of another's and then deciding to stand firm, yield, or reason further.

For all of this to happen, a man has to be teachable and willing to change, and that includes both actions and attitudes. And for that kind of change to happen, you must also be willing to relinquish pride and admit when you are wrong—a tall order for men who have difficulty with authority figures or for those with a distorted self-perception.

When you dare to be disciplined, you are connected to your destiny, which helps you break through whatever may stand in the way of your reaching God's ultimate goal for your life. Discipline attracts the blessing of God and moves you to a place of secured promise.

BARRIERS TO DISCIPLINE

Impatience, lack of commitment, or becoming discontent with God's process may tempt you to "help" God in a way that will inevitably draw you away from your true purpose. If you allow the voices around you to draw you away from being consistent and disciplined, you will become weary and stumble off course. "So let's not get tired of doing what is good. At just the right time we will reap a harvest of blessing if we don't give up" (Galatians 6:9, NLT).

DISCIPLINE AND THE RIGHT SEASON

Discipline is directly connected to an assigned season. There is a time and a season for every activity under heaven; a time to sow and a time to reap (read Ecclesiastes 3:1–8). Do not expect a time of harvest if you have not been consistent during the season of planting. Whenever I become impatient during a season of preparation for the harvest, I think of a particular doughnut commercial I've seen many times on television. The man who is responsible for making the doughnuts rises at 3 A.M. He doesn't really want to, but he knows it's time to carry out his responsibilities. The scene advances to the doughnut shop, where the lights are on, the coffee's brewing, and the doughnuts are cooking. People are pulling into the parking lot, knowing the doughnut man has shown up and done his job.

A man has to keep his vision in view to remain consistent and disciplined, even when he doesn't feel like it. Discipline has nothing to do with feelings; it has everything to do with fulfilling what you know to be your calling. What can keep you consistent in your commitment to vision when you are tempted by impatience or by less-committed voices around you? How can you overcome boredom when the slow process doesn't seem to be moving you closer to reaching your goals?

PREPARATION FOR POSSESSION

Understanding that God's process is less about reaching the goal and more about preparing you to handle the goal once it is reached can help you remain consistent through this developmental season. Throughout the Bible, God took people through certain tests and trials that seemed to have little to do with the ultimate goal. As you study God's process, however, you learn that each experience you must walk through develops and prepares you to possess your Promised Land.

Great men like Moses and David had to remain consistent, disciplined, and focused while less-committed voices appealed to their insecurities and pointed out seemingly insurmountable obstacles. Discipline will lead you to the open doors God has set before you, and the appearance of adversaries is merely a sign that you are making progress toward them. Only when the door of opportunity is open do the adversaries present themselves to try and keep you from moving into your destiny.

Staying disciplined and walking through that door of opportunity leads to more than just an immediate blessing. God's process and plan include the ability to sustain ourselves and to provide an inheritance for our progeny.

Joshua had been developed and prepared as Moses' aide. By the time the Israelites were ready to cross over the River Jordan and move into the Promised Land, he had learned to listen to God's voice and not be swayed by the fears of the people or the obstacles he saw before him. "Be strong and courageous," God told him, "because you will lead these people to inherit the land I swore to their forefathers to give them" (Joshua 1:6, NIV).

Because of Joshua's willingness to dare to be disciplined, many generations were impacted.

THE FRUIT OF DISCIPLINE IS OPPORTUNITY

"The steps of a [good] man are directed and established by the Lord..." (Psalm 37:23, AMP). Your discipline leads you to doors of opportunity, but the problem is God does not necessarily reveal where the doors are located. Instead, He ensures that if you are disciplined and willing to follow His direction, you will reach the doors of purpose and achieve the promise. "Trust in the LORD with all your heart; do not depend on your own understanding. Seek his will in all you do, and he will show you which path to take" (Proverbs 3:5–6, NLT).

A well-known parable tells of a monk who was instructed to plant a dry stick in the sand and water it daily. Since the spring was a great distance from his room, he had to leave the monastery in the evening in order to be back with water by the next morning. For three years he patiently fulfilled his revered teacher's command. At the end of this period, the stick suddenly put forth leaves and bore fruit. The teacher picked the fruit, took it to the church, and invited the monks to eat, saying, "Come and taste the fruit of obedience."

This monastic discipline involved being teachable, taking obedient action, and blending it with tremendous patience and personal sacrifice. Discipline often requires the passage of time for its fruit to be realized. In this instant microwave culture, the discipline of focused, active waiting is virtually extinct.

Think of active waiting spiritually, like preparing to board an airplane. You have your ticket, which tells you the flight time and number. Since possession of a ticket assures your passage on the flight, you begin packing and getting your various affairs in order. You are in active preparation to board the plane that will take you to your destination well before your airplane even reaches the airport.

HANDLING THE UNFORESEEN

Discipline allows a man to act favorably in unforeseen circumstances. Some people think discipline promotes closed-mindedness, but in truth, it creates an ordered, strategic way of living. Discipline actually gives you great flexibility, so that when the unexpected happens, you can respond rather than react to the situation. Discipline prepares you for divine interruptions. Instead of resenting them and allowing chaos to occur when the unscheduled happens, you grow to see these interceptions as divine opportunities.

Daring to be disciplined means scheduling what you can and preparing for what you know is ahead for that day, but at the same time expecting the unexpected. Then, when divine opportunities come, they will not be seen as intrusions. A miracle can be understood as a divine opportunity, and people often miss miracles because they have resented the intrusion into their normalcy.

Reaction is often unprepared, unplanned, and undisciplined action prompted by external forces—other people or circumstances. Response and responsibility (i.e., the ability to be responsive) derive from an internal discipline that has proactively prepared for the situation.

Understanding your season means knowing God's timing, which accomplishes His purposes in His way without regard for your wants and carnal desires. Discipline empowers you to set aside your personal agenda for God's priorities to guide your life.

You can observe the need for and the rewards of a disciplined life—as well as the consequences of being undisciplined—from men like Adam, Samuel and, of course, Jesus. The apostle Paul is a good example of a man dealing with the internal struggles everyone has to face. "For what I want to do I do not do, but what I hate I do. . . . For I have the desire to do what is good, but I cannot carry it out. For what I do is not the good I want to do; no, the evil I do not want to do—this I keep on doing" (Romans 7:15b, 18b–19, NIV).

Paul was fully aware of his shortcomings. A person living in denial cannot live simultaneously in discipline. Because Paul was victorious over his internal battles, toward the end of his life he could declare, "[T]he time has come for my departure. I have fought the good fight, I have finished the race, I have kept the faith" (2 Timothy 4:6b–7, NIV).

FOR WOMEN

HE MUST HAVE DISCIPLINE

A man without discipline—no matter how charming, daring, fun, or adventurous he may be—has real potential to hurt and frustrate you in the things that matter in life. A disciplined man may not generate the kind of excitement you have found appealing in the past, but what has been the result in those types of relationships?

As you look to a man for his "mate potential," realize that without internal discipline, a man will be unable to train or raise children or lead in a godly manner. Likewise, a man who cannot receive correction will not be able to correct or discipline others wisely.

A man who is disciplined will respond to situations rightly, without reacting to his feelings or yours. Don't get angry at him if he refuses to be swayed by emotional response. Encourage your man's steps toward being a man of discipline and do not hinder him inadvertently with subconscious manipulations.

RUNNING AWAY OR TOWARD?

Your destiny is your destiny, along with the events that shape you toward it. On the journey, however, the choice is yours whether you want to run away from the circumstances of your destiny or embrace it and run toward it.

While having great fame as a prophet, Elijah was not very disciplined. He ran, but instead of winning the race, he ended up on the mountain complaining to God about the circumstances that were blocking him from accomplishing his assignment. Elijah experienced one of the greatest victories in all of Biblical history. But despite just having witnessed the powerful hand of God at work, he became filled with fear and ran to hide in a cave.

While he was in hiding, Elijah had an interesting encounter with God. "What are you doing here, Elijah?" God asked. Elijah recounted his recent experiences and whined about how people were trying to kill him and how he felt as if he was the only one left who was willing to stand up for God (read 1 Kings 19). Elijah's lack of personal discipline allowed the circumstances of his life to cloud his vision and cause him to try to run away from his assignment instead of toward it.

Elisha, on the other hand, was prepared for his divine opportunity. When called by God to become Elijah's attendant, he quickly burned his oxen's yoke, cooked the oxen, and served steaks to the people of his village in preparation for his new assignment. He eventually realized that once he moved into this new season, he could not go back to his old life. He had no need to hang on to the remnants of his ending assignment.

Elisha must have been watching for his divine appointment, even as he worked at his daily tasks. Leaving the comfort of his home, his work, and the life he had known proved Elisha was a man who dared to be vulnerable. Elisha was loyal and faithful to his mentor, Elijah. And for his service, Elijah's protégé received a double portion of blessing. When he left the plow, Elisha had no idea where the path would lead him, but he was consistent and steadfast, trusting God through every circumstance.

Opportunities may be defined as time capsules that overflow with God's abundant grace according to His purposes and timing. Each opportunity confronts you with a choice: Dare to be disciplined in order to receive abundantly from God or squander His provision because of your lack of disciplined vision. Will you dare to be disciplined?

I dare you to be disciplined.

- Recognize and understand the season you are in.
- Make a commitment to be teachable and a learner for life.
- Prepare to respond instead of reacting to what's happening around you.
- Become teachable and receive correction with joy and receptivity.

26

DARE TO
BE VULNERABLE

*The insecurity required for love
is scary sometimes.*

ONE OF THE HARDEST THINGS to do is maintain what I call openness while handling disappointing relationships you have attempted to influence in a positive way. It's hard to stay positive when so much negativity is being played out around you. As a man, I have to guard against allowing the disappointments in life to produce a jaded attitude in me.

I know a lot of men who work in the criminal justice system. One of the consistent conversations I have had in the last few years is about how they remain detached from the attitudes of the prisoners and the environment in which they work. One of the biggest battles these men experience is leaving the mind-set needed for the prison environment at the prison when they leave work. They battle becoming cynical about the people and relationships on the outside.

They must protect their vulnerability. The power of environment is real. Often they spend more time at prison than in regular social settings and develop a suspicious mind-set for what they call civilians.

Those men in this line of work have to intentionally allow themselves to drop a well-developed defense mechanism so they can function normally with those they love and care for. If they do not intentionally endeavor to be vulnerable, the purpose for those relationships will be lost. A man who is not appropriately vulnerable will never reach his full potential and purpose.

Emotional vulnerability is an absolute necessity for a daring man, a man of purpose. I had to learn what this meant as I developed relationships with other men in ministry. I remember one young leader who came to me saying he wanted a father figure and mentor in his life. Staying true to my belief that God has called me to assist men in discovering their true calling and potential, I began to sow into this brother's life, sharing principles for success and sharing the things that would benefit his life, work, and family.

While I was experienced and successful in many areas of life, work, ministry, and relationships, I was inexperienced in this area of vulnerability. At that time, I did not understand that some I encountered through my work and ministry would use a façade of sincerity to conceal their self-centered agenda for gain or promotion.

As time progressed, I saw that he had not been honest with me about his reason for connecting himself to me. He realized that it would take more than just being in my physical proximity to duplicate the work God had produced in my life, and there was a distinct change in the way he related to me. I acknowledged the reservation God had placed in my spirit concerning this man. Because of my genuine desire to help and mentor, I was unable to discern the self-centered purpose and motives behind his veil of sincerity. The truth eventually surfaced and the relationship ended. But the experience taught me how to allow myself to be vulnerable despite the potential for hurt.

Admittedly, it was a painful experience, and I had to fight against completely shutting down emotionally, feeling and fearing that everyone who came to me for help would harbor this kind of deception. Going to God, I prayed concerning whether I would allow one incident to affect the way I related to other people.

My prayerful decision was to follow Jesus' example. Even though He'd had a Judas among His closest friends, Jesus dared to be vulnerable. He continued to be loving and giving in His relationships, knowing the very real potential for disappointment and betrayal.

Emotional vulnerability is a decisive action. My painful experience with the young minister taught me that. But I learned something else along my journey. The willingness to remain vulnerable also requires developing a higher level of communication, especially in the male-to-female relationship.

THE RISK OF VULNERABILITY

Choosing vulnerability will lead you to new discoveries in your intellect, emotions, and manhood. Vulnerability, or transparency, began in the Garden of Eden—the man and the woman were both naked and unashamed. Their sin changed them—they no longer were transparent and vulnerable with each other or with God. They tried to cover their nakedness and hide (read Genesis 2:25; 3:7–10).

God has always desired an open and transparent relationship with humankind. He sent His Son, Jesus, to reestablish the intimate connection that had been broken through humanity's sin. Our relationship with God allows the vulnerable places within us to be revealed and then filled with His love and strength.

Vulnerability allows you have intimacy with God, but it also allows you to be sensitive to the needs of others—gracious in times of trouble and compassionate with sensitive strength, wisely meeting the challenges you are called to face. Conversely, intellect can be unfeeling, calculating, without compassion. Until your vulnerability allows you to be sensitive to the needs of others, your earthly knowledge and wisdom are little more than a cold tool in the hands of a heartless potter. When you discover the strength to acknowledge your own vulnerabilities, you access a whole new dimension of understanding and ability in your decision-making process.

Contrary to contemporary thinking, vulnerability and sensitivity do not indicate that a man is weak or lacks strength. Once your intellect has been exposed to the power of the Holy Spirit, it connects you to transparent vulnerability that gives you the sensitivity you need for godly social interaction. It is no coincidence that the most creative individuals in this world—the greatest chefs, designers, builders, and architects—all reveal the creative side of a man.

Society does not encourage a man to be creative. As a matter of fact, when a man is extremely creative, his masculinity is generally questioned. But the premise that a man who is vulnerable and sensitive is less masculine than one who exhibits machismo is a misconception. God has created men to be strong and sensitive, intellectual and creative, masculine and vulnerable—all at the same time. All men are created to be strong as well as sensitive.

THE QUALITIES
OF EMOTIONAL VULNERABILITY

Machismo

Men expose their vulnerability in different ways. One of the most obvious ways is through their machismo. Wherever a man feels inadequate, he tends to overcompensate with exaggerated manliness—gestures, tones, or actions. Machismo is actually an effort, whether conscious or unconscious, to hide vulnerability. Show me a man who is overtly macho and I will show you a man who is not secure emotionally. An emotionally insecure man will have trouble trusting and loving another individual.

Love

Emotional vulnerability is directly related to a man's ability to love another person. The depth of a man's comfort with his own vulnerability determines the extent to which he is able to express love. Love desires God's best for the other person. By contrast, lust feeds on selfishness rather than godliness. Lust blocks vulnerability; love empowers it.

Trust

The more vulnerable a man allows himself to be, the more trust he endows to another. A man rarely gives his love without a high level of trust having been established in that relationship. He exposes his emotional vulnerability when he allows another to have direct influence over him. Since this influence can affect him either negatively or positively, it is an insecure place for a man to be. By nature, a man wants to be in control of his environment and especially of his emotions. When a man finds himself wanting to become more vulnerable in a relationship with a woman, it is because he is ready to commit more of his heart to her.

Commitment

Emotional vulnerability is directly related to the level of commitment to which a man commits himself. As I look back through life, I realize that those I loved most are the same people to whom I was most vulnerable, both intellectually and emotionally. They were able to influence my thinking, and the security of my emotions was in their hands. As a man, you can only have a healthy commitment to someone who has agreed to be as consistent in trust and love as you are.

Intimacy and Sexuality

Emotional vulnerability is essential to a healthy intimate relationship for a man. Contemporary society has encouraged men to become physical first, and then hope that emotional vulnerability will follow as their relationships develop. God's plan for you is to be intellectually, emotionally, and spiritually compatible before the relationship develops any further.

Most men are very physical at first and need time to develop emotional vulnerability. Men who seek to develop intellectually, emotionally, and spiritually enjoy a higher level of positive vulnerability and transparency. This begins to lay a foundation for spiritual intimacy, which is intertwined with our sexuality and emotions. Understanding God's plan and taking the time to cultivate a true relationship with a woman—intellectually, emotionally, and spiritually—will eventually produce true intimacy in the correct context of a relationship.

WHEN SHOULD I BE VULNERABLE?

All men have a tendency to choose a certain flavor in life. Flavor can be described as the type or preference you have in a woman. Unfortunately, if you are not careful how you choose your flavor, you can end up in a toxic relationship. Sometimes what you are attracted to is not a good match for you. When I was a teenager, I used to like women who were real fine and a little unpredictable, but what I really needed was a consistent woman whom I was attracted to for her inner beauty, not because she was the envy of my peers.

When I counsel a man whose vulnerability has left him emotionally injured and wanting to build a wall around him in defense, I lead him through a discussion about choices.

In the context of male-female relationships, sometimes the woman who desires your heart is not qualified for the assignment. Your inward desire to be appreciated and loved can push you to entrust an unworthy steward with a critical part of your life. You can form toxic relationships by connecting to people who are not good stewards of your intellect, emotions, or manhood.

Toxic relationships. There have been times when you lacked discernment on entering into a new relationship. As a result, you may have become entangled in a toxic relationship that not only hurt you but also poisoned other relationships that were healthy.

As a man dares to risk being vulnerable, what are some of the warning signs of a toxic relationship? Be forewarned if you discern that the other person:

- has an agenda for you
- becomes overly dependent on you
- wants to change you to your detriment
- provokes arguments instead of discussions with you
- talks incessantly and listens rarely
- flatters you instead of affirming you
- constantly finds fault and criticizes you and others
- resents or is jealous of your friendships with others

While not exhaustive, this list can help flag certain behaviors that reveal the potential for toxicity in relationships.

BEFORE YOU SHUT DOWN! When you are on the verge of shutting down your emotions, and therefore your vulnerability, I ask you to consider whether the relationship choices you have made have been consistent and similar, whether positive or negative. I am questioning whether you have chosen companions based only on physical attraction. Have you taken time to learn who the woman really is before trusting her with the sensitive side of your life? Have you been searching so intensely for that one special woman that you have exposed too much of yourself too quickly? The real question is not whether you should be vulnerable, but rather how you are choosing the women to whom you will be open and transparent.

The quickest way for you to overcome the wounding caused by a painful personal involvement is to accept your part in the equation. The reasons why relationships collapse are never one-sided. If you are pondering the reasons for a breakup, ask these questions:

- Did I choose correctly? If not, what caused me to choose incorrectly?
- What signs did I ignore that, after further analysis, are now painfully obvious?
- Which of these signs might have revealed this person's true character had I stopped to read them?
- What did I do (or fail to do) that brought me to this place of hurt?

Just as you learn that you cannot share your vision with everyone, it is critical to be selective about choosing people with whom you can be vulnerable.

The Bible says to submit yourselves to one another in the fear of

God (Ephesians 5:21). Lay a blueprint designed by God over the life of any individual who may be the focus of your future attention. Then determine to submit only to someone who consistently exhibits the character of God.

AVOID FLESH-TO-FLESH CONNECTIONS. We often connect the fallen part of our old man to the fallen part of another individual, setting ourselves up for mutual disappointment. If submission is an intellectual, emotional, and spiritual decision based on the character and consistent behavior of the other individual, that is someone you can be vulnerable to. Submitting to one another in reverential fear of God will be the safeguard needed to resume the willingness for emotional vulnerability.

If you have been hurt, don't let the past determine your future relationships. Dare to be vulnerable without setting aside discernment and wisdom. Risk new relationships, understanding that those associations can become significant ways for you to grow and mature, as well as opportunities for serving others.

FOR WOMEN

YOUR INFLUENCE

You have the capacity to greatly impact a man's willingness to be open, intimate, and vulnerable in relationship with you. If he does not exhibit these characteristics now, recognize that he can learn to be vulnerable, open, and intimate through your godly example.

Understand that he cannot tolerate or take the punishment for the toxicity of your past relationships, and is not likely to risk openness and vulnerability with you if your primary agenda is to manipulate or inappropriately change him.

He will, however, become open and vulnerable as trust and commitment grow in your relationship. Walk with him as he takes steps toward intimacy, openness, and vulnerability with you, realizing that as he opens his heart to God he becomes more willing to open his heart to you.

CHOOSE WISELY

Deciding on the right person to entrust with your vulnerability for a lifetime relationship requires looking into the person's life and character to determine whether she embodies certain principles of God. These traits address a man's relationship with a woman; however, they also are valued qualities for a woman to look for in determining when to become vulnerable.

1. **A strong commitment to spiritual things.** A woman without spiritual commitment lacks the qualities necessary to make it through difficult times. A woman's relationship with God cannot be casual, because it brings true balance to her life. A relationship with God is fundamental and foundational to qualifying as a safe person with whom to be vulnerable.

2. **Balanced organization in one's life.** Demonstrated crisis management is a trait you should look for in a woman. Inability to cope in a crisis usually signals that the individual does not possess the maturity needed to face the kind of difficult seasons that may arise in the relationship. Timeliness is a key indicator of an organized life.

3. **A structured life.** Predictability produces security in a relationship— the kind of security that leads to healthy vulnerability. Being in a

relationship with someone who has an unstructured life will always threaten the structure in your life. In the Bible, God tells His people to separate from individuals who exhibit a different drive or nature.

4. **Contemplative/planner.** A thoughtful orientation toward life helps to establish consistency and commitment in a relationship; both are needed. Does the potential woman in your life appear to have a life plan or is she living day to day? Even at a young age, the person should display some evidence of a sense of direction that leads down a definite path. If you attach yourself to someone (of any age) who is trying to "find herself," you are in for a bumpy ride that may culminate in her finding herself somewhere other than with you. There should be evidence of consistent structure.

5. **Balanced priorities.** A person with balanced priorities will also possess maturity and wisdom. A woman whose primary life concerns are in proper order has the ability to prioritize in the important relationship decisions—finances, job, children, religion.

6. **Ability to sacrifice for others.** This characteristic is the mark of an unselfish nature. A woman with a sacrificial heart performs true acts of benevolence; there is no hidden agenda. A woman who shares without an agenda is complete enough to humbly sacrifice for you. A woman with a sacrificial heart is safe to be vulnerable with. A relationship that demonstrates reciprocal sacrifice is essential to mutual fulfillment.

7. **Ability to care for herself.** A woman whose life experience has not included preparation to leave home or the ability to take care of someone other than herself in many cases is equipped to do little more than be physically present in a relationship. Your life partner must be willing to lend a helping hand; it is the helpmeet or counterpart principle.

8. **Positive self-image.** People with low self-esteem are often jealous, with an insatiable insecurity. Everyone is a little jealous at one time or another. But a jealous, insecure person who is limiting, isolating, imprisoning, and impossible to satisfy will usually necessitate that you give up part of yourself to remain in the relationship or friendship. This type of jealousy consumes time, work, friends, family, and career.

9. **Demonstrated fruitfulness.** You have to promise more than potential and big ideas. Productivity should be more than a dream. It should be exhibited as a lifestyle, not just a promise or a potential to be actualized in an indefinite future.

10. **Demonstrated wisdom.** A woman must have the ability to add to her own life in a rational, balanced way—counting the cost, not making ill-advised decisions that produce drama and havoc.

11. **Bounce-backability.** Inconsistencies are sewn into the fabric of life. Does she recover well from a crisis or does every testing situation cause her to respond, "I can't take it"? A person who demonstrates the ability to bounce back from adversity is better equipped to remain focused and consistent, come what may.

12. **Ability to subdue.** We all go through a season when multiple things seem to threaten the stability and structure we have worked so hard to maintain. The ability to bring back into control an out-of-control situation is a characteristic you want in a friend or mate.

13. **A sense of prohibition.** Does she have a principle of discipline? If not, you may inherit a dependent rather than a partner. Self-discipline is the fruit of trustworthiness.

14. **A good fit.** You don't have to be exactly alike, but you must agree on fundamental life principles and issues—finances, future, family, friends, and faith. God takes the rib from Adam, gives him Eve in its place. She fits into the place made vacant for her.

15. **Healthy family relationships.** Does the woman have an adult relationship with her parent? Does she get along with her siblings? A good predictor of her behavior in the relationship can be seen in her relationship with her family, especially her parents. People who are rude, unfeeling, selfish, or disrespectful to their parents will usually conduct themselves the same way with you.

16. **Proven loyalty.** Real commitment is learned and refined when it is tested. It does not come suddenly, with nothing more than a verbal assertion as its foundation.

17. **Transparency.** The right kind of love interest can handle your negative past. The right kind of love, the "safe place" kind of love, is uniquely equipped to handle the mistakes of your past, as long as they are not representative of the present. If you must hide who you used to be or where you came from, it will be almost impossible to totally commit to that person. Likewise, is she transparent about who she is? A person who feels she should hide parts of her life silently anticipates rejection.

18. **A responsible work ethic.** An inability to obtain and maintain employment is a sign of immaturity, and very often a feeling of entitlement. You don't want to become a safety net for someone's lifestyle. Very often, a person with a poor work ethic also has a "buy what you want, beg for what you need" mentality.

Vulnerability is a choice. It is your responsibility to look for the right qualities and characteristics in the person with whom you will be open and transparent. No one is perfect, and taking a "checklist" approach to relationship could cause you to miss a wonderful opportunity for bonding, partnership, and intimacy. In general, though, the person you choose to make yourself vulnerable to should demonstrate maturity and wisdom in the critical areas of life.

I dare you to choose to be vulnerable.

- Learn from but also set aside past hurts and disappointments in relationships.
- Risk new relationships while being discerning and wise.
- Choose healthy relationships over toxic ones.
- Be willing to commit, love, trust, and be open.

27

DARE TO
BE BOLD

Search for the future inside of you.
It's in the deposit called your strength.

D ARING TO BE A MAN requires courage and boldness on your
part. Boldness and courage are integral to every dare that
has been issued in the preceding chapters. Boldness requires
courage and a willingness both to risk and to change.

Men of faith are often asked to step into unstable situations.
When called by God to move into such a position, you may find that
the majority of men who heard the same command will choose to stay
behind. At this point in time, boldness and faith are the only two
things of which we can be certain. Those you trusted for wisdom and
strength in the past may not have the boldness to step out or the faith
to move into this new realm of authority. Many times the most sig-

nificant doors leading to manhood are ones you must walk through alone. Those you thought would accompany you are standing in the distance watching to see if the risk you have taken this time is too great.

BOLDNESS TO ENTER FULL MANHOOD

This season of growth into manhood requires boldness and faith to do or achieve something that you have never accomplished before. One of the great dilemmas and drawbacks, of course, is fear—not fear that Christ will let us down but fear that we will not be able to do what the Lord has called us to do.

Christ speaks of a boldness needed to approach Him in just such times of need. But there seems to be a certain ambiguity within the spiritual community—the thing we need is the very thing we are hesitant to bring in our approach to God. For example, God tells us He will supply all our needs (Philippians 4:19), yet we resist asking for them, choosing instead to believe that material blessings are not of God. The truth is, God tells us that when we need something that we can come boldly to the throne and ask Him for what we need (Hebrews 4:16).

There is a spiritual dynamic that a man who dares to be a man must accept: boldness is needed where fear exists, and faith is needed when the situation is beyond your natural capabilities. Boldness, like faith, allows you to step outside the realm of your natural capability and gives you strength to travel down a path that seems uncharted and unfamiliar.

Boldness, however, is not to be confused with recklessness. Boldness is based on a calculated move into a dimension of faith where you may have limited or no experience but one that you know God has called you into. When you dare to be bold, you continue to reach higher vistas and deeper dimensions in your life. David understood this principle. Psalm 138:3 (NIV) declares, "When I called, you answered me; you made me bold and stouthearted."

When you dare to be bold, you may also need to determine to be different from your ancestors in certain areas of your life—in education, vocation, and most often, your spiritual life. God will give you the desire to boldly forge into new dimensions and the courage to enter into a new land.

Boldness is a definite prerequisite for you or any man to step into full manhood.

Boldness springs out of integrity.

Inner purity and truthfulness give you the courage to face any earthly power or dark spiritual attack. The prophet Daniel displayed these traits as a key to his boldness. On his web site (www.edcole.org), Ed Cole offers several attributes that describe Daniel's character: unashamed boldness, uncommon standard, unearthly protection, unhindered persistence, unblemished faith, unusual test, immeasurable blessing, unlimited influence.

When you live in the knowledge that you have nothing to fear, nothing to lose, and nothing to hide, you will dare to be bold. Daniel had no fear of earthly rulers because his authority and power came from God. He had nothing to lose because his life was a living sacrifice before God. He had nothing to hide because his inner man was pure.

Want to take a bold move in your life to become like Daniel? Follow this command: "Because we have these promises, dear friends, let us cleanse ourselves from everything that can defile our body or spirit. And let us work toward complete holiness because we fear God" (2 Corinthians 7:1, NLT).

BOLDNESS TO HANDLE RESISTANCE

Boldness is needed in the face of unusual resistance. Paul said, "I press on toward the goal to win the prize for which God has called me heavenward in Christ Jesus. All of us who are mature should take such a view of things" (Philippians 3:14–15a, NIV). The Amplified Bible adds, "So let those [of us] who are spiritually mature and full-grown have this mind and hold these convictions."

There are some goals you will reach easily because they are well within your physical, intellectual, and emotional capabilities. Other goals are set for you by God, and will meet with great resistance. Just as physical strength cannot be attained or maintained without using the muscles to push against a stronger force, spiritual growth requires exercise to grow to meet and overcome resistance.

PRESS FORWARD TOWARD THE GOAL! The disciples were told to meet Jesus on the other side of the lake. Only halfway to their goal, they found themselves in a storm in the darkest part of the night. "He saw the disciples straining at the oars, because the wind was against them" (Mark 6:48, NIV). They were literally pulling with all their might.

You may find yourself midway between where you started and where you need to be. That's where the resistance threatens to stop you from reaching your goal. At that point, you must pull with all your might, believe with all your faith, and press boldly into the darkness toward the goal. When you are able to press into the interference that stands between you and your goals, you will find yourself consistently victorious.

Focus! Boldness requires you to focus aggressively on your goal as you patiently and steadfastly press on toward the finish line. At those times you confidently declare the truth, revealing an inner courage to stand your ground and continue toward your Promised Land.

When boldness attaches itself to your vision and combines with the expectation that God has revealed, you will move forward at a miraculous rate. Your boldness will birth courage, then the vision will pull and the revelation will push you far beyond what you ever thought you were capable of accomplishing.

BOLDNESS TO CONFRONT FEAR

Two of the greatest inhibitors to pushing through to the goal are fear and public opinion. Courage is a choice, which means boldness is also a choice. When David chose to fight Goliath, he did so fully aware of the giant's size and might. Certainly, he had some measure of fear when the giant stood before him. But what drove David to victory was that he saw the giant as a fear to be confronted, whereas Saul and the Israelites saw the giant as a fear to be avoided.

In order to be courageous, you have to decide that God's truth is greater than the facts presented by the circumstances and the crowd. The facts may tell you, "This situation is too big for you to handle," but the truth tells you, "For I can do everything through Christ who gives me strength" (Philippians 4:13, NLT). The spectating crowd points out the impossibility of the situation, but truth reminds you that all things are possible to him who believes (Mark 9:23).

When you get into a situation where fear arises and you have to make a choice to be bold and courageous, your belief in the truth of God will overcome the facts of the situation and the voices of the disbelieving crowd.

BOLDNESS TO STEP OUT

Peter obviously was a bold and outspoken man, even before he became a disciple of Jesus. The Lord wanted to develop this boldness in him so Peter would become the powerful leader he would need to be once Jesus returned to His Father. We see this bold courage portrayed when the disciples were in the middle of the lake one night without Jesus. Of the twelve, only Peter had the courage to challenge what might have been a ghost walking toward them on the water, to see if it was really their Teacher. "Lord, if it's you," he said, "tell me to come to you on the water."

Not only did he boldly confront the ghostly figure, but when Jesus invited him to come, he had the courage to actually step out of the boat and defy gravity. "Then Peter got down out of the boat, walked on the water and came toward Jesus" (Matthew 14:25–30, NIV).

Peter was an experienced fisherman. He knew full well that the sea was capable of sucking him in like a sponge, but his faith in the truth of Jesus as the Son of the living God moved him to boldness and inspired the courage that enabled him to step out of that boat. Boldness and courage are always enhanced by truth.

MAKE A RADICAL CHANGE

There may be some character traits, some circumstances, or some dimensions of your life that need radical change. After reading this book, you may have identified those areas and now know that God has given you the authority and the ability to overcome every challenge in your life.

Now is the time to take your new faith and establish a new reality in your life. Courageously face any challenge before you, whether emotional, intellectual, spiritual, or situational.

316 DARE TO BE A MAN

FOR WOMEN

BALANCE BOLDNESS

Boldness in a man is a trait that most women seek in a candidate for relationship or marriage. But it has become increasingly difficult for a man to exercise boldness. Society does not encourage it. If a man desires to meet his responsibilities, the demands of the modern corporate era necessitate the sacrifice of some traditional expectations for both men and women.

Women are, mainly out of necessity, taking on responsibilities men were created to fulfill. Sometimes, out of sheer frustration, a man will pull away with an "Okay, you got it" attitude. Instead of running into boldness, he runs away from it.

In his heart, every man, including your man, wants to fulfill the role that God has designed for him. You can encourage him to do so by not becoming an obstacle to his journey toward boldness. Affirm the steps he chooses to take. Don't try to dictate his journey. Be patient as God reveals his destiny and he learns to use the tools he has already been given to equip him for victory.

Dare to be the woman a man needs so that he can dare to be all that God has called and equipped him to be. Celebrate his small successes, keeping in mind that in ultimately stepping into his destiny he achieves victory for you both!

I dare you to boldly press forward to the victory that God has already assigned to your life, by seeking to change the areas that have been revealed to you.

- Step outside the realm of your natural capabilities.
- Have the desire to forge a new path and have the faith that God will provide one for you.
- Focus on your goals and press on toward your Promised Land.
- Believe that the truth of God will overcome the facts of the situation.
- Live in the knowledge that you have nothing to fear.

TAKE THE
DARE *NOW*

I have compiled for you a summary checklist of all the daring challenges made to you in this book. Prioritize them. Check them off as they become part of your action and daily mind-set.

Dare to move forward . . . change . . . grow . . . mature!

- [ ] Understand you are like Him. God ~~is~~ ~~X~~ not a projection of *your* image.
- [ ] Know you are sovereignly empowered to take dominion and subdue the earth. ~~take~~ *wrong* "dominion" over your own thoughts+ choices
- [ ] Obey all He requires of you to be and to do.
- [ ] Realize that <u>consistent obedience matures</u> and disciplines you.
- [ ] Discover that God, not you or others, knows what's best for you.

- ☐ Take initiative and control instead of being passively reactive to life.
- ☐ Forgive others as God has forgiven you.
- ☐ Take up and exercise the authority and sovereignty God has given you.
- ☐ Usher God's presence into your life.
- ☐ Come face-to-face with God. *through His Words.*
- ☐ Become an example to others of a man who lives a praise-filled life.
- ☐ Break with the traditions of men so that you can seize a breakthrough with God.
- ☐ Face God.
- ☐ Be transformed by God's ~~image.~~ *Word*
- ☐ Come before God in humility.
- ☐ Be uncovered in His presence.
- ☐ Become transparent.
- ☐ Believe God for a creative miracle in becoming a new man in Christ. *Read + Do*
- ☐ Be a man after God's own heart.
- ☐ Discover that your uniqueness empowers you to achieve success within the realm of your capabilities.
- ☐ Know that faith will take you through God's process to ~~receive His blessing.~~ *Live and Learn all that He would have you lear*
- ☐ Listen to God's promises for you.
- ☐ Learn about God's timing and plans for you.
- ☐ Declare the good news of His promises.
- ✳ ☐ Discover that circumstances and situations are designed to reveal your character to you.
- ☐ Come out from pagan authority over your life.
- ✳ ☐ Separate from troublesome relatives and associates.
- ☐ Be willing to wait within your waiting. Seek God's destiny, which clothes you with uniqueness and worth, potential and prestige.

- [ ] Separate from the boys. ✳
- [ ] Refuse another man's coat of destiny.
- [ ] Remember the promise of the coat, even when others strip it from you.
- [ ] Return to the Father's arms, as He wants to reestablish your identity, authority, and position.
- [ ] Put on Christ. ✳
- [ ] Risk vulnerability.
- [ ] Embrace intimacy with Abba Father.
- [ ] Abandon doubt of God while risking trust through a leap of faith.
- [ ] Love God passionately—with all your mind, heart, soul, and strength.
- [ ] Worship relationally in spirit and truth, not ritualistically or religiously.
- [ ] Love and accept others unconditionally. *ask! God doesn't!!*
- [ ] Use God's standard of covenant for relating instead of relying on contractual relationships. *Only God makes covenants!*
- [ ] Communicate effectively by listening and seeking to understand others. ✳
- [ ] Use the three-question process to communicate.
- [ ] Understand that others may not comprehend your nonverbal communication. *&*
- [ ] Move from childless ways to maturity.
- [ ] Release unrealistic expectations of your biological father.
- [ ] Form a personal, intimate relationship with the Father.
- [ ] Understand the process of maturing from trials to character.
- [ ] Become a "son" mentored by a father who dwells in the Father's likeness.
- [ ] Live out the character qualities of the Father. *wow! That would be something!*
- [ ] Take up your responsibility following Jesus. ✳

- [ ] Lose your self-centeredness and serve God ~~and others.~~
- [ ] Accept various and multiple responsibilities ~~at work,~~ in your family, and in spiritual and ~~societal leadership.~~
- [ ] Become fruitful; multiplying, subduing, and taking dominion of your sphere of influence. (*marriage + family*)
- ✳ [ ] Evaluate and prioritize your multitude of responsibilities.
- [ ] Hear and receive revelation from God for your fruitfulness. — *The W*
- [ ] Speak out what you hear from God. *Speak the Word.* *is THE rev*
- ✳ [ ] Respond to what God has said to you in obedience and bear good fruit in your relationships, work, and personal spiritual maturation.
- ✳ [ ] Set aside all jealousy, domination, manipulation, and intimidation.
- [ ] Exercise authority over your environment. *Poppycock!*
- [ ] Seek God's direction for exercising your authority.
- [ ] Receive authority from your relationship with the Father. *Dangero*
- [ ] Anticipate the outcome before you act or speak in authority.
- [ ] Grow from each time you dare to exercise authority and dominion. *"exercise"* (*God is the only Good*) —
- [ ] Risk hurt and become vulnerable.
- [ ] Refuse to be jealous.
- ✳ [ ] Choose your friends wisely.
- ✳ [ ] Choose with whom you will be vulnerable by building partnerships only with those who share your kingdom values.
- [ ] Learn from disappointments, but refuse to allow them to become hindrances to future friendships.
- [ ] ~~Become a warrior.~~
- ✳ [ ] Break away from a parent's identity and embrace God's identity for you.
- [ ] ~~See yourself as a conqueror, not~~ as defeated or crushed.
- ✳ [ ] Confront your real feelings, do not suppress them.
- ✳ [ ] Recognize and understand the season you are in.
- ✳ [ ] Make a commitment to be teachable and a learner for life.

✱ ☐ Become teachable and accept correction with joy and receptivity.

☐ Prepare to respond instead of reacting to what is happening around you. *With the Word.*

✱ ☐ Learn from, but also set aside past hurts and disappointments in relationships.

✱ ☐ Risk new relationships while being discerning and wise.

✱ ☐ Choose healthy relationships over toxic ones.

✱ ☐ Be willing to commit, love, trust, and be open.

✱ ☐ Be quick to listen, slow to speak, and slow to anger.

✱ ☐ Decide to understand what the person is really saying before you respond.

✱ ☐ Ask questions that get to the root issues of problems, relationships, and situations.

✱ ☐ Understand a̶ ̶w̶o̶m̶a̶n̶'̶s̶ *your wife's* patterns of communication.